The Missing Tax Accounting Guide

A Plain English Introduction to ASC 740 Tax Provisions

THE MISSING TAX ACCOUNTING GUIDE – A PLAIN ENGLISH INTRODUCTION TO ASC 740 TAX PROVISIONS

Copyright ©2022 Tax Director Services, Inc. All rights reserved.

Edition 2.0

No part of this publication may be copied, reproduced, translated, stored in a retrieval system, or transmitted in any form or by any means, electronic, mechanical, photocopying, recording or otherwise, without prior written permission from the author.

ISBN: 979-8-9868657-0-6

For information, contact:
Tax Director Services, Inc.
1273 Horsham Way
Apex, NC 27502

www.nctaxdirector.com

Table of Contents

1 **PRELIMINARY MATTERS** 9
    1.1   ABOUT THE AUTHOR 9
    1.2   REVIEW AND EDITING 9
    1.3   OTHER BOOKS AND CPE COURSES BY THE AUTHOR 9
        "Alteryx™ for Accounting, Tax and Finance Professionals." 9
        Additional information 10
    1.4   COPYRIGHT INFORMATION 10
    1.5   TRADEMARKED TERMS 10
    1.6   LEGAL DISCLAIMER 10
    1.7   NASBA COMPLIANT TAX ACCOUNTING AND OTHER CPE 11
    1.8   UPDATES FROM EDITION 1.0 11

2 **AN INTRODUCTION TO TAX PROVISION WORKPAPERS** 13
    2.1   LEARNING OBJECTIVES 13
    2.2   TAX PROVISION EXAMPLE #1 - BACKGROUND AND ASSUMPTIONS 13
    2.3   FINANCIAL STATEMENTS (5) 14
        Balance sheet 14
        Income statement 15
        Income taxes footnote 15
    2.4   THE PROOF OF PRETAX BOOK INCOME (1600, 1000 AND 5) 16
    2.5   THE TOTAL TAX EXPENSE (OR "PROVISION") CALCULATION (1000) 16
    2.6   THE EFFECTIVE TAX RATE RECONCILIATION (5 AND 1000) 17
    2.7   TAX ADJUSTING JOURNAL ENTRIES (50 AND 1600) 18

3 **TAX ACCOUNTING VS. TAX COMPLIANCE CONCEPTS** 21
    3.1   LEARNING OBJECTIVES 21
    3.2   TAX COMPLIANCE DEFINED 21
    3.3   TAX ACCOUNTING DEFINED 21
    3.4   THE TOTAL TAX EXPENSE (OR PROVISION) IS THE SUM OF CURRENT AND DEFERRED TAXES 23
    3.5   THE TAX PROVISION VS. THE TAX PROVISION WORKPAPERS 23
    3.6   INCOME TAXES VS. NON-INCOME TAXES 24

4 **THE MAIN PURPOSES OF THE TAX PROVISION** 25
    4.1   LEARNING OBJECTIVES 25
    4.2   KEY ELEMENTS OF A PUBLIC ACCOUNTING FIRM'S FINANCIAL STATEMENT OPINION 25
    4.3   THE FOUR MAIN PURPOSES OF A TAX PROVISION WORKPAPER PACKAGE 25
    4.4   WHAT ARE NOT THE MAIN PURPOSES OF A TAX PROVISION? 26

5 **RELATIONSHIPS BETWEEN THE TAX PROVISION AND OTHER TAX CONCEPTS** 29
    5.1   LEARNING OBJECTIVES 29
    5.2   THE DIFFERENCE BETWEEN TAX PROVISION AND TAX RETURN TIMING 29
    5.3   THE RETURN TO PROVISION (OR "RTP") PROCESS 30
    5.4   THE RELATIONSHIP BETWEEN THE CURRENT TAX EXPENSE (PER THE FINANCIAL STATEMENTS) AND TAXES PER THE TAX RETURN 30

5.5	THE RELATIONSHIP BETWEEN A W-2 AND A TAX RETURN	31
5.6	THE RELATIONSHIP BETWEEN THE UNADJUSTED TRIAL BALANCE AND THE TAX PROVISION	31
5.7	TAX WITHHOLDINGS, ESTIMATED TAXES, AND TAX EXPENSE ACCRUALS ARE NOT THE SAME AS THE TOTAL TAX EXPENSE (OR PROVISION)	32
	Individual estimated income taxes	*32*
	Corporate estimated income taxes	*32*
	The relationship between estimated taxes and tax expense	*32*
	An example	*33*
	Summary	*33*
5.8	WHAT IF DATA AND INFORMATION CHANGES IN THE MIDDLE OF THE TAX PROVISION PREPARATION PROCESS?	33
	A change to pretax book income will impact the tax provision calculation	*33*
	Despite potential trial balance movement, start the tax provision process as soon as possible	*34*
	Start the tax provision "as soon as possible" with an advanced draft of the unadjusted trial balance	*34*
	What this looks like in practice	*35*
	A "hard close" in advance of the provision	*35*

6 A METHODICAL REVIEW OF THE TAX PROVISION PREPARATION PROCESS (EXAMPLE #1) 37

6.1	LEARNING OBJECTIVES	37
6.2	YOUTUBE VIDEO	37
6.3	A REVIEW OF COMPANY BACKGROUND AND ASSUMPTIONS	37
6.4	OBTAIN A TRIAL BALANCE FROM THE ACCOUNTING GROUP (1600)	38
	The company's trial balance is the starting point	*38*
	Observations from reviewing the trial balance	*39*
6.5	THE "WHY" BEHIND THE NEED FOR QUALITY TAX PROVISION WORKPAPER DESIGN AND REFERENCING	39
	Key questions workpapers need to answer for a reviewer	*39*
	Comments to preparer's on workpaper design and referencing	*40*
	The "why" behind the importance of quality workpapers	*40*
	The consequences of an organized or disorganized tax provision workpaper package	*41*
	Summary – The "Truck Rule"	*42*
6.6	KEY EXCEL WORKPAPER CONVENTIONS	42
	Add a title and a description to each workpaper	*42*
	Create a reference number for each workpaper	*42*
	Shade formulas	*43*
	"Not used"	*43*
6.7	COMPUTE PRETAX BOOK INCOME (1600)	44
6.8	COMPUTE THE TAX PROVISION (1000)	45
	Pretax book income is the starting point of the tax provision	*45*
	Identify and calculate book/tax differences	*45*
	Calculate taxable income and the current tax expense	*45*
	Calculate deferred taxes and the total tax expense	*46*
	Make tax provision calculations clean and relevant	*46*
	Why superseded data persistently stays in tax provision calculations	*47*

The process of cleaning up tax provision workpapers 47
Keep the return to provision ("RTP") process in mind.. 48
6.9 **DETERMINE THE YEAR-END TAX ADJUSTING ENTRY (50, 1000, 1600)** 48
6.10 **COMPLETE THE TAX PAYABLE ROLLFORWARD (50, 60, 1600)** 50
Tax journal entry observations.. 50
Calculate the ending taxes payable and the related tax adjusting entry 50
6.11 **REVIEW THE TAX ADJUSTING ENTRY AND PROVIDE IT TO THE ACCOUNTING GROUP (50, 1600)** .. 51
6.12 **REVISITING THE TRIAL BALANCE AFTER ADJUSTING ENTRIES HAVE BEEN BOOKED**....................... 53
6.13 **VERIFY TAX AMOUNTS ARE CORRECT IN THE FINANCIAL STATEMENTS (5, 1600)** 55
The tax provision workpapers support the tax-related figures in the financial statements 55
A review of non-tax financial statement figures.. 55
A review of tax-related financial statement figures 57
6.14 **WRITE THE TAX FOOTNOTE AND OTHER TAX-RELATED DISCLOSURES (5)** 57
6.15 **DRAFT FINANCIAL STATEMENTS CAN NOW BE COMPLETED** 59
6.16 **ADDRESS AUDITOR QUESTIONS ON THE TAX PROVISION CALCULATION AND THE RELATED CONTROLS** 59
Tax specialists will audit the tax provision.. 59
Internal controls are also audited 60
6.17 **THE FINANCIAL STATEMENTS ARE ISSUED (AND THE CONSEQUENCES OF AN INCOME TAX-RELATED ERROR)** 60
The financial statements are issued after the audit is complete 60
Tax provision errors can result in a restatement of the financial statements 61
6.18 **PARTING THOUGHTS ON THE TAX PROVISION PROCESS** 62

7 THE FINANCIAL STATEMENT AUDITOR'S PERSPECTIVE OF THE TAX PROVISION........... 63
7.1 **LEARNING OBJECTIVES** 63
7.2 **THE TAX SPECIALIST'S APPROACH TO AN AUDIT**... 63
Verify tax-related figures on the 'face' of the financial statements 63
Prove out pretax book income 64
Be aware of changes to pretax book income and other financial data 64
Take time to review entity trial balances on a line-by-line basis 65
Verify the company's technical tax positions.. 66
Determine that tax accounting rules are properly applied.. 66
Document and support your audit assertions with verifiable evidence.......................... 67
Tie out and support the financial statement footnotes & management discussion and analysis ("MD&A").. 68
Beware of "SALY" 68
7.3 **APPLYING AUDIT CONCEPTS TO EXAMPLE #1** 69
Sample audit questions and client information requests... 69
Client responses to questions... 70
7.4 **OBSERVATIONS FROM THE EXAMPLE #1 CLIENT AUDIT** 72
Clients don't want to be audited.. 72
A corporate Tax Group's view of an audit... 72
You don't have to find a problem to be a good auditor... 73
First ask the Assurance/Audit Team, and then follow up with the client 74
Carefully manage how you handle client questions 75

Invest time and effort to improve audit efficiency 75
    7.5   AUDIT TERMINOLOGY RELATED TO TAX PROVISIONS 76
"Material" and "materiality" 76
"De minimis" 76
Company approaches to recording audit findings that are above de minims but below the materiality threshold 77
Illustrating the considerations for making a late adjustment for an immaterial amount . 77
Restatements and material weaknesses from an auditor's point of view 78

8   AN INTRODUCTION TO BOOK/TAX DIFFERENCES 81
    8.1   LEARNING OBJECTIVES 81
    8.2   BOOK/ TAX DIFFERENCES EXIST BECAUSE OF DIFFERENT RULES AND OBJECTIVES FOR FINANCIAL AND TAX REPORTING 81
    8.3   BOOK/TAX TERMINOLOGY – "SCHEDULE M'S" AND "M-1'S" 82
    8.4   GAAP FINANCIAL DATA IS THE STARTING POINT FOR DETERMINING TAXABLE INCOME 83
    8.5   INCOME (AND NOT BOOK/TAX DIFFERENCES) GIVES RISE TO INCOME TAXES 83
"Income" gives rise to "income taxes" 83
Book/tax differences can be favorable or unfavorable 83
    8.6   THE SOURCES FOR IDENTIFYING AND CALCULATING BOOK/TAX DIFFERENCES 84
Source #1 - Unmodified (or "pure") trail balance amounts 84
Source #2 - Modified trial balance (or GL) amounts 85
Source #3 - Special tax calculations 87
Source #4 - Tax credits 88
    8.7   THE RELATIONSHIP BETWEEN BOOK/TAX DIFFERENCES AND TEMPORARY AND PERMANENT DIFFERENCES 89

9   PERMANENT DIFFERENCES AND TAX PROVISION EXAMPLE #2 91
    9.1   LEARNING OBJECTIVES 91
    9.2   PERMANENT DIFFERENCES DEFINED 91
    9.3   FAVORABLE VS. UNFAVORABLE PERMANENT DIFFERENCES 91
    9.4   TAX PROVISION EXAMPLE #2 – PERMANENT DIFFERENCES 91
Updated background and assumptions 92
The trial balance (1600) 92
The tax provision (1000) 93
M-1 calculation summary (1200) 93
Financial statements (5) 93
The effective tax rate ("ETR") reconciliation (5) 94
Permanent differences DO impact the effective tax rate 94

10   TEMPORARY DIFFERENCES AND AN INTRODUCTION TO DEFERRED TAXES 97
    10.1   LEARNING OBJECTIVES 97
    10.2   TEMPORARY DIFFERENCES DEFINED 97
    10.3   AN ILLUSTRATION OF TEMPORARY DIFFERENCES REVERSING OVER TIME 98
    10.4   TEMPORARY DIFFERENCES GIVE RISE TO DEFERRED TAXES 100
GAAP is an accrual-based (vs. a cash basis) concept 100
Tax accounting is an accrual-basis (vs. a cash basis) GAAP concept 101
    10.5   DEFERRED TAXES – AN INTRODUCTION 102
An example of deferred taxes 102

  Year 1 journal entries and observations *103*
  Year 2-5 journal entries and observations *103*
  Other helpful ways to think about deferred tax expenses and liabilities *104*
 10.6 Favorable vs. unfavorable temporary differences 105
  Taxable temporary differences (deferred tax expenses and liabilities) *105*
  Deductible temporary differences (deferred tax benefits and assets) *106*
 10.7 Sources of temporary differences 106
  Timing differences *106*
  Business combinations *106*
  Indefinite differences *106*
 10.8 Temporary differences are measured by book vs. tax basis differences 107
  ASC 740 refers to temporary differences as a balance sheet concept *107*
  Basis and adjusted basis *107*
  Tax vs. book basis – Assets – Accelerated tax expenses *108*
 10.9 Tax basis balance sheets 110
  Book (GAAP) journal entries *111*
  Tax journal entries *112*
  Observations on the book vs. tax income statements *112*
  Observations on the book vs. tax basis balance sheets *113*

11 DEFERRED TAX LIABILITIES/EXPENSES AND DEFERRED TAX ASSETS/BENEFITS............ 115
 11.1 Learning objectives 115
 11.2 Current tax expense/payable vs. current tax benefit/receivable 115
  Current tax expense and taxes payable *115*
  Current tax benefits and taxes receivable *116*
 11.3 Deferred tax expenses/liabilities vs. deferred tax benefits/assets 116
  Deferred tax expenses and deferred tax liabilities *116*
  Deferred tax benefits and deferred tax assets *118*
 11.4 Tax vs. book basis differences with assets and liabilities 119
  Assets – Book basis exceeds tax basis = Deferred tax liability (and expense) *119*
  Assets – Tax basis exceeds book basis = Deferred tax asset (and benefit) *120*
  Liabilities – Book basis exceeds tax basis = Deferred tax asset (and benefit) *121*
  Liabilities – Tax basis exceeds book basis = Deferred tax liability (and expense) *123*
 11.5 Valuation allowances and deferred tax assets 123
 11.6 Parting thoughts on deferred tax assets and benefits 124

12 TAX PROVISION EXAMPLE #3 – TEMPORARY DIFFERENCES AND DEFERRED TAXES.... 127
 12.1 Learning objectives 127
 12.2 Updated background and assumptions 127
  The trial balance (1600) *128*
 12.3 The tax provision (1000) 128
 12.4 Schedule M calculation summary (1200) 129
 12.5 Tax payable/receivable (60) 130
 12.6 Tax journal entry (50) 130
 12.7 Financial statements (5) 131
 12.8 The effective tax rate ("ETR") reconciliation (5) 131
 12.9 Deferred taxes related to timing "normalize" the effective tax rate 132

  12.10 TAX PROVISION EXAMPLE #4 – COMPREHENSIVE EXAMPLE (PERMANENT AND TEMPORARY DIFFERENCES 133

13 AN INTRODUCTION TO STATE INCOME TAXES 135
  13.1 FIRST COMPLETE THE STATE TAX PROVISION (1100) 135
  13.2 THE NEXT STEP IS TO COMPLETE THE FEDERAL TAX PROVISION (1000) 136
  13.3 STATE INCOME TAXES IN THE FINANCIAL STATEMENT FOOTNOTES (5) 138
  13.4 STATE INCOME TAXES IN THE EFFECTIVE TAX RATE RECONCILIATION (5) 138
    The presentation of income taxes in the ETR reconciliation 138
    Understanding the difference between income taxes in the ETR reconciliation and elsewhere in the financial statements 139
    "State taxes net of the federal benefit" 140
  13.5 STATE TAXES AND THE TAXES PAYABLE ON THE BALANCE SHEET (5 AND 60) 140
  13.6 THE USE OF BLENDED TAX RATES 141
    In general 141
    Balancing volume, the related complexity, and materiality 142

14 STATE TAXES – PERMANENT AND TEMPORARY DIFFERENCES 143
  14.1 AN EXAMPLE OF A PERMANENT DIFFERENCE AND STATE TAXES 143
    Current tax provision – State taxes (1100) 143
    Current tax provision – Federal taxes (1000) 144
    Taxes payable rollforward (60) 145
    The financial statement balance sheet (5) 145
    The income tax table in the financial statement footnotes (5) 146
  14.2 STATE TAXES AND THE EFFECTIVE TAX RATE RECONCILIATION 146
    The ETR reconciliation – In general (5) 146
    State taxes and the effective tax rate reconciliation 147
    The rationale for the presentation of state taxes in the financial statements 149
  14.3 A SIMPLE EXAMPLE OF A TEMPORARY DIFFERENCE AND DEFERRED TAXES THAT INCLUDES STATE TAXES 150
    A progressive introduction to temporary differences and state taxes 150
    Pretax book income (5 and 1600) 150
    The current state income tax expense (1100) 151
    The deferred tax calculations for state income taxes (1320) 151
    The current federal income tax expense (1000) 153
    The deferred tax calculations for federal income taxes (1310) 154
    The financial statements and the footnotes (5) 155
    The mistake of netting the tax rate when computing deferred state income taxes 157
  14.4 A MORE REALISTIC EXAMPLE OF A TEMPORARY DIFFERENCE AND DEFERRED TAXES THAT INCLUDES STATE TAXES 159
    The company has pretax book income and a tax expense 159
    The current state income tax expense (1100) 159
    The current federal income tax expense (1000) 160
    The deferred tax calculations for state income taxes (1320) 161
    The deferred tax calculations for federal income taxes (1310) 161
    The income tax table in the financial statements (5) 161
    The taxes payable rollforward (60) 162

The tax adjusting journal entry ("tax AJE") (50) 163
The effective tax rate reconciliation (5) 164
    14.5   APPENDIX 5 – COMBINING PERMANENT DIFFERENCES, TEMPORARY DIFFERENCES AND STATE TAXES 165

A significant milestone 165

15 CONCLUSION 167
    15.1   FEEDBACK AND CORRECTIONS 167
    15.2   RECEIVE NOTIFICATIONS FOR FUTURE BOOKS, CPE SEMINARS AND WEBINARS 167

16 APPENDIX – EXAMPLE #1 – A BASIC TAX PROVISION WORKPAPER PACKAGE 169

17 APPENDIX – EXAMPLE #2 – PERMANENT DIFFERENCES 181

18 APPENDIX – EXAMPLE #3 – TEMPORARY DIFFERENCES & DEFERRED TAXES 193

19 APPENDIX – EXAMPLE #4 – PERMANENT AND TEMPORARY DIFFERENCES 207

20 APPENDIX – EXAMPLE #5 – COMPREHENSIVE EXAMPLE – PERMANENT AND TEMPORARY DIFFERENCES PLUS STATE TAXES 221

1 Preliminary Matters

1.1 About the author

Trent Green is an author, continuing professional education (CPE) developer, instructor, conference speaker, and Fortune 500 corporate tax contractor and consultant through his company, Tax Director Services (www.nctaxdirector.com).

Before starting Tax Director Services, Trent was the Head of Tax for PROS, a $160M publicly traded company. Before joining PROS, he was a Tax Director with PwC. Before joining PwC, Trent was the Head of International Tax for SAS, a $2.7 billion multinational corporation operating in more than 50 countries.

Trent began his career in public accounting with Coopers & Lybrand (PwC) working on a variety of corporate, partnership, and individual income tax issues. He has a Bachelor of Arts, a Business Minor, and Master of Accounting degrees from UNC-Chapel Hill. Trent has taught CPE and presented at conferences since 2009, and in 2016 he received a "5.0 Speaker Award" from the North Carolina Association of CPAs. Finally, Trent has extensive experience working with youth through The Church of Jesus Christ of Latter-day Saints, coaching baseball, and community service. He lives with his family in Apex, North Carolina.

Trent's full professional profile is at linkedin.com/in/trentgreen.

1.2 Review and editing

The author would like to thank Thomas Klein, a Distinguished Teaching Professor at the University of Arizona, and his students for their review of certain material contained in this guide. Mr. Klein is the managing member of Thomas D Klein CPA PLLC, an accounting firm specializing in the preparation of tax provisions for private and public companies. His full professional profile can be found at linkedin.com/in/thomaskleincpa.

1.3 Other books and CPE courses by the author

"Alteryx™ for Accounting, Tax and Finance Professionals."

Dealing with massive amounts of messy data as part of Microsoft Excel™ calculations has traditionally been an enormously labor-intensive and time-consuming challenge for accounting, tax and finance professionals. This book explains how Alteryx™ can be used to address these challenges in a progressive, fully illustrated manner.

- Learn how to import data from Excel and other sources into Alteryx using the Input Data tool.

- Develop Alteryx "workflows" to quickly and systemically organize, format, cleanse and analyze large amounts of data using tools such as Select Records, Dynamic Rename, Select, Filter, Unique, Text to Columns, DateTime and several others.
- Cleanly and accurately combine separate datasets using the Join and Union Tools.
- Learn advanced techniques for manipulating data presented in rows and columns using the CrossTab and Transpose tools.
- Use the Summarize tool to perform calculations and to aggregate data in rows.
- Export data that you've cleaned and organized to Excel using the Output Data tool for further computations and analysis.
- Review methods and techniques for taking advantage of the speed and power of Alteryx while simultaneously strengthening internal controls.

All of the material presented in this book is explained in the context of financial and other examples that matter to accounting, tax and finance professionals. If you've been searching for a better, faster and more accurate way to organize large amounts of data that feed into and support complex Excel calculations, this is the guide you've been looking for.

Additional information

See www.nctaxdirector.com/cpe-courses for additional information and updates on Trent's publications, CPE courses, and YouTube training videos.

1.4   Copyright information

No part of this material has been authorized for free download, transmission, or any form of copying (paper or electronic) by professionals, firms, students, or any other person or organization. Further, this material may not be used to teach continuing or professional education courses without the express written permission of the author. In plain English, I'm happy to share with you what I know about Alteryx through this book, I just ask that you pay the list price for the book in exchange.

1.5   Trademarked terms

All references to "Excel" refer to Microsoft Excel™, a software product created and maintained by Microsoft Corporation.

1.6   Legal disclaimer

This material is sold with the understanding that the author is not engaged in the rendering of accounting, tax, legal, or other professional services or advice through its publication. Numerous simplifying assumptions have been made in this material (and in the accompanying examples) in an effort to more clearly illustrate complex tax accounting topics and concepts. As a result, this material should not be applied to a company's specific financial data, facts and circumstances without more in-depth analysis of tax laws, regulations and U.S. GAAP. This material is not intended to be used or relied upon by any person or entity, nor can it be, for the purposes of avoiding tax penalties.

1.7 NASBA compliant tax accounting and other CPE

If you would like to enroll in NASBA compliant CPE webcasts:

- Sign up to my mailing list on my website's homepage at nctaxdirector.com for announcements and
- See my courses page at nctaxdirector.com/cpe-courses.

1.8 Updates from Edition 1.0

The main updates from edition 1.0 to edition 2.0 are as follows.

- Sentence clarifications and grammatical corrections.
- Chapter 14 – An Introduction to State Income Taxes.
- Chapter 15 – State Taxes – Permanent and Temporary Differences.
- Appendix 5 – A comprehensive example of a provision with permanent and differences that includes the impact of state taxes.

In summary, prior to this edition, a simplified federal and state blended rate was used as the basis for examples and explanations in the text. This edition builds on those concepts by explaining through commentary, illustrations, journal entries, and a comprehensive example in the appendix how state taxes work in tax provision calculations. These additions related to state taxes are important because they complete the foundation you need to understand and apply more advanced tax accounting concepts.

2 An Introduction to Tax Provision Workpapers

Before proceeding with more in-depth explanations of tax provision concepts, we will first review a basic set of tax provision workpapers which will be referred to as "Example #1." This will provide context to information that is presented later in the material.

The full set of all Example #1 tax provision workpapers is found in the Appendix at the back of the material starting on page 169. Various sections in this chapter refer to these workpapers. For example, "Financial Statements (5)" means the financial statements of the company can be found in Example #1, workpaper #5, and so on.

2.1 Learning objectives

- Become familiar with foundational tax provision concepts and workpapers in the context of financial statements.

2.2 Tax provision Example #1 - Background and assumptions

The company background and the assumptions that form the basis of the tax provision calculation for Example #1 are as follows.

- This is the company's first year of operations ("Year 1").
- The company was started on January 1 with $1,000,000 of capital.
- This is a stand-alone U.S. C corporation with no domestic or foreign subsidiaries.
- While the company has elected the accrual method of accounting, except for income taxes, all revenue has been collected, and all expenses have been paid in cash.
- This company's Year 1 annual financial statements were released sometime in February of Year 2.
- The company will file its annual tax return for Year 1 in October of Year 2.[1]
- The total tax expense (or provision) in Example #1 is only comprised of current taxes; there are no deferred taxes (the meaning of current and deferred taxes will be explained in detail later in the material).
- Related to the previous point, the current taxes calculated in the tax provision represent the estimate in the company's financial statements (issued in February

---

[1] The due date for IRS Form 1120 (a corporate tax return) is October 15th for a calendar year corporation.

of Year 2) of the company's Year 1 tax liability. In other words, the company expects to settle its Year 1 tax liability in cash when it files its tax return on October 15 of Year 2.[2]

- In this example, state taxes are not shown separately. When you see the term "federal tax," it includes state taxes. The combined federal and state tax rate of the company is 25%.
- There is no "other comprehensive income" in this example; all income and expenses are part of continuing operations.

With this outline of the company's legal form and operations, we are now ready to review the tax provision workpapers of Example #1, as well as make observations that will help bring tax accounting issues more into focus as we progress through the material.

2.3 Financial statements (5)

We will start our review of Example #1 with the financial statements, beginning with the balance sheet.

Balance sheet

- An important convention used throughout this book is that hard coded figures are unshaded and calculated figures (or those pulling from elsewhere) are shaded yellow.[3]
- The balance sheet is in balance; assets are equal to liabilities and shareholder equity ($1,125,000). All other non-tax-related assets and liabilities are grouped together as "Other Assets" and "Other Liabilities."[4]
- There is a taxes payable liability of $31,250 on the balance sheet.

Consolidated Balance Sheet	Amounts
Other Assets (this includes all non-tax-related assets)	$1,125,000
Deferred Tax Asset - Federal	$0
Total Assets	$1,125,000
Liability - Tax Payable - Federal	$31,250
Other Liabilities (this includes all non-tax-related liabiilities)	$0
Equity - Common Stock & APIC	$1,000,000
Equity - Retained Earnings	$93,750
Total Liabilities & Stockholders' Equity	$1,125,000

---

[2] In practice, it's highly unlikely this would be the case. The company would normally pay estimated taxes in Year 1, an extension payment in April of Year 2 to true-up any tax balance due, meaning there may be little to no cash payment needed upon the filing of the tax return in Year 2. However, as previously noted, there are numerous simplifying assumptions in this material designed to make the tax provision concepts clear.

[3] That being the case, you can see that all figures on the balance sheet (all in all parts of the financial statements) are computed elsewhere in workpapers that will be presented in more detail as we progress through the example.

[4] This grouping of non-tax related asset and liability accounts is a simplification to make it easier to focus on tax accounting issues without dealing with extra "noise." A similar convention is used throughout the workpapers.

- Retained earnings of $93,750 ties to the rollforward at the bottom of workpaper 5 in the Appendix.

Income statement

- Pretax book income ("PTBI"), or income before tax ("IBT"), is $125,000; it's formally referred to in the financial statements as "Income/(Loss) Before Income Tax Provision."
- The total income tax expense (or "provision") of the company is $31,250.
- As noted in the assumptions above, there is no "Other Comprehensive Income;" all income and expenses are part of continuing operations.

Consolidated Statement of Comprehensive Income/(Loss)

Revenue	$340,000
Expenses (Pretax)	($215,000)
Income/(Loss) Before Income Tax Provision	$125,000
Income Tax (Provision)/Benefit	($31,250)
Net Income	$93,750
	In Balance
Other Comprehensive Income	$0
Comprehensive Income/(Loss)	$93,750

Income taxes footnote

Following are observations on the income taxes footnote (which would be one of many of the company's footnotes in the financial statements).

- The total tax expense is comprised of $31,250 in current taxes; there are no deferred taxes (see the illustration below).
- The company's income tax expense of $31,250 is what we would expect based on the following reasoning:
    - $31,250 is equal to 25% of pretax book income ($125,000 x 25%).
    - The company's effective tax rate of 25% is equal to the statutory tax rate of 25% (as noted in the assumptions).

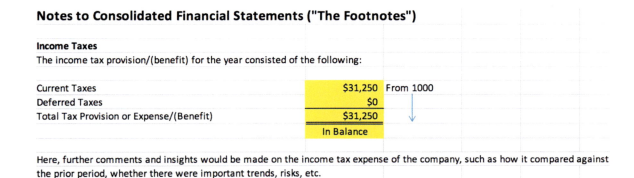

Notes to Consolidated Financial Statements ("The Footnotes")

Income Taxes
The income tax provision/(benefit) for the year consisted of the following:

Current Taxes	$31,250	From 1000
Deferred Taxes	$0	
Total Tax Provision or Expense/(Benefit)	$31,250	
	In Balance	

Here, further comments and insights would be made on the income tax expense of the company, such as how it compared against the prior period, whether there were important trends, risks, etc.

2.4 The proof of pretax book income (1600, 1000 and 5)

Pretax book income ("PTBI") is the starting point of the tax provision calculation. Therefore, it's critical to ensure that PTBI is the same (or "ties") in the following sections of the Example #1 workpapers.

- The trial balance (workpaper 1600) – See the "Pretax Book Income Calculation" at the top of page 2 of 2 of workpaper 1600. Here PTBI is proven by using two different methods which we'll refer to as Option 1 and Option 2 (these will be discussed in more detail later on).
- The tax provision calculation (workpaper 1000) – PTBI of $125,000 is the starting point of the tax provision calculation at the top of workpaper.
- The financial statements (workpaper 5) – "Income/(Loss) Before Income Tax Provision" is $125,000.

Again, pretax book income should be the same for all of the above, and the one that's the most important is the last bullet. In other words, it's *crucial* that PTBI per the financial statements ties to the tax provision calculation (workpaper 1000) and all other applicable tax provision workpapers.

2.5 The total tax expense (or "provision") calculation (1000)

Having confirmed the correct starting point of the tax provision (PTBI of $125,000), we can move on to reviewing the tax provision calculation itself for Example #1 (see the illustration).

Pretax Book Income	$125,000
Permanent Differences	
Permanent Difference - GL-related Items - Revenue	$0
Permanent Difference - GL-related Items - Expenses	$0
Permanent Difference - Special Tax Calculation	$0
Temporary Differences	
Temporary Difference - GL-related Items	$0
Temporary Difference - Depreciation	$0
Tax Return Calculations	
Subtotal: Pre-NOL Federal Taxable Income	$125,000
Times: Federal Tax Rate	25.00%
Subtotal: Federal Tax Before Credits	$31,250

- Pretax book income of $125,000 for GAAP purposes is equal to taxable income of $125,000. In other words, there are no book/tax differences (also referred to as "Schedule M's,").
- Taxable income of $125,000 is multiplied by the statutory rate of 25% resulting in a current tax expense of $31,250. (Recall for purposes of this example that the "Federal Tax Rate" of 25% includes state income taxes).

- In this example, we will assume the current tax expense is the amount of *cash tax* the company expects to owe when it files its tax return for Year 1 (which must be by October of Year 2).
- There are no deferred taxes in this tax provision (the concept of deferred taxes will be covered in later chapters). As a result, the $31,250 total tax expense of the company is equal to the current tax of $31,250.

2.6 The effective tax rate reconciliation (5 and 1000)

Once you understand a company's tax calculation, your next question should be, "Is the tax expense (or provision) of the company in line with what I would expect based on the statutory (tax) rate?" This question is answered by the Effective Tax Rate (or "ETR") reconciliation in the financial statement footnotes as shown in the following illustration.

Description	Dollar	Rate
Expected Tax Provision/(Benefit) at the Statutory Tax Rate	$31,250	25.00%
Nondeductible Meals	$0	0.00%
Income Tax Provision/(Benefit)	$31,250	25.00%

Note that this reconciliation is shown in both dollar and percentage terms. Further interpreting our example, it shows that the *expected tax* of the company is $31,250 ($125,000 of PTBI times 25%) and the *expected tax rate* is equal to the statutory rate of 25%. It's also noteworthy to mention that because there is no difference between GAAP and taxable income in Example #1, the *actual* tax provision and ETR of the company, $31,250 and 25% respectively, are equal to the *expected* amounts. This is practically unheard of in practice, but it's a good starting point to gain an intuitive understanding of tax provisions before we move on to more complex examples.

The first line of the tax provision workpaper at 1000 (shown below) is the source of the expected amounts in the ETR reconciliation.

	Tax Provision Current Year	Dollar Amt. Current Year	ETR Current Year
Pretax Book Income	$125,000	$31,250	25.00%

- Here we can see that the "expected tax" on pretax book income of $125,000 is $31,250 (or $125,000 of PTBI times the 25% statutory rate).
- As noted above, in percentage terms you can see that the "expected tax rate" of the company is equal to the statutory rate of 25% ($31,250 divided by $125,000).

2.7 Tax adjusting journal entries (50 and 1600)

The tax provision is an important part of supporting the figures in a company's financial statements. However, the tax provision calculation (referring to workpaper 1000) does not by itself adjust the company's general ledger ("GL") accounts to what they need to be to close the books and finalize the financial statements.[5] For this, refer to workpaper 50, the "Tax Journal Entry Summary" (see the illustration).

Account Description	Opening Balance From 1600[1]	Calculated Balance "Plug"[2]	Adjusting (Tax) Journal Entry Carries to 1600[3]
Liability - Tax Payable - Federal	$0	($31,250)	($31,250)
Liability - Tax Payable - State	$0	$0	$0
Liability - Deferred Tax Liability - Federal or State	$0	$0	$0
Expense - Income Tax - Federal - Current Exp./(Ben.)	$0	$31,250	$31,250
Expense - Income Tax - State - Current Exp./(Ben.)	$0	$0	$0
Expense - Income Tax - Federal or State - Deferreded Exp/(Ben)	$0	$0	$0
Totals / Check Figure (should be zero)			$0

- The above excerpt from workpaper 50 shows what the tax-related accounts were on GL before the tax provision process ("Opening Balance"), what they should be at the end (the "Calculated Balance"), and the "Adjusting Entry" needed to get there (debits are positive and credits are negative).
- Note that the tax adjusting journal entry ("AJE") is in balance; it foots to zero because total debits (positive) are equal to total credits (negative).

Now refer to the tax-related accounts on the company's trial balance at workpaper 1600 (see a condensed version in the next illustration that follows).

- The figures in the "Unadjusted Opening Trial Balance" were provided by the Accounting Group to the Tax Group in order to calculate the company's total tax expense (or tax provision). As far as tax-related accounts are concerned:
    - The opening taxes payable liability was zero.
    - The opening income tax expense was also zero.
- The "Tax Adjusting Entries" in the middle column come from the "Tax Journal Entry Summary" at workpaper 50. These are the amounts needed to adjust the tax accounts on the GL to what they need to be in the "Closing Trial Balance" column on the far right.
    - The ending tax payable needs to equal $31,250 tax payable.

---

[5] The general ledger (GL) is the base level of an accounting system, and it is where accounting entries are booked. In practice, you might hear the term, "That figure ties back to the GL," referring to a trial balance account or a number from the financial statements.

- o The ending income tax expense also needs to equal $31,250.
- The adjusted (or final) trial balance is the source of the figures on the financial statements on workpaper 5, including the income tax expense of $31,250 and the tax payable of $31,250.
  - o This is a very important point – the final trial balance supports the financial statements, and tax provision workpapers support the tax-related figures in the final trial balance (and the financial statements!).

Account Description	Unadjusted Opening Trial Balance	Tax Adjusting Entries	Closing (or "Final") Trial Balance
Liability - Tax Payable - Federal	$0	($31,250)	($31,250)
Expense - Income Tax - Federal - Current Exp./(Ben.)	$0	$31,250	$31,250
Check Figure (should be zero)	$0	$0	$0

3 Tax Accounting vs. Tax Compliance Concepts

Now that we have reviewed some of the core workpapers that make up a tax provision, we will now cover some important tax accounting concepts.

3.1 Learning objectives

- Learn key tax accounting terms and how to understand and discuss them in practice.
- Get introduced to the concept of deferred taxes as part of the concepts of the total tax expense of a company.
- Be able to differentiate between above-the-line and below-the-line taxes.

3.2 Tax compliance defined

To know what "tax accounting" means, it's first important to understand the concept of "tax compliance." The tax compliance process can be summarized in these steps.

1) Analyzing the GAAP (or "book") financial information of a company (e.g. the trial balance workpaper 1600 in Example #1).
2) Converting GAAP income to taxable income based on the rules of the Internal Revenue Code and the accompanying IRS-authored Treasury regulations.[6]
3) Computing taxable income, typically on IRS Form 1120 (along with any other required forms, elections and disclosures) and
4) Filing these forms with the IRS and paying any applicable tax.[7]

From an accounting point of view, tax compliance can be thought of as a cash basis method of accounting, i.e., it tells you how much tax you owe with your tax return based on your taxable income.

3.3 Tax accounting defined

The tax accounting rules for US GAAP are found in the FASB Accounting Standards Codification in the section, "ASC 740 – Income Taxes."[8] All income tax-related expenses, benefits, assets, and liabilities recorded in the general ledger of a company and

---

[6] Said another way, GAAP financial data (income and balance sheet items) is the starting point for determining taxable income.
[7] While the above explanation is in the context of filing U.S. federal tax returns with the IRS, the same concepts apply to filing state and foreign income tax returns.
[8] These rules were previously known as "FAS 109," and it's possible that you may still hear that term used in practice.

reported in its financial statements must be materially correct and calculated according to the rules of ASC 740 to be in conformity with US GAAP.

Unlike tax compliance, which focuses on how much *cash tax* a company owes for a given year, tax accounting is a more expansive accrual-basis GAAP concept. In other words, tax accounting is not only concerned with how much tax a company will owe with its tax return for the current period's financial activity ("current taxes"), but also how much tax it will owe in the *future* based on the same period's financial activity ("deferred taxes").

As a theoretical example of a more straightforward expense, let's say that in Year 1 a company signs a legally binding contract to purchase supplies of 100. However, during Year 1 the company only pays for 70 of the supplies. Because GAAP is an accrual-based concept, the Year 1 expense for supplies is 100. This is because GAAP not only measures how much cash was paid for supplies in Year 1 (70), but how much the company is legally obligated to pay for supplies in Year 2 and beyond (30) based on its Year 1 activities (i.e. the signing of the contract which gave rise to the 100 of expense happened in Year 1).

Accounting for income taxes follows a similar pattern. Let's say, for example, that a company generates income in Year 1 that will result in a tax expense of 100. However, because the income is tax-favored, only 70 of tax will be due with the Year 1 tax return and the remaining 30 of tax will be payable in the future. For GAAP, the tax expense will be 100, and it will be broken down as a current tax expense of 70 and a deferred tax expense of 30. Thus, even though 30 of the tax will be paid in Year 2 or later, it is counted as a Year 1 expense because that is the period which gave rise to the tax expense. These concepts are illustrated in the table below.

Description	Supplies	Income Taxes
Cash Expense	70 – This portion of the supplies expense equals the cash paid to the vendor in the current period (Year 1).	70 – This is a "current tax expense," or the cash tax due with the Year 1 tax return. If the tax is due but not yet paid there will be a "taxes payable" on the balance sheet.
Accrued Expense	30 – There is an accrued supplies liability for the amount legally owed to the vendor but not yet paid.	30 – There is a "deferred tax expense" to account for the "deferred tax liability" that will be due in the future based on Year 1 activities.
Total GAAP Expense	100	100

As noted in the table above, tax accounting does not just involve calculating tax-related income statement expenses (current and deferred tax expenses); it also has rules to calculate balance sheet items, such as income taxes payable and deferred tax liabilities.[9]

3.4 The total tax expense (or provision) is the sum of current and deferred taxes

One of the main questions the rules of ASC 740 answers is, "What is the tax expense of a company?" As introduced previously, for tax accounting purposes the total income tax expense of a company is comprised of two parts: current taxes *and* deferred taxes. Also, each of the following terms you might hear in practice is synonymous with a company's "total income tax expense."

1) Tax expense
2) Tax provision (or "the provision")
3) Total tax provision
4) Tax accrual
5) Income tax expense
6) Total income tax expense

The term "tax benefit" can also mean "tax provision" in the sense that a company might record *income* from taxes, meaning they are recording a tax refund due (or a negative expense) rather than a tax expense for the period.[10]

Because of the many different things that "tax expense" can mean, it can be helpful to take a step back and clarify what is being asked or discussed. For example, if someone from the Accounting Group asks in a meeting, "What was our tax for the year?" an appropriate response to clarify might be, "Are you referring to the tax we owed with the tax return or are you referring to the GAAP tax expense for the year?"

3.5 The tax provision vs. the tax provision workpapers

Suppose someone asks, "Where is the tax provision?" In this context, "the tax provision" refers to the workpaper package used to calculate and support the total income tax expense of the company. These workpapers most often reside in Excel or tax accounting software but, in a broader sense, the tax provision workpapers also include all of the research, memos, emails, and other documents used to support the total tax expense of a company as reported in the financial statements.

---

[9] The accrual-basis aspects of tax accounting are expanded on more fully starting at page 101, "Tax accounting is an accrual-basis (vs. a cash basis) GAAP concept."

[10] For more clarification on this point, along with an example, see page 116 under the heading, "Current tax benefits and taxes receivable."

3.6 Income taxes vs. non-income taxes

Non-income tax items such as sales taxes, property taxes, and value-added taxes (VAT) are outside the scope of ASC 740. In other words, the total tax expense of a company per GAAP financial statements does *not* include taxes related to any of these items.

In this context, it's also helpful to understand the concept of "above the line" and "below the line" tax expenses. Consider the following example:

Description	Amount	Explanation
Sales	1,000	
Property Taxes	(100)	"Above the line" taxes - outside the scope of ASC 740
Subtotal: Pretax Book Income	900	
Total Tax Provision	(225)	"Below the line" taxes calculated pursuant to ASC 740
Net Income from Operations	675	

As shown in the illustration, property taxes of 100 are an "above the line" tax expense for financial statement purposes because they factor into the calculation of pretax book income. This is important because above the line expenses are part of EBITDA,[11] which is a metric often followed by financial analysts and senior management. Income taxes of 225 are considered a below the line expense, meaning they factor into net income from operations, but not pretax book income.

---

[11] "EBITDA" stands for "earnings before income taxes, depreciation, and amortization."

4 The Main Purposes of the Tax Provision

4.1 Learning objectives

- Name the four main purposes of a tax provision workpaper package.

4.2 Key elements of a public accounting firm's financial statement opinion

To understand the main purposes of the tax provision it's helpful to review the key assertions an accounting firm makes when auditing a company's financial statements:[12]

- "In our opinion, the consolidated financial statements…present fairly, in all material respects, the financial position of [Company X]…in conformity with accounting principles generally accepted in the United States of America (i.e. U.S. GAAP)."
- "It is also in our opinion that [Company X] maintained, in all material respects, effective internal control over financial reporting…"

In summary, an audit firm attests to the following:

1) A company's financial statements are <u>materially correct</u>.
2) The financial statements are reported in accordance with <u>U.S. GAAP</u> and
3) The company maintains sufficiently effective <u>internal controls</u> so that potential material misstatements can be detected and avoided.

4.3 The four main purposes of a tax provision workpaper package

The four main goals or purposes of a tax provision workpaper package in order of importance are as follows:

---

[12] These assertions above assume that the accounting firm is issuing a "clean opinion," i.e. there is no going concern issue, there are no material misstatements or material weaknesses in the control environment, and so on.

1) *To support the tax-related figures and explanations in the company's financial statements* (or Form 10-K[13]), the footnote disclosures, and any related management discussion and analysis.
2) To calculate the tax journal entries necessary to close the books on an accounting period. In other words, the tax provision workpapers compute and support the "tax entry" that's provided to the company's Accounting Group (think of the middle column of workpaper 50 in Example #1).
3) To follow and document a sound process while completing items #1 and #2 that meets internal controls (or "SOX")[14] requirements.[15]
4) To complete all of the above accurately and on time so that the financial statements can be issued on schedule with no tax-related material misstatements (accuracy) or material weaknesses (SOX control deficiencies).

4.4 What are NOT the main purposes of a tax provision?

While the following items are important parts of the tax provision preparation process, *by themselves* they are inadequate, incomplete, and do NOT fulfill the main purposes of a tax provision workpaper package as outlined in the previous section.

1) Calculating the tax provision – While determining the tax provision of a company is significant (e.g. the $31,250 tax expense computation per workpaper 1000 in Example #1), the Tax Group is responsible for *much more* than just calculating the total tax expense of a company. For example, the Tax Group also needs to compute balance sheet information such as taxes payable.
2) Calculating the effective tax rate ("ETR") – There is no question that a company's ETR is an important metric. However, the tax provision workpapers also need to support the *reasoning* behind effective tax rate. In other words, the Tax Group

---

[13] For a public company, the financial statements are often referred to as "the 10-K." A Form 10-K is an annual report a company must prepare as required by the U.S. Securities and Exchange Commission ("SEC"), and its purpose is to provide a comprehensive summary of a company's financial performance for a given period (typically one year).

[14] "SOX" refers to The Sarbanes-Oxley Act. This law was passed by Congress in 2002 to protect investors of publicly traded companies by, among other things, setting forth standards designed to improve financial reporting disclosures and to strengthen internal controls.

[15] For internal controls, remember that it's the *process* and supporting *documentation* that is being tested by auditors, not just the mathematical outcome of a calculation or its level of materiality. Said another way, the tax provision you compute and report in your financial statements may be materially correct, but if your method for getting there is flawed and your workpapers are a disaster then you could still get hit with a material weakness finding by your financial statement auditors. Why? Because your process was so flawed that it *could have* resulted in a material weakness.

needs to explain *what* specific items drive the ETR higher or lower than the statutory rate, as well as *why* that is the case. In addition, the Tax Group must compute and explain numerous other tax-related figures that appear in the financial statements.

3) To produce a "clean workpaper package" – The GAAP financial statements are the end-product, <u>not</u> the tax provision workpapers (no matter how well-organized and put together they are). In other words, having clean tax provision workpapers without thinking about how they support specific figures in the financial statements would be like preparing tax return calculations in spreadsheets without considering how those figures would be reported on specific forms for the tax return filing.

5 Relationships Between the Tax Provision and Other Tax Concepts

With an understanding of core relationships between the tax provision and tax compliance, as well as the main purposes of the tax provision, we will now explore the relationship between a company's tax provision and other tax concepts.

5.1 Learning objectives

- Know the difference between tax provision and tax return timing.
- Understand the basics of the return to provision (or "RTP") process.
- Recognize the following relationships:
  - The current tax per the financial statements and the tax liability per the tax return.
  - A W-2 for individual income tax purposes and an unadjusted trial balance for tax provision purposes.
  - Estimated taxes, tax accrual, and the total tax (or provision).
- Learn why it's important to start the tax provision process as soon as possible, as well as different ways this is done in practice.

5.2 The difference between tax provision and tax return timing

What is the difference between tax provision and tax return timing? Here is what it might look like for a typical company with a December 31st (or calendar) year-end.

- The financial statements of the company will be filed in mid to late February or early March (sometime in the first quarter following its year-end).
- The tax provision is prepared as part of the year-end closing process to calculate and support the tax-related figures reported in the financial statements.
- The company will likely file a tax return extension in April with plans to complete and file its tax return by late summer or early fall, but no later than the October 15th extended due date.[16]

---

[16] As a practical matter, those preparing state tax returns will want the federal return done before the due date. For example, if a company has to file in 25 states, the SALT (or "State and Local Tax") Team may want the federal return completed by September 15th (or earlier) so there is a sufficient amount of time to do the state filings.

In summary, as part of the tax provision process in late January and early February, the Tax Group will (among other things) estimate the tax they will report on the company's tax return later in the year (October).

5.3 The Return to Provision (or "RTP") process

The return to provision ("RTP") process is "truing up" the company's tax liability from what it was estimated to be at the tax provision (e.g. in February) as opposed to what it turned out to be upon the filing of the tax return (e.g. in October).[17]

For example, using reasonable estimates based on the information that was available at year-end, you estimated the company's total tax expense to be 100 for financial statement purposes.[18] However, later in the year when you do all the calculations and other work necessary to prepare the company's tax return, you determine the actual tax liability to be 103. If that's the case, in the quarter the tax return is filed, you would make the following RTP adjusting entry:

Current Tax Expense   3
   Tax Payable   3[19]

Ideally, RTP entries are small and considered "changes in estimate" rather than "errors." In other words, in the example above, a true-up adjustment of 3 is likely small enough for senior management and your financial statement auditors to accept and move on. However, if the RTP entry were 30 rather than 3, it suggests that the tax expense reported in the year-end financial statements may have been materially misstated, and that could result in a difficult conversation with your auditors about what happens next.[20]

5.4 The relationship between the current tax expense (per the financial statements) and taxes per the tax return

Earlier, we defined the total tax expense (or provision) of a company as the sum of current and deferred taxes. Assume that a company's tax provision breaks down as follows:

---

[17] This can also be referred to as the return to accrual (or "RTA") process.
[18] For purposes of this example, we are assuming the company's tax return liability (i.e. "current tax") is the only component of its total tax expense.
[19] The entry is 3 and not 103 because 100 of tax expense had already been booked as part of the year-end close. Thus, only a true-up of 3 is needed to bring the previously estimated tax expense of 100 to its actual balance of 103.
[20] See page 61 for further details on the implications of a large RTP adjustment under the heading, "Tax provision errors can result in a restatement of the financial statements."

Current Tax Expense	1,000
Deferred Tax Expense	300
Total Tax Expense	1,300

The company's expected tax return liability for the year at the time the financial statements were issued is embedded in the current taxes figure of 1,000. Note that the 1,000 does not *only* consist of a company's expected cash tax liability per the tax return, because other items can also be classified as current taxes.[21] Generally speaking however, a company's current tax expense is mostly comprised of a company's tax return-related liabilities (i.e. the cash tax).

5.5 The relationship between a W-2 and a tax return

To better understand tax provision concepts, it can also be helpful to relate them to individual income tax concepts. For example, on an individual level, just because you've received your W-2, 1099's for interest and dividends, mortgage interest statement, and your charitable contribution "thank you" letters does not mean you automatically know your tax liability for the year. You still have to do the work of using this information to complete Form 1040 and related forms to determine whether you have a tax refund or a balance due, and that can be a time-consuming and involved process depending on the complexity of your situation.

5.6 The relationship between the unadjusted trial balance and the tax provision

As with individual income tax, The Tax Group of a corporation must have information about the income and expenses of a company to prepare the tax provision (and, later, the company's tax return). Thus, your starting point is to obtain a "preliminary" (or unadjusted) trial balance from the Accounting Group. This trial balance is an organized record of all the income, expenses, assets, and liabilities of a company that have been finalized *except* for income tax-related items (which is why it's a "preliminary" or "unadjusted" trial balance).

Using the unadjusted trial balance (and other information), it's your job (assuming you are a member of the Tax Group) to prepare the tax provision. As part of this process, you will generate the tax entry necessary to close the books, thus finalizing the company's trial balance (which will be used to construct the financial statements). Finally, just as you keep your W-2's and other supporting information on file in the event of an IRS

---

[21] Tax contingencies, which are not covered in this introductory material, are one example of another item that is classified as part of current (as opposed to deferred) taxes.

audit of your personal tax return, you will use your tax provision workpaper package as evidence to support all of the tax-related figures and assertions in the company's financial statements.

5.7 Tax withholdings, estimated taxes, and tax expense accruals are NOT the same as the total tax expense (or provision)

Individual estimated income taxes

In theory, as an individual you are supposed to project your total tax at the beginning of a given year (i.e. compute an "individual tax provision"). You are then supposed to set your Year 1 withholdings using federal Form W-4 (and the state equivalent) to have taxes withheld over the course of the year that equal exactly what you expect to owe in total. Thus, when you file your Form 1040 (and state return) for Year 1 by April 15th of Year 2, the amount of tax you compute on your return should (ideally/theoretically) be exactly equal to your withholdings, meaning you will neither owe tax nor get a refund.

Corporate estimated income taxes

Relating this to a corporation, assume in January-February of Year 1 you project that your cash tax due for the year will be 1,200. If that is the case, you should make quarterly estimated tax payments during Year 1 of 300. Thus, when you file the corporate tax return for Year 1 in October of Year 2, it will show that your tax for the year is 1,200 (assuming your projection was perfectly accurate). However, that tax will be fully offset by the 1,200 paid during Year 1 (300 in estimated tax payments x 4 quarters). As a result, when you file the corporate return, the company will neither owe tax nor be due a refund.

The relationship between estimated taxes and tax expense

Obviously, the scenarios outlined above rarely work perfectly in practice. An individual or corporation's income tax is almost always higher or lower than the amount they project through withholdings or estimated tax payments (sometimes significantly so). Thus, while it is certainly important to take estimated tax payments into account when determining your income tax refund or balance due, your *tax withholdings (300 x 4 = 1,200) during the year have NO bearing on the calculation of your total tax.*

Similarly, when you look at a company's unadjusted trial balance, it may show that income tax has already been accrued during the year as current and/or deferred taxes. However, whatever the company has (or has not) accrued for taxes to date bears no impact on the overall tax provision (or total tax expense) of the company. The tax accrued to date does, however, impact how much additional tax expense you will need to accrue in the current period to adjust it to the correct amount.

An example

That was a lot of English. Let's look at some math and journal entries to illustrate the relationship between a company's estimated taxes and its tax expense. As a simplification, assume that a company's cash tax and tax provision are the same (meaning there are no deferred taxes). The company initially projected its Year 1 income tax expense (or provision) to be 800. Thus, prior to the preparation of the Year 1 tax provision at the beginning of Year 2, the company had accrued 800 of tax expense and made estimated tax payments of an equal amount. However, as part of tax provision work at the beginning of Year 2, the company updated its Year 1 tax expense projection to 1,000. Following are the tax journal entries that would be recorded in connection with this fact pattern.

Tax expense accrued during Year 1 prior to the preparation of the tax provision
Tax Expense   800
  Tax Payable   800

Estimated taxes paid in cash during Year 1
Tax Payable   800
  Cash   800

Additional accrual at the tax provision (at the beginning of Year 2, but related to Year 1) to bring the total tax expense to 1,000

Tax Expense   200
  Tax Payable   200

Summary

The point of the example is to show that the amount of tax accrued during Year 1 (800) had no bearing on the total tax expense of the company per the tax provision calculation (1,000); the tax provision calculation was going to be the same (1,000) regardless of how much tax the company did or did not accrue during the year. However, the amount of tax the company expensed during the year (800) did impact how much additional tax needed to be accrued (200) at the tax provision to bring the total tax expense to the correct balance (1,000).

5.8 What if data and information changes in the middle of the tax provision preparation process?

A change to pretax book income will impact the tax provision calculation

If you are preparing an individual's income tax return and their W-2 changes, meaning their salary and wages turn out to be different than what you were expecting, then the tax return will clearly be affected. Likewise, if the Accounting Group changes the trial balance by booking additional entries that impact pretax book income (or balance sheet figures that are "tax sensitive," meaning they are part of tax calculations), it will affect the tax provision calculation as well.

Despite potential trial balance movement, start the tax provision process as soon as possible

If changes by the Accounting Group to the trial balance will affect the tax provision calculation, wouldn't it make sense to wait until the trial balance is "truly final" before starting the tax provision? While that sounds good in theory, it is rarely realistic or advisable in practice. Due to the tax provision process being so involved and complex, there is usually not enough time to wait until the trial balance quits moving to start with the tax provision calculation and the supporting workpapers. This is because once pretax book income is finalized, the last item to fully close the books is normally the tax entry.

Start the tax provision "as soon as possible" with an advanced draft of the unadjusted trial balance

Because of the ordering of the closing process, the Tax Group is almost always under a substantial amount of pressure to finish the tax provision "as soon as possible."[22] As a result, you should start the tax provision process early on by obtaining an advanced draft of the unadjusted trial balance. And while it's true that subsequent changes in the trial balance will cause some additional work, by starting earlier rather than later you can:

1) Get a jump on setting up the tax provision workpapers.[23]
2) Test the tax provision model to ensure that it's working properly.[24]
3) Get a preview of additional data and information you will need to complete the tax provision (something that can be hard to see without getting into the details of the tax provision model).

---

[22] There is diversity in practice on what is considered a realistic timeframe for the Tax Group to provide the tax entry necessary to close the books to the Accounting Group after pretax book income has been finalized. However, expectations such as "just update the spreadsheet", "push a button", or "a day" are too fast and invite errors due to not taking into account all that goes into ensuring that the tax provision calculations are accurate.

[23] The point here is that many workpapers may be manageable on a stand-alone basis in terms of size and complexity, but a key element of the tax provision process is *speed*. Thus, if you save work for crunch time that you could have done earlier, then you're inviting (or at least flirting with) failure.

[24] The complexity (and importance) of this step should not be underestimated, whether you use tax provision software or an Excel-driven process. Trying to get the tax provision model working *after* the books close will *dramatically* increase the difficulty (and pressure) of the tax provision process.

"The Missing Tax Accounting Guide – A Plain English Guide to ASC 740 Tax Provisions"
@ 2022 Tax Director Services, Inc.
All rights reserved

4) Begin the documentation process (researching and writing memos of tax positions, SOX controls support, etc.).

What this looks like in practice

An example of applying these concepts in practice would be completing a draft of the tax provision based on a preliminary trial balance while the Accounting Group is working to close the books. Essentially, the idea is to carry the tax provision calculation all the way to the end as if it were final. This exercise will accomplish each of the steps outlined above, which will allow you to surface unanticipated problems, complexities, and issues so that they can be researched and resolved to the extent possible *before* the finalization of pretax book income. In summary, the further you take the tax provision process before pretax book income is finalized, the faster you will be able to accurately complete the tax provision and produce the entry necessary to close the books.

A "hard close" in advance of the provision

Taking the above concept a step further, some Tax Groups will complete a "hard close" a month or two in advance of year-end tax provision work. For example, a Tax Group might compute their tax provision and the accompanying workpapers based on November as a test to ensure that the tax provision process is in order and they're not "figuring things out" during the crush of live year-end tax provision work.

Is this a lot of work, to essentially have two year-end closes for tax provision purposes? The answer is yes. In theory, eleven months' worth of the work should be done if you do a November hard close, leaving "just December" to do at year-end. In practice, however, even with a hard close, there is still a lot of re-work that goes into computing the year-end tax provision. In addition, a Tax Group will often push off some work to year-end as part of a hard close (SOX documentation, for example, is a likely candidate).

So why make the effort to do a hard close tax provision given that it's not a very efficient approach? The answer is that it's not about efficiency, it's about speed and accuracy. For example, if you implement (or change) your tax provision software during the year, you will want to surface issues early so you have time to address them *before* year-end (vs. during the "real" closing of the books in January). Similarly, if the company's made an acquisition or engaged in a complex transaction, a hard close can be a great way to address those issues early on so you only have "normal issues" to work through at year-end.

6 A Methodical Review of the Tax Provision Preparation Process (Example #1)

Previously, we examined Tax Provision Example #1 ("Example #1") from a reviewer's standpoint, got an overall understanding of the key workpapers, and went over how they related to one another. In this section, we will once again review Example #1, but this time we will do so from a preparer's standpoint, going over how to construct a tax provision workpaper package from the ground up.

6.1 Learning objectives

- Know how to start the tax provision preparation process and how pretax book income fits in.
- Review key tax provision workpaper conventions and why they are important.
- Be able to compute a basic tax provision and how this one component relates to the overall tax provision workpaper package.
- Learn how the tax payable rollforward and the tax adjusting relate to each other, the tax provision, the final trial balance and the financial statements.
- Recognize the work needs to be done after you complete the tax provision workpaper package as part of the preparation of the financial statements.
- Gain insight into how your financial statement auditors think about tax provision workpapers.
- Learn the ramification of making an error in tax provision calculations.

6.2 YouTube Video

I have created a YouTube video that provides an overview of Chapter 6.

- See https://nctaxdirector.com/videos.
- Find the "Tax Accounting" section.
- Click on the link, "An Introduction to ASC 740 Tax Provisions (22:30)."

6.3 A review of company background and assumptions

Before getting back into the details of Example #1, let's once again review the company's background and the assumptions:

- This is the company's first year of operations ("Year 1").
- The company was started on January 1 with $1,000,000 of capital.
- This is a stand-alone U.S. C corporation with no domestic or foreign subsidiaries.
- While the company has elected the accrual method of accounting, except for income taxes, all revenue has been collected, and all expenses have been paid in cash.
- This company's Year 1 annual financial statements were released sometime in February of Year 2.
- The company will file its annual tax return for Year 1 in October of Year 2.
- The total tax expense (or provision) in Example #1 is only comprised of current taxes; there are no deferred taxes (the meaning of current and deferred taxes will be explained in detail later in the material).
- Related to the previous point, the current taxes calculated in the tax provision represent the estimate in the company's financial statements (issued in February of Year 2) of the company's Year 1 tax liability. In other words, the company expects to settle its Year 1 tax liability in cash when it files its tax return on October 15 of Year 2.
- In this example, state taxes are not shown separately. When you see the term "federal tax," it includes state taxes. The combined federal and state tax rate of the company is 25%.
- There is no "other comprehensive income" in this example; all income and expenses are part of continuing operations.

Now that you've been reminded of the company's legal form and operations, the situation is this: Year 1 has ended, it is early to mid-January of Year 2, and you have been tasked with preparing the company's tax provision package.

6.4 Obtain a trial balance from the Accounting Group (1600)

The company's trial balance is the starting point

You cannot do any meaningful work on the tax provision until you have information on the company's income, expenses, assets, and liabilities. With this in mind, your first step is to obtain an unadjusted opening trial balance for Year 1 from the Accounting Group.[25] The financial figures related to this trial balance are in the far-left column on workpaper 1600.

For the purposes of Example #1, you can assume that all income and expense figures in the unadjusted opening trial balance are final EXCEPT for tax-related figures.

---

[25] As noted earlier, if it is not possible to obtain a final trial balance early on, start the tax provision as soon as you can with an advanced draft.

Calculating and supporting the tax-related amounts for the final trial balance is *your job*, and it's one of the main purposes of preparing tax provision workpapers.

Observations from reviewing the trial balance

With the trial balance in hand, let's examine it more closely (see the illustration):

- The trial balance foots to zero (see the "Check Figure" at the bottom), which means that total assets is equal to liabilities plus shareholder's equity. This should *always* be the case, and if it's not then immediately contact the Accounting Group for clarification.
- This trial balance has been kept simple so that it's easier to filter out "noise" and zero in on tax provision issues.

Account Description	Unadjusted Opening Trial Balance
Asset - Cash (after cash income tax payments)	$1,125,000
Asset - Tax Receivable - Federal	$0
Asset - Fixed Assets	$0
Asset - Accumulated Depreciation	$0
Asset - Deferred Tax Asset - Federal	$0
Asset - Other	$0
Liability - Accrued Expenses	$0
Liability - Tax Payable - Federal	$0
Liability - Deferred Tax Liability - Federal	$0
Liability - Other	$0
Equity - Common Stock & APIC	($1,000,000)
Equity - Retained Earnings (beginning of year)	$0
Revenue - Standard	($340,000)
Revenue - Permanent Item	$0
Expense - Standard	$215,000
Expense - Permanent Item	$0
Expense - Temporary Item	$0
Expense - Depreciation - Book	$0
Expense - Income Tax - Federal - Current Exp./(Ben.)	$0
Expense - Income Tax - Federal - Deferred Exp./(Ben.)	$0
Check Figure (should be zero)	$0

6.5 The "why" behind the need for quality tax provision workpaper design and referencing

Key questions workpapers need to answer for a reviewer

Before covering additional specifics of preparing a tax provision, I feel it's important to explain the thought process of a reviewer as they look at any tax provision workpaper. They will ask themselves questions such as the following:

1) *What is the workpaper that I'm looking at telling me, and why is it part of the tax provision package?*
2) *There are a lot of figures and information on this workpaper, so:*
   a. *What key figure(s) is it calculating, or what numbers should I be paying attention to?*
   b. *What other information in this workpaper is important, and why?*
3) *How do the figures and information in this workpaper tie back to the overall tax provision calculation?*

To answer these reviewer questions quickly and efficiently, a preparer needs to thoughtfully assemble and reference workpapers in a manner that's clear, organized, logical, methodical, and consistent.

Comments to preparer's on workpaper design and referencing

Some preparers take pride in their work and design great, well-referenced workpapers, while others seem to lack such skill and commitment. Here are a few reasons that drive the differences between these two groups of people:

1) Laziness/sloppiness – Let's be frank: in addition to taking time, creating good, thorough, well-conceived, and well-referenced workpapers takes thought, diligence, concentration, and attention to detail. Unfortunately, some preparers aim to do the minimum amount of work possible, and they will not put forth the effort to create good workpapers unless it's practically forced on them.
2) Shifting responsibility – Sometimes preparers cut corners in creating and referencing workpapers to meet their own individual budgets and timelines, but by doing so they make it harder for reviewers to meet their own. For example, assume that an Analyst has 40 hours to prepare a tax provision and a Manager has 15 hours to review the work. By skimping on design and referencing, an Analyst might be able to meet *their* budget goal and deadline. However, because the workpapers will be harder to follow without a logical framework and good referencing, the Manager may struggle to do a timely and accurate review. The better course may be for the Analyst to take an extra 3-4 hours to clean up the workpapers, which will likely make the Manager's review far more efficient and effective.

The "why" behind the importance of quality workpapers

Each of the above explanations assumes that while the preparer understands the importance of preparing well-referenced workpapers and how to do so, they are being neglectful or inconsiderate of the needs of their colleagues. However, another reason a preparer may not take the time to create polished workpapers is the "why" behind the need to do so has never been explained to them.[26] To help with this, I am now going to address you as if you're a preparer.

In practice, the tax provision files you work on and develop can be huge. In fact, it is not unusual for tax provisions to have multiple Excel workbooks, some of which can have 50-100 tabs. With all of the tax provision's size, complexity, and nuances, *you have the best idea of how it works*. Why? Because *you* prepared it! *You* are the one who gathered the data, created the Excel workbooks, and organized the tabs within each workbook.

---

[26] A key leadership principle is if you are ever going to ask your troops to storm the fortress, they will be a lot more focused, motivated, loyal, and effective if they know the reason why.

You are the one who created individual workpapers, developed formulas for the many calculations, and linked them all together. Furthermore, you almost certainly worked many hours over a sustained period of time to do this.

Because of the time and effort you put in, as well as your understanding of your own thought process, nobody has a better grasp of the tax provision workpapers than you do…*whether you took the time to do good referencing or not*. In other words, as the preparer, good referencing is not necessarily that important, because you already know your way around the calculation. But – and this is the key – *the workpaper referencing is not for you; it is for the reviewer(s)!*[27]

The consequences of an organized or disorganized tax provision workpaper package

This is what this all boils down to: without clear referencing, it's easy for even a smart, experienced reviewer to get lost in a tax provision calculation. At worst, the reviewer will not be able to follow your work, resulting in frustration and a loss of time for everyone (which will be intensified by the pressure everyone will be under to finish the tax provision accurately and on time). And at best, a knowledgeable, talented reviewer will eventually be able to decipher your (lousy) workpapers, but only after slowly, painfully, and methodically slogging through them, doing a lot of their own numerical tie-outs and referencing work along the way.

If your reviewer has a difficult time going through your workpapers, how do you think they will remember your contributions? Do you think you will get recognized for all the "hard work" you put into preparing the tax provision? I wouldn't count on it. On the other hand, what if you provide your reviewer with a clean, well-referenced workpaper package that is a pleasure to review? Then, even if you make some mistakes, the reviewer should be able to quickly spot and correct them. That way, even if your calculations aren't perfect, you may still get significant amount of positive recognition for your contributions to the tax provision team due to the high quality of your work. The bottom line is simple: every reviewer likes to review great workpapers.

---

[27] I can tell you from experience that, as a preparer, it's possible to get lulled into complacency because you can follow and understand complicated tax provision workpapers that you created "today." However, as time goes on your memory will fade, and eventually you will have difficultly following your own work (yes, *your own* work) in the future if your workpapers are poorly referenced and organized. So, the lesson is that you not only want to prepare good workpapers for your manager today, but you also want to create a good trail for yourself to follow in the future. Remember, experience is the best teacher. The only question in this matter is whether you want to learn from my experience… or yours.

Summary – The "Truck Rule"

To summarize, remember that preparing a good workpaper package is less about how smart and talented you are as it is to adhering to the "Truck Rule." That is, if a truck runs over you on your way back from lunch, are your workpapers sufficiently well organized and referenced for a reviewer to be able to make sense of them in a reasonable amount of time *without you present?* If the answer is yes, then you are almost certainly doing it right.

6.6   Key Excel workpaper conventions

Now that you understand that "why" behind preparing a quality tax provision workpaper package, *how* do you do that? The full answer is another book in itself, but the following key Excel workpaper conventions will get you off to a good start.[28]

Add a title and a description to each workpaper

Your first order of business is to add a clear, accurate title to each workpaper. Most preparers already do this for their own benefit, whether asked to or not, so this likely isn't news to you. However, in my experience, few preparers follow-up later by adding *a clear description at the top of each workpaper* that answers the reviewer's all-important question, "What am I looking at, and why is this workpaper in the tax provision package?"[29]

To write your workpaper descriptions, I strongly recommend that you use the "Text Box" feature from the Excel ribbon's "Insert" menu (see the illustration). This is because a text box can easily be moved or resized, the text wraps, and it's easy to format (bold, underline, color, etc.). In addition, because a text box "floats above" an Excel worksheet, it doesn't impact spreadsheet data in rows or columns.

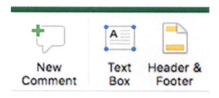

Create a reference number for each workpaper

The larger and more involved a tax provision is, the more important it is to have a consistent, logical workpaper numbering system. This reference number should be in the name of the Excel tab where it resides for ease of online review. For consistency, this

---

[28] Even if you use software specifically designed to compute a tax provision, it's highly likely that you depend on Excel to some degree or another to support tax provision calculations. If that's the case, then all the commentary in this section applies to those Excel workpapers.

[29] See the workpapers in the Appendices for numerous examples of workpaper descriptions.

numeric reference should also be part of the workpaper title. Lastly, at the risk of stating the obvious, I recommend that you keep your Excel tabs in numerical order.

Shade formulas

I have found that it is very helpful to follow the pattern of shading cells that contain formulas and to leave hard-coded cells unshaded. This tells a reviewer (and you as the preparer!) where source data is entering into the tax provision calculation (unshaded) vs. what is calculating (shaded). This formatting makes the review, as well as tracking down issues and source data, much quicker and more efficient. I use this shading method in ALL of my Excel workpapers, whether they are part of this book or whether I am doing consulting work.

"Not used"

To organize yourself further, put the title "Workpaper not used in the tax provision calculation" in large letters at the top of any workpaper that is not being used to support the overall tax provision calculation (see the illustration for an example).

Workpaper not used in the Tax Provision Calculation

Example #1 - A Basic Tax Provision Workpaper Package
1800 - Tax Credits Summary
US Parent

The purposes of this workpaper is to summarize various federal and state tax credits.

You might be asking yourself, when might this be the case? Why would I ever have a workpaper in the tax provision that isn't needed? An example might be that you started the tax provision with one trial balance and you did a significant amount of work using it. However, further in the process, the Accounting Group made some entries, pretax book income changed, and they provided you with an updated trial balance to incorporate into the tax provision. It's possible (for a variety of reasons) that you may not want to delete the old trial balance from the tax provision file even though you're linking up the calculation to the new one (this is a judgment call). If that's the case, I recommend the old trial balance be labeled as shown in the preceding illustration.[30]

What does this accomplish? The clear message to a reviewer (and you) is, "I thought it was important to keep a record of this workpaper in the tax provision, but you do not need to spend any time reviewing it." This is important because I (and a host of other reviewers) have spent 30 minutes or more trying to understand the purpose of a workpaper in the tax provision calculation only to discover that it's not even being used!

---

[30] To take things a step further, you could also add a note such as, "This workpaper is no longer being used in the tax provision calculation *because* [add the explanation]."

There are numerous other Excel, workpaper, formula and presentation conventions used in the Example #1 workpapers, but a full description is beyond the scope of this material.

6.7 Compute pretax book income (1600)

Getting back to the tax provision calculation, after you obtain the unadjusted trial balance, the next step is to compute pretax book income. In Example #1, this is found on workpaper 1600 below the trial balance section and appears as shown in the following illustration.

First, note that pretax book income is computed two different ways, which will be referred to as "Option 1" and "Option 2." The rationale behind each method is as follows:

Pretax Book Income Calculation

	From Unadjusted Opening Trial Balance	From Closing (or "Final") Trial Balance
Option 1 - Revenue & Expense Excluding Income Taxes		
Pretax Book Income/(Loss)	$125,000	$125,000
Option 2 - Net Income with Taxes Added Back		
Current Year Net Income/(Loss)	$125,000	$93,750
Add: Current Tax Expense/(Benefit) - Federal	$0	$31,250
Add: Deferred Expense/(Benefit) - Federal	$0	$0
Equals: Pretax Book Income/(Loss)	$125,000	$125,000
	In Balance	In Balance

1) Option 1 – You calculate pretax book income ("PTBI") by summing all income and expenses on the trial balances *except for* income-tax related expenses. That summation, by definition, is pretax book income, or net income before tax expenses.
2) Option 2 – You sum ALL income and expense items to calculate net income and then you ADD BACK income tax expenses to arrive at pretax book income.

I recommend calculating pretax book income using both methods to ensure you get the same answer for the following reasons:

1) Pretax book income is the starting point of the tax provision calculation, so it's vitally important to take extra steps to ensure that it's calculated correctly.
2) With Option 1, on a large trial balance, it's easy to inadvertently pick up or miss an income tax account in a summation formula, particularly if all tax expense accounts are not grouped together.
3) With Option 2, you may accidentally miss certain tax expense accounts to add back to net income in calculating PTBI.

Again, if you compute PTBI using both methods and you get to the same answer ($125,000 in our example), you can be comfortable that it's correct. While this may seem like overkill, getting pretax book income is so important in a tax provision calculation that it's worth taking a little extra time to make sure that it's right.

6.8 Compute the tax provision (1000)

After you have confirmed pretax book income, you're ready to start computing the tax provision itself (workpaper 1000). Following is a review of tax provision mechanics.

Pretax book income is the starting point of the tax provision

Pretax book income is the starting point of the tax provision calculation. In our example, you will see the $125,000 we just proved out on workpaper 1600 at the top of workpaper 1000.

Identify and calculate book/tax differences

Pretax book income is determined pursuant to the rules of U.S. GAAP. If there were no differences between book and tax, pretax book income would equal taxable income. However, for the tax provision computation you must examine income, expense, and balance sheet accounts on the trial balance at 1600 to determine if any amounts should be modified based on the Internal Revenue Code and the accompanying rules and regulations to arrive at taxable income.

If there are differences between how an item of income or expense is calculated for GAAP (or "book") vs. tax purposes, it is referred to as a "book/tax difference." For example, let's say that the book depreciation for a piece of equipment in Year 1 is $1,000, but the tax depreciation for that same piece of equipment in Year 1 is $1,500. This means there will be a book/tax difference of $500 ($1,500 minus $1,000) between the company's GAAP pretax book income and its taxable income attributable to depreciation. As shown on workpaper 1000, book/tax differences are further subdivided between "permanent" and "temporary" differences.

- Book/tax differences are explained in further detail starting on page 79.
- Permanent differences are explained starting on page 91.
- Temporary differences (and deferred taxes) are explained starting on page 95.

For Example #1, we will assume there are no permanent or temporary book/tax differences. In other words, we will make the simplified assumption for now that U.S. GAAP pretax income ($125,000) is equal to taxable income (also $125,000).

Calculate taxable income and the current tax expense

Now that we have determined taxable income for the company ($125,000), we can project the cash tax we expect to be due with the tax return. For now, we will continue to assume that the cash tax of the company is the only component of its current tax expense, and we will also assume that this expense will be settled when the tax return is filed (vs. through estimated or extension payments). Also, referring to the assumptions for Example #1, the federal and state tax rate is 25% on a combined basis. Based on these factors, the current tax expense of the company is $31,250 ($125,000 PTBI x 25%).

Calculate deferred taxes and the total tax expense

Because the concept is so important, it bears repeating that the total tax expense (or provision) of a company is the sum of current and deferred taxes. In this simplified example, the company's total tax expense ($31,250) is equal to the current tax expense (also $31,250) only because deferred taxes are zero.[31]

Summary of Current and Deferred Taxes

Current Tax Expense/(Benefit) - Federal	$31,250
Deferred Tax Expense/(Benefit) - Federal	$0
Total Tax Provision	$31,250

Make tax provision calculations clean and relevant

Recalling our earlier discussion, as you work on the tax provision the model can become very large, containing worksheet after worksheet in multiple Excel workbooks. Because of this complexity, as well as the difficultly of seeing the end of the tax provision calculation from the beginning, it's not uncommon for preparers to add data and calculations to tax provision workpapers that end up NOT being used. These "dead data sets" (referring to the illustration that follows from the bottom of workpaper 1000) can end up staying in the provision file for a couple of reasons.

A Random, Unnecessary Calculation in the Tax Provision that has no Bearing on Anything

Who knows where this number is coming from	$8,417	Delete these kinds of side calculations from your
Less: Some other seemingly random number	($1,217)	tax provision file to reduce "noise"
Equals: Yet another number you cannot tie to anything	$7,200	

First, it takes time to streamline a tax provision file, and preparers are often strained during the tax provision preparation process to "create perfect workpapers" while also meeting budgets and deadlines.

Second, it's not just a question of time, but of timing. For example, assume that a well-intentioned preparer plans to go back after the provision is done to clean up the files. The challenge is that not long after the year-end tax provision:

- Tax return extensions need to be filed.
- Quarterly estimated taxes need to be calculated and paid.
- The first quarter financials (with quarterly tax provisions) also come up quickly.
- Not long afterwards, the tax return (compliance) filing process needs to be started.
- In addition to all of the above, there will be a stack of issues in email to go through that weren't possible to address during the intensity of year-end.

The point here isn't to be discouraging, but realistic. If you plan to "come back later" to clean up your tax provision workpapers it's very unlikely to happen. It's far better to

---

[31] As noted previously, deferred taxes (along with temporary differences) will be discussed in more detail starting on page 95.

follow sound organizational practices such as those I've outlined while you're in the thick of the work. Then, each year going forward, you build on your work and incrementally improve your processes until you've created a well-oiled machine.

Why superseded data persistently stays in tax provision calculations

With all of the above in mind, let's assume that you make it a priority to clean up and streamline the tax provision in whatever ways you can as part of your year-end preparation procedures. In doing so, you discover data and calculations in the file that at first appear to be irrelevant, but you find they actually link to the tax provision calculation in less obvious, forgotten, or unexpected ways. As a result, if you were to wantonly delete such data and calculations you would be running the risk of "blowing up" the entire tax provision file. This is one of the main reasons that outdated, superseded, and duplicate information stays in tax provision calculations, because you and everyone else believes that "somebody else" might have an important reason for it to be there.

The process of cleaning up tax provision workpapers

While the challenges of finding the time and dealing with the intricacies of tax provision workpapers are real, it's still important to consistently invest time in streamlining the tax provision workpapers. As previously noted, while it may not be realistic to clean up a tax provision file all at once, the incremental improvements you make over the course of time will make a difference in managing the complexity of the calculation.

The alternative approach is to do nothing, and to continue to add layer after layer of calculations into the model each year. The danger of that choice (because doing nothing *is* a choice) is that the tax provision calculation will grow in complexity until it eventually collapses under its own weight. In other words, it will get to the point that the calculation is almost entirely unworkable because it's so difficult and time consuming to update, work with, link up, prove out, follow, and review.

What all this means is that at some point you (or somebody!) need to exercise the initiative and the leadership to go deep into the tax provision file while you still have preparation momentum and say, "What is this calculation doing and why is it in the workpapers?" If data or calculations are relevant and support the overall tax provision calculation then link it up and ensure it's referenced in a manner that's clear, concise and accurate. On the other hand, if you determine that a tax provision calculation (or workpaper, file, memo, document, etc.) does NOT support the tax provision calculation because it is old, irrelevant, superseded, or otherwise not needed then *delete it*.[32]

---

[32] Be methodical and SAVE any tax provision file BEFORE you delete something in case you inadvertently blow up the calculation!

Keep the return to provision ("RTP") process in mind

As a final note on the tax provision calculation (referring specifically to workpaper 1000), know that you will complete a return to provision (or "RTP") analysis later in the year in connection with preparing the corporate tax return. In the RTP analysis, you will calculate and explain the differences between your tax provision calculations and what you ultimately report on the tax return.

To illustrate, on workpaper 1000 you're projecting the current tax expense to be $31,250. If that turns out to be the company's actual tax liability when you file the return then it means your tax provision calculation was accurate. However, if there is a large difference between what you project for income taxes at the provision vs. what you report on the tax return, it could raise concerns with your auditors (and senior management) about whether the financial statements were materially accurate at the time they were filed. For these reasons, it is important to approach the tax provision process as thoroughly and carefully as possible, because *you will be held accountable for how accurately you project the tax return as part of the tax provision process*.[33]

6.9 Determine the year-end tax adjusting entry (50, 1000, 1600)

After you calculate the total tax expense of the company ($31,250 – see workpaper 1000), the next step is to determine the year-end tax adjusting entry needed for both current and deferred taxes. The question is this: if the total tax expense for the year is $31,250, what amount of tax needs to be expensed as part of the year-end closing process to balance the books?

To get to the answer, you need to know how much income tax expense has *already* been accrued over the course of the year. For example, let's say that a company estimates its tax expense to be $2,500 a month.[34] This means that by the end of December the company would have accrued a total tax expense of $30,000 ($2,500 x 12 months), and the cumulative journal entry would look like this:

Current Tax Expense	$30,000	
Income Tax Payable		$30,000

Since we know that the ending GL balance for tax expense needs to be $31,250, the year-end tax adjusting entry would look like this:

---

[33] This concept is also summarized on page 30 under the heading, "The Return to Provision (or "RTP") process.".

[34] For purposes of this example, we are continuing to assume that the company (per Example #1) has current tax only, and no deferred tax expense.

Current Tax Expense	$1,250
Income Tax Payable	$1,250

A key point here is that just because you calculate a company's total tax expense to be $31,250 does not mean you automatically "book an expense of $31,250." The amount of tax expense you book (e.g., the $1,250 in the adjusting journal entry above) is equal to how much you need to adjust the current balance ($30,000) so that the ending balance ($31,250) ties to the tax expense per the provision calculation (workpaper 1000).

Now that you understand the rationale for adjusting to the correct tax expense, we will go to the tax provision workpapers in Example #1 to determine what the tax adjusting entry needs to be. In doing so, we will refer to the following:

1) 50 – Tax Journal Entry Summary
2) 1000 – Tax Provision Summary
3) 1600 – Trial Balance

First, per the *unadjusted* trial balance (the far-left column on workpaper 1600 – see the illustration), we can see that there was *no* income tax accrued over the course of the year.

Expense - Income Tax - Federal - Current Exp./(Ben.)	$0
Expense - Income Tax - Federal - Deferred Exp./(Ben.	$0

On the tax provision at workpaper 1000, we confirm once again that the total tax expense of the company is $31,250.

Now refer to workpaper 50 (see the illustration that follows). Here we see the opening balance of the current tax expense was zero (as confirmed by workpaper 1600), and the "calculated balance," or the total tax expense for the year, is $31,250 (as confirmed by workpaper 1000). That means the adjusting tax journal entry (or "tax AJE" for short) needs to be $31,250, which is the amount we see in the "Adjusting Entry" column.

Account Description	Opening Balance From 1600[1]	Calculated Balance "Plug"[2]	Adjusting (Tax) Journal Entry Carries to 1600[3]	Notes/Explanation/Reference
Asset - Deferred Tax Asset - Federal	$0	$0	$0	Calculated at 1310 - Tax-effected deferred tax rollforward
Asset - Tax Receivable - Federal	$0	$0	$0	Calculated at 60 - Tax Payable (or Receivable) Rollforward
Liability - Deferred Tax Liability - Federal	$0	$0	$0	Calculated at 1310 - Tax-effected deferred tax rollforward
Liability - Tax Payable - Federal	$0	($31,250)	($31,250)	Calculated at 60 - Tax Payable Rollforward
Expense - Income Tax - Federal - Current Exp./(Ben.)	$0	$31,250	$31,250	Calculated at 1000 - Tax Provision Summary
Expense - Income Tax - Federal - Deferred Exp./(Ben.	$0	$0	$0	From 1000 - Tax Provision Summary
Totals / Check Figure (should be zero)			$0 In Balance	Total debits and credits should net to zero

"The Missing Tax Accounting Guide – A Plain English Guide to ASC 740 Tax Provisions"
@ 2022 Tax Director Services, Inc.
All rights reserved

In summary, unlike the first example in this section where we assumed that tax expense was accrued during the year ($30,000), in Example #1 we see that no taxes were accrued. As a result, the entire tax expense ($31,250) needs to be booked as part of the year-end closing process.

6.10 Complete the tax payable rollforward (50, 60, 1600)

Tax journal entry observations

Before reviewing how to complete the tax payable rollforward (workpaper 60), it's important to briefly re-review the tax journal entry summary (workpaper 50). The purpose of tax entry workpaper 50 is to adjust all income tax-related GL balances from what they currently *are* (the "Opening Balance" column) to what they *should be* (the "Calculated Balance") column.

In the preceding section, we proved out what the ending tax expense ($31,250) and the related adjusting entry should be (a debit of $31,250). Note, however, that that is only *one side* of the tax entry. As we all know, basic accounting principles say that a tax entry must have *two sides*, and the total debits must equal the total credits.

This point touches on one of the things that make working with tax provisions so challenging. With sales you credit revenue and immediately (and automatically) debit the offsetting accounts receivable (or cash). Or if you have an expense accrual you can simply debit the expense and credit an offsetting liability. In both situations, your accounting entries are in balance right away. However, because of the complexity and multifaceted nature of a tax provision, it's often necessary to calculate one side of a tax entry at a time. Thus, if you make a mistake *anywhere* in the tax provision it can throw the journal entry out of balance and it can be *very challenging* to figure out what's causing the difference. So, helping the tax journal entry process go smoothly is yet another important reason to have a clean, well-organized, well-referenced workpaper package.

Calculate the ending taxes payable and the related tax adjusting entry

Since we now know that one of the main purposes of the tax provision workpaper package is to calculate the ending (or closing) GL balances for each income

Liability - Accrued Expenses	$0
Liability - Tax Payable - Federal	$0
Liability - Deferred Tax Liability - Federal	$0
Liability - Other	$0

tax-related account, we will now examine the "Taxes Payable" amount on the unadjusted trial balance (see the illustration above from far-left column on workpaper 1600). Here we see the opening taxes payable balance is zero. With that as the starting point, following is a condensed version of the taxes payable rollforward from workpaper 60 of Example #1:

    Taxes payable – Beginning balance $0 (workpaper 1600)
    Add: Current tax expense per the provision $31,250 (workpaper 1000)
    Taxes payable – Ending balance $31,250 (workpaper 60)

Consistent with this rollfoward, refer to the tax journal entry at workpaper 50 (see the following illustration). Here we see that the "Opening Balance" of the tax payable is $0 (per the unadjusted trial balance at 1600) and the "Calculated Balance" for the end of the year is $31,250 (per workpaper 60 above). This means the "Adjusting Entry" in the far-right column needs to be a debit entry of $31,250.

Liability - Tax Payable - Federal	$0	($31,250)	($31,250)
Expense - Income Tax - Federal - Current Exp./(Ben.)	$0	$31,250	$31,250
Totals / Check Figure (should be zero)			$0
			In Balance

6.11 Review the tax adjusting entry and provide it to the Accounting Group (50, 1600)

From earlier in the material, we learned one of the main purposes of the tax provision is to calculate the tax adjusting journal entry (the tax "AJE") necessary to close the books on an accounting period and to provide it to the company's Accounting Group.[35] As previously noted, this tax journal entry is found at workpaper 50. In the previous steps, we focused on calculating the individual components of the tax journal entry (i.e. the tax expense and the tax payable), but now we're looking at the entry as a whole. Note the following from the illustration:

[This space was intentionally left blank].

---

[35] See page 25 under the heading, "The four main purposes of a tax provision."

Account Description	Opening Balance From 1600[1]	Calculated Balance "Plug"[2]	Adjusting (Tax) Journal Entry Carries to 1600[3]
Asset - Deferred Tax Asset - Federal	$0	$0	$0
Asset - Tax Receivable - Federal	$0	$0	$0
Liability - Deferred Tax Liability - Federal	$0	$0	$0
Liability - Tax Payable - Federal	$0	($31,250)	($31,250)
Expense - Income Tax - Federal - Current Exp./(Ben.)	$0	$31,250	$31,250
Expense - Income Tax - Federal - Deferred Exp./(Ben.	$0	$0	$0
Totals / Check Figure (should be zero)			$0 In Balance

1) It is good practice to list ALL tax-related accounts in the left-hand column, whether they have activity or not (see the "Account Description" column). This provides a comprehensive way to review and check all tax accounts each period.[36]
2) Note that total debits (positive $31,250) equal total credits (negative $31,250), and the "Check Figure" for the tax entry foots to zero (the "In Balance" proof).
3) It's important that all tax provision workpapers are clean and well referenced, but this is especially true of the tax journal entry summary.[37] In our example, you can find support in the workpapers for the "Opening Balance" and the "Calculated Balance" amounts for each tax account:
    a. The opening balances are from the unadjusted trial balance at workpaper 1600.
    b. The support for the calculated balance for the tax payable is at workpaper 60 (the tax payable rollforward).
    c. The support for the calculated balance of the current tax expense is at workpaper 1000 (the tax provision calculation).

---

[36] Reviewing all tax-related accounts on the tax journal entry workpaper is important because you might assume a given tax account didn't have any activity for the period simply because the Tax Group didn't book anything to it. However, if you don't check the account balance, you may miss that *someone else* (without your knowledge or mistakenly) made an entry that impacted an income tax-related account. For example, what if someone mistakenly booked a large sales tax refund receivable to an income tax account? If you don't check the income tax receivable/payable balance you will miss the opportunity to catch and correct such errors.

[37] If you look at the numbers on this workpaper 50, that is just what they are – numbers. For SOX (or control) purposes, you need to carefully reference each figure back to the tax provision workpapers to show auditors and other reviewers that there is clear trail to the applicable support.

4) After examining the remaining tax accounts, you determine there are no more tax entries to make.

After you complete the tax entry, you provide a copy (meaning a copy of workpaper 50) to the Accounting Group. They will then book it, meaning they will enter the debits and credits you provide into the general ledger. After they do so, the books will be closed, the Accounting Group will produce a final trial balance, and that will be used to support the figures in the financial statements.

6.12 Revisiting the trial balance after adjusting entries have been booked

We'll now review the trial balance at workpaper 1600 to see how the tax adjusting entry fits in (see the illustration that follows). The explanation for each column in the trial balance is as follows:

- "Account Description" – This is a listing of each of the company's GL accounts on the trial balance.
    - In practice, each GL account is normally assigned an "account number." For example, "Cash" might be account 1000, Accounts Receivable might be account 2000, and so on.
- "Unadjusted Opening Trial Balance" – This is the trial balance the Accounting Group provided you to prepare the tax provision. In Example #1, all account balances were final except those that were tax-related (tax payable, current tax expense, etc.).
- "Tax Adjusting Entries" – Amounts in this column come from workpaper 50. They adjust the account balances from what they were ("unadjusted balances") to what they should be (the "final" balances in the column at the far-right).
- "Closing (or 'Final') Trial Balance" – After booking the tax adjusting entry, the Accounting Group "closes the books" and produces the final trial balance. These amounts serve as the basis for the figures reported in the company's financial statements (see workpaper 5).

[This space was intentionally left blank].

Account Description	Unadjusted Opening Trial Balance	Tax Adjusting Entries	Closing (or "Final") Trial Balance
Asset - Cash (after cash income tax payments)	$1,125,000		$1,125,000
Asset - Tax Receivable - Federal	$0	$0	$0
Asset - Fixed Assets	$0		$0
Asset - Accumulated Depreciation	$0		$0
Asset - Deferred Tax Asset - Federal	$0	$0	$0
Asset - Other	$0		$0
Liability - Accrued Expenses	$0		$0
Liability - Tax Payable - Federal	$0	($31,250)	($31,250)
Liability - Deferred Tax Liability - Federal	$0	$0	$0
Liability - Other	$0		$0
Equity - Common Stock & APIC	($1,000,000)		($1,000,000)
Equity - Retained Earnings (beginning of year)	$0		$0
Revenue - Standard	($340,000)		($340,000)
Revenue - Permanent Item	$0		$0
Expense - Standard	$215,000		$215,000
Expense - Permanent Item	$0		$0
Expense - Temporary Item	$0		$0
Expense - Depreciation - Book	$0		$0
Expense - Income Tax - Federal - Current Exp./(Ben.)	$0	$31,250	$31,250
Expense - Income Tax - Federal - Deferred Exp./(Ben.)	$0	$0	$0
Check Figure (should be zero)	$0	$0	$0
	In Balance	In Balance	In Balance

As a parting thought, it's vitally important not to treat the tax journal entry as an afterthought. *Developing and then balancing the tax AJE can be one of the most complex, elusive, and time-consuming elements of preparing the tax provision.*

At the risk of restating the obvious to drive home a key point, no matter how good your tax provision workpapers are, if you don't supply the Accounting Group with a tax AJE they're all for nothing. The GL accounts (or "the books") won't magically correct themselves. It's *your job* to make that happen, and you do that by supplying the Accounting Group with a tax AJE that's supported by a clean and comprehensive tax provision workpaper package. That's why all of this is called <u>tax accounting</u>, because you're applying your tax knowledge and expertise to help the Accounting Group to update the GL and to produce materially accurate financial statements.

6.13 Verify tax amounts are correct in the financial statements (5, 1600)

The tax provision workpapers support the tax-related figures in the financial statements

The purpose of preparing tax return workpapers is to produce and file a timely and accurate tax return. In other words, the *tax return is the final product*; that's what the IRS sees, it's what they care about, and that's what they view as the final, official tax position of the company. Likewise, the primary purpose of the tax provision workpaper package is, "To support the tax-related figures and explanations in the company's financial statements (or Form 10-K), the footnote disclosures, and any related management discussion and analysis."[38]

Said another way, no matter how clean, correct, well-referenced, and well-organized the tax provision workpapers are, *if the financial statements are wrong then you will have failed to deliver*. The financial statements of the company are the final product; they're what investors, management, the Board, Wall Street analysts, the SEC, and the public accept as the final, official financial position of the company. Therefore, above all else, it's vital to ensure that the tax-related figures and disclosures on your company's financial statements are correct, and it's through well-prepared tax provision workpapers that you accomplish this goal.

A review of non-tax financial statement figures

It's not normally the responsibility of the Tax Group (or tax auditors) to review the *non-tax* elements of the financial statements, but we will do so for a complete understanding of Example #1, as well as to add context to our review of the company's tax-related figures and disclosures.[39] The observations below relate to the balance sheet illustration that follows:

[This space was intentionally left blank].

---

[38] See page 25 under the heading, "The four main purposes of a tax provision."
[39] Tax professionals are more effective when they have a sound understanding of the following aspects of a company: accounting policies and practices, business operations, the industry, risks, opportunities, the competitive environment, and management strategies.

Consolidated Balance Sheet	Amounts	Notes/Explanation/Reference
Other Assets (this includes all non-tax-related assets)	$1,125,000	From 1600 - Closing trial balance (third column on page 1 of 1)
Deferred Tax Asset - Federal	$0	From 1600 - Closing trial balance and 1310 Deferred tax rollforward
Total Assets	$1,125,000	Ties to the company's published financial statements
Liability - Tax Payable - Federal	$31,250	From 1600 (closing trial balance) and 60 (tax payable rollforward)
Other Liabilities (this includes all non-tax-related liabilities)	$0	From 1600 - Closing trial balance (third column on page 1 of 1)
Equity - Common Stock & APIC	$1,000,000	From 1600 - Closing trial balance (third column on page 1 of 1)
Equity - Retained Earnings	$93,750	See the "Retained Earnings Rollforward" on 2 of 2
Total Liabilities & Stockholders' Equity	$1,125,000	Ties to the company's published financial statements
	In Balance	

- On the balance sheet, "Other Assets" of $1,125,000 comprises all non-tax related assets (PP&E, cash, AR, etc.), and this amount ties to the final trial balance on workpaper 1600.
- "Common Stock & APIC" of $1,000,000 ties to workpaper 1600.
- The support for the retained earnings balance of $93,750 is in the "Supporting Calculations" section at the bottom of workpaper 5. It's equal to retained earnings at the beginning of the period ($0), plus net income ($93,750), less distributions ($0).

Having reviewed the balance sheet, we'll now turn our attention to the income statement (see workpaper 5, or the illustration below):

Consolidated Statement of Comprehensive Income/(Loss)		
Revenue	$340,000	From 1600 - Closing trial balance (third column on page 1 of 1)
Expenses (Pretax)	($215,000)	Same
Income/(Loss) Before Income Tax Provision	$125,000	Ties to pretax book income per 1600 (page 2 of 2)
Income Tax (Provision)/Benefit	($31,250)	See the "Income Taxes" footnote on page 2 of 2
Net Income	$93,750	
	In Balance	"In Balance" - Ties to net income per 1600 (page 2 of 2)
Other Comprehensive Income	$0	
Comprehensive Income/(Loss)	$93,750	Ties to the company's published financial statements

1) The $340,000 is referred to as "Revenue – Standard" on the trial balance at 1600. For our purposes, this is GAAP revenue that is also tax revenue (i.e. revenue where there are no book/tax differences).
2) The $215,000 is referred to on the trial balance at 1600 as "Expenses – Standard." These are GAAP expenses that are also allowable as tax deductions (i.e. expenses where there are no book/tax differences).

3) Pretax book income (referred to as "Income/Loss before Income Tax Provision") per the financial statements is $125,000. This ties to the "Pretax Book Income Calculation" on page 2 of 2 of workpaper 1600.
    a. In that proof, Options 1 and 2 both show PTBI to be $125,000.
4) "Net Income" and "Comprehensive Income" are both $93,750, meaning there is no "other comprehensive income" in Example #1.

A review of tax-related financial statement figures

With an understanding of the non-tax items in the financial statements (and referring to the prior illustrations), we're now ready to review the tax-related figures on the "face" of the financial statements (meaning those that are on the balance sheet and income statement).[40]

1) The tax payable of $31,250 on the balance sheet ties to the following:
    a. The final trial balance at workpaper 1600.
    b. The tax payable rollforward at workpaper 60.
2) The $31,250 tax expense of the company (referred to as "Income Tax (Provision)/Benefit") ties to the following:
    a. The final trial balance at workpaper 1600.
    b. The tax provision calculation at workpaper 1000.

6.14 Write the tax footnote and other tax-related disclosures (5)

While the CEO and CFO (with the assistance of the Chief Accounting Officer or Controller) have overall responsibility for the financial statements, the Tax Group is generally expected to write and provide the figures necessary to support the "Income Taxes" section of the "Notes to the Consolidated Financial Statements." A simple example of a tax footnote for Example #1 is as follows.

Notes to Consolidated Financial Statements ("The Footnotes")

Income Taxes
The income tax provision/(benefit) for the year consisted of the following:

Current Taxes	$31,250	From 1000
Deferred Taxes	$0	
Total Tax Provision or Expense/(Benefit)	$31,250	
	In Balance	

Here, further comments and insights would be made on the income tax expense of the company, such as how it compared against the prior period, whether there were important trends, risks, etc.

---

[40] While all tax-related figures in the financial statements are important, those reported on the face of the financial statements (vs. those reported in the footnotes) are most important with respect to materiality.

Note the following from the tax footnote illustration:

1) The breakout between current ($31,250) and deferred taxes ($0) is shown in arriving at the total tax expense of the company ($31,250).
2) The total tax expense per the footnote ($31,250) ties to both the tax expense on the face of the financial statements as well as the tax provision workpapers at 1000.
3) Refer to the language at the bottom of the footnote ("Here, further comments would be made…"). Obviously, that's not the language you would see in an actual footnote. What's important to understand is that the financial statement footnote should provide "plain English" summaries and insights on the company's material income tax-related facts, figures, trends, policies, and positions.[41]

Now we will review the company's "Effective Tax Rate Reconciliation," which is a component of the company's tax footnote.

Description	Dollar	Rate	
Expected Tax Provision/(Benefit) at the Statutory Tax Rate	$31,250	25.00%	From 1000
Nondeductible Meals	$0	0.00%	
Income Tax Provision/(Benefit)	$31,250	25.00%	
	In Balance	In Balance	

The effective tax rate ("ETR") is the percentage of income tax a company pays on its *pretax book income*. You calculate the ETR (25%) by dividing the total tax expense ($31,250) by the pretax book income in the financial statements ($125,000).[42] Here is how to interpret the ETR reconciliation:

1) On the first line, we see $31,250 and 25%. The 25% is the statutory tax rate and the $31,250 is the *expected tax* of the company's pretax book income at the statutory rate. (Normally the federal rate of 21% is used as the statutory rate, but to simplify Example #1 we're using a combined federal and state rate of 25%).
2) "Nondeductible Meals" is an example of a permanent book/tax difference that may cause a difference between the *expected* tax of the company vs. the total tax

---

[41] Despite the fact that there are SEC disclosure guidelines for the tax footnotes, there is significant diversity in practice on how companies approach footnote disclosures: how long they are, the use of technical vs. plainer language, how much detail they provide, how much they rely on tables vs. written explanations, etc.

[42] Companies normally present their ETR reconciliations in dollars OR percentages but, in our example, we show both.

expense per the provision. In Example #1, meal expenses and other potential book/tax differences which could impact the ETR are zero.[43]

3) The third line shows the ETR of the company (25%). Again, this is computed by dividing the total tax expense ($31,250) by pretax book income ($125,000).

In summary, the purpose of the ETR reconciliation is to show what drives the difference between the *expected* tax at the statutory rate ($31,250) and the company's *actual* tax expense ($31,250). While there are no such differences in Example #1, there will be in examples later in the material.

6.15 Draft financial statements can now be completed

Now that you have verified the tax-related figures on the face of the financial statements, written the tax footnote, and confirmed that everything ties back to the tax provision workpapers, you're now ready (from a tax perspective) for the Accounting Group to finalize the financial statements.[44]

6.16 Address auditor questions on the tax provision calculation and the related controls

Despite the work done to this point, the financial statements will not be issued by the company until the financial statement auditors are satisfied that everything is in order (with a "clean opinion" being the company's goal).[45]

Tax specialists will audit the tax provision

The accounting firm's audit partner will normally assign tax specialists to audit the tax provision. The role of the tax auditors is to ensure that the tax-related figures, footnotes, and other disclosures in the financial statements are materially correct and follow the tax accounting rules of ASC 740 (and applicable SEC guidelines if it's a public company). As part of this process, you will provide the auditors with the tax provision workpapers, answer their questions, and provide all requested documentation to support your tax conclusions and calculations.

As you work with the accounting firm's tax specialists, remember that *their work is subject to "audit"* as well, through both internal firm quality reviews as well as by the

---

[43] Nondeductible meals and entertainment will come into play in Example #2 as part of the discussion on "permanent differences" starting on page 91.

[44] There may be an "SEC Reporting Group" within the Accounting or Finance Group charged with this responsibility.

[45] For a reminder of the auditor's objectives and responsibilities with respect to the financial statements, refer back to page 25 under the heading, "Key elements of a public accounting firm's financial statement opinion."

PCAOB if they audit a public company.[46] These levels of oversight are designed to ensure that tax specialists perform their audit procedures and analysis in a thorough manner and that they obtain sufficient, verifiable evidence to support their audit assertions. As a result, while auditors are expected to be polite and professional towards their clients, Tax Groups should also expect them to exercise professional skepticism, as well as to be demanding and persistent when it comes to information requests for material tax calculations and positions taken by the company.

Internal controls are also audited

In addition to making sure the tax provision is materially correct (i.e. that you got sufficiently close to the "right answer"), the audit team will also determine if your internal (or SOX) controls are adequate. In other words, they will evaluate tax provision documentation and processes to determine if they were sufficiently robust to prevent a material misstatement of income tax-related items (i.e. that you do not have a "material weakness" in your tax controls).

To understand the implications of an audit of your controls, consider a situation where you make an error in the tax provision, the auditors catch it through their examination procedures, and you correct the error before the financial statements are issued. Wouldn't this be a "no harm, no foul" situation because your financial statements were corrected before they were issued? Isn't it true that the audit firm is responsible for catching a company's mistakes? No. While the company's financial statements may be materially correct when issued due to the correction, you can still be hit with a *tax-related material weakness that must be disclosed in the financial statements* as part of the audit opinion. This is because the audit showed that your controls, processes, and procedures for preparing the tax provision failed to catch an error that <u>could have</u> caused a material weakness.

6.17 The financial statements are issued (and the consequences of an income tax-related error)

The financial statements are issued after the audit is complete

After your company completes the financial statements and the auditors render their opinion, the financial statements are formally issued. Now you're *finally* done, and you can take a much-deserved break, right? Assuming your financial statements are materially correct the answer would be yes…but keep reading.

---

[46] "The Public Company Accounting Oversight Board is a nonprofit corporation established by Congress to protect investors and the public interest by promoting informative, accurate, and independent audit reports and to oversee the audits of public companies…" Source: https://pcaobus.org.

Tax provision errors can result in a restatement of the financial statements

If a material tax-related (or other) error is discovered *after* the financial statements have been issued, it will result in what is referred to as a "restatement." In other words, the company must reissue (or correct) their financial statements, along with an explanation of what happened, why it happened, what changed, and by how much.

Why is a tax-related restatement considered a big deal? Among other things, one concern of senior management is the impact a tax-related restatement could have on investor confidence, as well as the company's stock price. On the latter point, research shows that "…investors and dealers react negatively to restatements and are *more concerned with revenue recognition problems than with other financial reporting errors* (emphasis added)."[47] In other words, while no restatement is considered good news to investors, a silver lining is that revenue recognition rather than tax or other areas is the main area of concern (presumably because revenue figures are generally more closely tied to the valuation of the company).[48]

Does this mean that tax-related restatements don't matter, because they tend not to be a primary focus of investors? The answer is no. To one degree or another, companies and audit firms consider a restatement of any kind to be embarrassing and undesirable because it is a "public admission" of a mistake. Also, as noted above, there is the concern that a restatement of any kind can erode confidence in the financial reporting of the company. Because of these consequences, the possibility of a restatement increases the pressure on the Tax Group (and the audit firm) to ensure that the tax provision is materially correct.[49] Unfortunately, none of this is helped by the fact that the tax provision is one of the most complex (if not *the* most complex) aspects of the financial statements for many companies.[50] To top things off, if the Tax Group makes an error in the tax provision that results in the financial statements being materially misstated, it

---

[47] See "The Effect of 10-K Restatements on Firm Value, Information Asymmetries, and Investors' Reliance on Earnings", a research study performed by Kirsten L. Anderson and Teri Lombardi Yohn of Georgetown University.

[48] This statement assumes that any tax-related error is not *hugely* material. In other words, sophisticated financial statement readers know that taxes are complex, and they are likely not surprised when there is a periodic need for a tax-related correction to the financial statements. But again, if the tax issue has a major financial impact, that would likely make more of a difference in investor perception.

[49] This is especially true of public companies, because the mistake (via the restatement) must be openly admitted to Wall Street analysts, investors, the company's employees, and "everyone else."

[50] One high level way to gauge the level of tax complexity at a company is to compare the length and sophistication of the tax footnote to the company's other financial statement footnotes.

almost always means the auditors will also report a finding of a material weakness in the tax controls.[51]

6.18 Parting thoughts on the tax provision process

Before moving on to other topics, I want to make one final observation on the tax provision preparation process. Even though the company's facts, figures, and assumptions in Example #1 are *simplified and very straightforward*, preparing, documenting, understanding, and explaining even a basic tax provision is a *very involved process* that requires considerable time, care, precision, and attention.

---

[51] Reviewing a concept covered earlier, this is another way of saying that the auditors assert in their written opinion that the tax provision processes were not sufficiently strong enough to prevent a material misstatement.

7 The Financial Statement Auditor's Perspective of the Tax Provision

7.1 Learning objectives

- Learn what a tax provision looks like from an auditor's standpoint.
- Gain an understanding of vital practices, processes, and the mentality to adopt as an auditor.
- Review an example of how to apply audit principles and procedures (based on Example #1).
- Gain insight into how Tax Groups view the audit process as a means to better understand and more effectively interact with them.
- Be able to articulate the meaning of key audit terminology.

7.2 The tax specialist's approach to an audit

Even if you prepare rather than audit tax provisions, it's very important to understand a financial statement auditor's perspective so that you can anticipate and prepare for questions and issues that are important to them. <u>This chapter is written to and for financial statement auditors</u>.

If you're a tax specialist on the audit team, your main goal is NOT to "tick and tie" client workpapers, or to simply make sure that the tax provision is mathematically accurate. As a tax specialist of the Audit Team, your job is to help the auditors (specifically the audit partner) get comfortable that *the tax-related aspects of the financial statements are materially correct, and that there is sufficient, verifiable evidence to support that assertion.*

Verify tax-related figures on the 'face' of the financial statements

First and foremost, you need to ensure that the income tax-related figures on the face of the financial statements tie to the tax provision workpapers. The "face" of the financial statements (as opposed to the footnotes, discussed further below) refers to:

- The balance sheet
- The income statement
- The statement of cash flows
- The statement of shareholder's equity

While tracing tax-related items on the face of the financial statements back to the tax provision workpapers is your primary goal, it's important to note that the financial statements (or even a draft of them) may not be available until late in the audit process.

Therefore, to meet the audit deadlines required for the financial statements to be issued on time, during the first part of the audit you should focus on confirming that the figures in the tax provision workpapers tie to the company's trial balance (and other accounting data) based on the assumption that those amounts will ultimately tie to the financial statements.

Prove out pretax book income

One of the first things you should check as an auditor is that pretax book income per the company's financial data and the tax provision are equal.[52] If that's the case, it's a strong indicator that the financial data population used to calculate the tax provision is complete and accurate. However, if pretax book income per the tax provision and the company's financial data do NOT agree, contact the company's Tax Group and your Audit Team immediately. If you fail to do so, you risk wasting a substantial amount of time (and exceeding your budget) by performing audit procedures on a tax provision that is incomplete or populated with old data.

Be aware of changes to pretax book income and other financial data

Given these factors, during the audit it's very important to stay in close communication with both the audit team (of which you are a member) and the company's Tax Group, and it needs to be clear to everyone that you should be informed of any changes in pretax book income. But you might ask yourself, under what circumstances would pretax book income change? For one thing, it's not uncommon for companies to make late entries to their books as they wrap up their year-end close (even after the audit has started). Also, your audit team may find information during their review which would require entries to be made. Here are specific things to keep in mind:

1) Income Statement – Any change to income statement accounts will change pretax book income (and the tax provision along with it) unless it's a reclass from one income statement account to another. Even in such cases, you need to ensure that tax-sensitive accounts are not impacted.[53]
2) Balance Sheet – Most balance sheet changes will not impact the tax provision, but they will if the accounts are a component of a tax provision calculation (i.e. they are tax sensitive accounts).

---

[52] If the client hasn't already created one, I highly recommend that you prepare a "Proof of Pretax Book Income" similar to what's shown on page 2 of workpaper 1600 of Example #1. This isn't a super-complicated exercise, but it's VITALLY important that you confirm your starting point is correct. If it's not, *nothing else will be!*

[53] A "tax-sensitive" account is one that impacts calculations in the provision. For example, if there is a reclass of $20,000 from one general expense account to another, it will not impact the tax provision. However, if $20,000 of general expense is reclassed to meals (a tax sensitive account), then it WILL have an impact on the tax provision calculation.

Finally, as an auditor it's always important to remember when verifying pretax book income (and other accounting information) that *your final product is a set of audited financial statements*. Thus, while you will start off auditing trial balances and other client workpapers, in the final analysis the most important thing is that the tax-related figures in the financial statements are accurate and supportable. Therefore, get a copy of the draft financials once they're available to ensure they meet your expectations, and monitor them for accuracy until they're issued because it's the final version that counts!

Take time to review entity trial balances on a line-by-line basis

After you verify your pretax book income starting point, a common next step is to start reviewing and tying out the book/tax differences in the client's tax provision calculation. This is the wrong approach. Why? I don't know the details of your particular firm's audit procedures or the "traditions" that are followed by your audit team, but I can tell you that if you just start following a client's work then it will lead you to where they say it goes. That's not auditing – that's rubber stamping…and that's not the job.

The point here isn't that a client's tax provision is wrong. No, the point is your responsibility is to objectively verify it's materially correct. A simple but powerful way to gain knowledge, understanding and a sense of independent thought at the beginning of a client tax provision review is to carefully look at their trial balance on a line-by-line basis. What will you see? I can't say for sure because, of course, it will vary by company, as well by divisions, lines of business, and entities within the same company. But one thing I do know is this: *you'll see a lot*. For example:

- You'll know the level of sales, and whether they come from tangible goods, services or from some other source.
- You'll know the material categories of assets.
    - Is the company fixed asset intensive or not?
    - Is inventory a significant component of the company's operations?
- You'll see whether there are intangibles or goodwill on the balance sheet, and how significant those amounts are.
- You'll get a sense for where the reserve accounts are and how much is booked to them.
- How is the company capitalized?
- Is there a significant amount of debt?

I could go on and on with the insights you will gain. But again, my point is simple: LOOK at the trial balance in detail. Even if it's 500 lines long, it just won't take you that much time to go through it, to become familiar with it, and to identify the material areas to pay attention to. That small investment of time will pay enormous dividends as you move forward. So, armed with the understanding of what the client's trial balance looks like, THEN start your audit of their tax provision. As you do so, you will be amazed at how much more grounded and informed you will be than had you started into the process entirely from a "tax perspective."[54]

Verify the company's technical tax positions

A tax provision (and a tax return) isn't just about doing numeric calculations in a vacuum. Companies take a host of technical positions that impact their taxable income:

1) How to classify an asset for purposes of depreciation.
2) Whether certain activities qualify for the R&D credit.
3) Whether activities in a state or country rise to the level of creating a tax filing requirement and paying tax (e.g. "nexus" or "permanent establishment").
4) Whether a transaction is tax-free or not.

These are just a few of *many* possible examples. The point is that, as an auditor, you need to examine the tax positions a company has taken and determine whether they're reasonable, defensible, and supportable. In addition, it's not enough to evaluate issues that are directly brought to your attention or provided to you in writing (such as a memo). You need to be sufficiently observant, objective and thorough to identify potential transactions, structures, fact patterns, and issues with tax implications that the company may not have been aware of (or did not bring to your attention).

Determine that tax accounting rules are properly applied

As previously noted, a tax provision is not a tax return. Tax provisions and the accounting entries that are derived from them must be in accordance with U.S. GAAP (i.e. ASC 740). So, it's not only important to make sure that tax calculations in a tax provision are correct, but that those tax calculations are *accounted for correctly*. For example, a company may plan to take a deduction of $1,000 on their tax return. However, they know that $300 of this deduction is very aggressive and is unlikely to be sustained upon audit. Based on tax accounting rules related to uncertain tax positions, a company can only claim a financial statement (or tax accounting) benefit of $700, regardless of the position they take on their tax return.

There are many areas that might need to be considered when evaluating a company's tax provision: valuation allowances, APB 23 and the deferral of foreign earnings, business combinations, and so on. The point is that, as an auditor, you are evaluating more than just the projected taxable income and cash tax liability of a company, but also their accounting positions based on their tax profile, the nature of their transactions, and so forth.

---

[54] I know much of I've said in this section may seem obvious. That said, I'm aware of numerous instances of tax professionals working in the details of a provision in some capacity (auditing or otherwise) who have NO IDEA what the overall trial balance looks like because they just haven't taken 30 minutes to an hour to study it.

Document and support your audit assertions with verifiable evidence

"I love you."
"Do you have evidence to support your assertion?"[55]

As an auditor, it's important that you obtain verifiable evidence to support your audit assertions. But before we go any further, what is an "audit assertion"? For one, it includes any figure that's part of the tax provision. For example, assume the client gives you an Excel spreadsheet that's neatly organized and calculates a certain tax-related figure. Is it enough to skim through it, make sure it's mathematically correct, and then confirm the amount it's calculating ties to the tax provision file? The answer is no. How do you *know* the figures on the spreadsheet are correct? That's the key. After all, anyone can create a neatly organized spreadsheet. As an auditor, your job is to *verify* that the figures presented to you in spreadsheets, memos and other support are correct. Here are some ways to do that:

a. Where possible, agree figures in tax provision calculations and workpapers to the company's trial balance (which your Assurance colleagues are auditing).
b. If that's not possible, tie figures in tax provision calculations to other objective, verifiable data (e.g. W-2 wage data for the R&D calculation).
c. Separately obtain and review workpapers for "pure tax calculations" (the R&D credit, the foreign tax credit, etc.), ensuring that these calculations follow the tax rules and that the figures used to calculate them are verified according to the guidelines above.

The main point is to not accept any tax provision figures, spreadsheets, and workpapers and other support at face value; *trace everything to source data and documentation*. This same principle applies to auditing a company's tax positions. In other words, you shouldn't just accept that a transaction is tax-free, or qualifies for a preferential tax rate, or that some other benefit applies just because "the client says so" (even if it's documented in a memo on their letterhead). You should understand the facts of a company's tax positions, find verifiable evidence supporting those facts, and objectively evaluate whether the company's positions are sustainable based on how existing tax law and regulations are applied in practice based on your own knowledge and professional judgment.

Does all of that sound challenging? It is. And not only does it require a substantial amount of technical experience, but there is an art to auditing effectively without provoking a client to the point that they hate your guts. When dealing with company personnel it's unhelpful to come across as doubting, combative, or cynical ("All companies are hiding something"). Instead, be polite and trust your client, but establish a

---

[55] This is from a quote I saw tacked up in a corporate tax department.

sufficiently professional distance and manner that makes it clear that you expect support for everything they give you.[56]

Tie out and support the financial statement footnotes & management discussion and analysis ("MD&A")

While tax-related figures on the face of the financial statements carry the most weight, it's also important to tie out each tax-related figure or percentage that appears in the financial statement footnotes and the MD&A[57] to the tax provision workpapers.[58] Additionally, with respect to the financial statement footnote and the MD&A, you need to check the following:

1) The written explanations in the financial statements on tax-related matters cover areas required by SEC (for public companies) or other applicable disclosure requirements.
2) The tax-related summaries and explanations are accurate based on your understanding of the company's tax profile, positions, and activities.
3) The information provided is sufficiently robust to be meaningful (as opposed to glossing over or obscuring important matters).
4) The explanations are sufficiently clear and understandable to non-tax readers of the financial statements.

In summary, when auditing tax provisions, avoid getting lost in spreadsheets, memos, and other details, and always keep your focus on verifying the accuracy of the financial statements.

Beware of "SALY"

"What did the accountant cross the road?"
"Because that's what the workpapers called for last year." – Unknown

When auditing, should you build on the work of the prior year to gain efficiencies? Should you pay attention to how things were done? Should you build on the experience that was gained? Should you be on the lookout for the same issues? If there have been no major changes in the business, should you expect things to be similar overall to the prior year?

---

[56] As an example, you might say, "Thank you for providing Calculation X. I have checked it, and everything looks correct, but please show me where Figure Y came from."

[57] MD&A stands for the "Management Discussion & Analysis" section of SEC Form 10-K. This is where management provides an overview of a company's business, operations, and performance.

[58] Ideally, the client will have a summary workpaper that contains all the figures from the tax provision which ties to the financial statements (i.e. a "10-K tie-out" workpaper).

The answer is yes to all of these questions. HOWEVER, in all that you do as an auditor, be careful not to fall robotically into the well-worn groove of the same-as-last-year (or "SALY"[59]) mentality. If things really haven't substantively changed then following the prior year makes perfect sense. But ask questions. Pay attention and decide on your own if things have changed. Give familiar things a fresh look before diving into the details of ticking, tying and documenting. Follow the facts.

To illustrate the dangers of the SALY trap, I'll offer just one example. Let's say that in auditing a tax provision you assume that the book/tax differences are a) exactly what the client told you they were per their workpapers and b) are the same as they were last year. Based on this approach, you sailed through your audit procedures in record time and coming in well under budget. Everything appears great until it becomes clear that you never took more than a cursory look at the client's trial balance. Had you examined it in any detail, you would have discovered that the client created a new account where they booked a material reserve. Further, the client booked an expense in connection with the reserve *and* they counted it as a deduction to taxable income on their provision, when in fact the expense was non-deductible. In summary, because you assumed everything was the same as the prior year you missed an important audit finding, and such a mistake in the face of plain and available evidence can have serious ramifications.

7.3 Applying audit concepts to Example #1

Now that we've covered the theory of auditing tax provisions, we'll apply these concepts to Example #1. "Wait a minute," you might say. "Example #1? There's hardly anything going on! The balance sheet is simple, there are no book/tax differences (taxable income is the same as pretax book income), the effective tax rate is the same as the statutory rate, and there are just a few workpapers. What can there possibly be to audit?" To best answer these questions in context, let's examine them under a hypothetical scenario. I will act as the auditor, and you will be my client.

Sample audit questions and client information requests

The column on the left shows my thought process as an auditor, and the column on the right shows the corresponding questions, data, information and follow-up questions I will (or will not) request from you as the client.

The Audit Issue/Question	The Client Question/Information Request
"This company has $340,000 in revenue and $215,000 in expenses. While they're not very large now, it seems unlikely the company would have *no* book/tax differences. I need to get a more detailed	"I noted in the financial data you previously provided that many balance sheet and income statement items had been combined. Please provide a trial balance that has a detailed breakdown of assets, liabilities, income, and expenses."

---

[59] This is pronounced like "Sally."

breakout of the trail balance and review it on a line-by-line basis."	
"The company is using a 4% state tax rate in calculating the tax provision, which perfectly matches the rate of the state in which they operate. But do they have operations in other states (or countries)? And if so, could those activities cause the company to have additional tax filing requirements?[60]"	"Please provide a breakout of sales by location (state and country). Also, please provide a breakdown of payroll and fixed assets by location (state and country)."
"I wonder whether revenue is generated from one product or service, or whether there are multiple lines of business? Also, what's driving expenses? Are the company's expenses tied directly to revenue generation or do the spending patterns suggest the company is investing in other areas?"[61]	I don't have any client questions for now on these points. I will first examine the more detailed trial balance (see my request above) and that information will tell me what (if any) follow-up questions I need to ask.
"Based on the high-level financial data previously provided, operations appear to be straightforward. Also, this is the company's first year of operations, which increases the likelihood they're not doing anything out of the ordinary. However, I wonder if there is anything going on within the business that may not be evident from looking at the trial balance."	"Aside from your standard operations, is there anything going on with the business that you feel is worth discussing? Briefly describe your overall strategy. Has it changed during the year, or do you anticipate changes in the near to medium-term? If so, how might that affect your revenue, expenses, and your overall operations?"

Client responses to questions

Here are the additional facts and issues that were surfaced in response to the questions in the previous section:

- The company is trying to stretch their money during the start-up phase so they can pursue as many initiatives as possible. As a result, the Controller (who has limited tax experience) prepared the company's tax provision with no outside assistance because "it was simple and fairly straightforward."

---

[60] If a company has "nexus" in a state, it means their activities have risen to a level where they need to file returns and pay tax. In an international tax context, this is known as having a "permanent establishment" (or a "PE") in another country.

[61] The issue here is that a company's source(s) of revenue and how it spends its money can have significant tax implications.

- As part of their Year 1 marketing strategy, the client spent money entertaining prospective customers. Entertainment expenses are 100% non-deductible.[62]
- The company plans to file a tax return on the federal level, as well as for their home state (where their HQ is established). However, the company also has sales in three other states, as well as the UK. In addition, while most of the employees work at the company's HQ facility, employees in two other states work from home offices. Each of these employees has a laptop, a second monitor and a printer that shows up on the company's fixed asset system. These facts suggest the company may have filing requirements in more than just their home state[63]
- The company is selling services, but it turns out that they also have a small manufacturing operation that sells tangible property. This means the company has inventory, which brings a set of different tax considerations.[64]
- The manufacturing equipment the company is developing is cutting edge, so it appears that some of their expenses may qualify for the R&D tax credit.
- Company management believes their product has huge sales potential, but they're also concerned that unless they rapidly bring it to market they could lose their competitive advantage. As a result, senior management has targeted a potential company to acquire in an effort to quickly bring in customers, and serious talks have already occurred (with outside counsel involved). Senior management is also engaged in talks with banks and private equity firms about financing. These activities suggest that some of the company's expenses could be nondeductible IRC 263(a) costs.
- Given the additional information above, *there could be a material error(s) in the tax provision. If so, it could also suggest there may be a material weakness in the company's tax controls.*

Is it realistic that all of these issues would come out based on the audit inquiries? Probably not. However, it's also true that none of the issues that were detected were unrealistic given the company's tax profile, and any one of them could cause audit-related concerns. The point is, as an auditor, *do not simply accept what you are given (or told) at face value.* Instead, exercise professional skepticism by doing the following:

1) Make observations
2) Form expectations
3) Ask questions
4) Obtain objective and verifiable information (following-up as needed)
5) Perform analysis

---

[62] For this exercise, it's not necessary to know the rules behind all the tax issues raised by the client responses. The more important point is that the questions revealed several important items that were not immediately obvious but need to be addressed.

[63] You also need to follow up on the UK sales activity to ensure that the company did not trigger a tax filing requirement by creating a permanent establishment.

[64] IRC 263A is an issue to be aware of, but it wouldn't come into play in this simple example because the figures are so small.

After using any and all of the above techniques, document and support your audit assertions.

7.4 Observations from the Example #1 client audit

"Do I paint a correct picture…or do I exaggerate?"
Mr. Potter to George Baily in, "It's a Wonderful Life"

Clients don't want to be audited

As an auditor, there is something important you need to understand: *your client doesn't want to be audited.* Yes, the members of senior management all have advanced degrees, and they're well aware of the theory that audits add value because they give markets greater confidence in the company's financial position. In addition, a company's management subject themselves to audits because their shareholders, Wall Street, a lender, a regulatory body, or some other entity or group requires it. But at the ground level – with the company's accounting and tax personnel – there's no upside to an audit.

As a best case scenario, company personnel may glean some meaningful strategies, practices, and insights from their auditors based on their observations and experiences at other companies. But, relative to how much time they consume, audits don't help with the day-to-day operations of the company. Instead, they're often viewed by company personnel as something to get through so they can get back to the real work of getting things done.

A corporate Tax Group's view of an audit

Focusing specifically on the Tax Group's perspective, let's consider the possible outcomes of an audit:

1) The tax provision is materially correct. While this is a significant achievement at a company that has any degree of complexity (and the more the complex, the more significant the achievement), "perfection" in the tax provision may already be "expected" by senior management because it's a "routine" annual occurrence (like filing a tax return).[65] In short, there may be no significant reward for the Tax

---

[65] In other words, a Tax Group may only be considered to add value to a company to the extent that they meaningfully reduce the ETR or generate significant cash savings by engaging in complex tax planning. While this view sounds reasonable and understandable on the surface, it doesn't recognize the fact that taxes persist in being the cause of a significant percentage of company restatements, which speaks to their challenging nature and complexity (especially when you consider how many specialists prepare or review the various parts of a tax provision). Thus, in my view, Tax Groups (and outside firms) that consistently do high quality tax provision and compliance work add significant value in the form of reduced financial statement and audit risk. And, of course, Tax Groups that also engage in successful tax planning add *even more* value.

Group in successfully completing the tax provision beyond maintaining the status quo in terms of their present positions, their level of compensation, etc.

2) Significant and/or meaningful (but not material) issues are found with the tax provision. At a minimum, this will cause discomfort within the Tax Group, but it could also impact raise, bonus, stock compensation, and promotion decisions. The severity of the outcome will generally be decided on the overall performance of the Tax Group (i.e. has the Tax Group's work been trending down, staying the same, or getting better?). Another important factor is the strength of the Tax Group's relationship with senior management, the auditors, and other decision-makers.

3) A material error is found in the tax provision. This outcome could range from bad to catastrophic. At a minimum, the Tax Group is going to get called out and be the focus of negative attention. That *will* happen; the real question is what happens from there. It's highly likely that a material error will weigh heavily into any performance evaluation, and it's not uncommon for senior members of the Tax Group to lose their jobs over a material error (or a finding of a material weakness) in the tax provision.[66]

In summary, as an auditor, it's important to understand that when you examine a company's tax provision that their Tax Group faces significant risks and pressures. In summary, they have a lot to lose if any significant (or material) issues are found, and there's often little in the way of reward or upside if things turn out satisfactorily.[67]

You don't have to find a problem to be a good auditor

With the Tax Group's perspective of an audit firmly in mind, I want to make it absolutely clear that you don't have to find a problem, mistake, error or uncover some kind of nefarious cover-up to be a good auditor. Said another way, your job as an auditor isn't to find something *wrong*, your job is to independently confirm and document with verifiable evidence that a company has done things the *right way* from an accounting point of view, both in terms of how they have applied US GAAP (following the rules) as well as how accurately they have done so (being materially correct from a financial point of view). That's it – that's the job.

---

[66] The term "Tax Group" in this context also applies to an outside firm that the company may have hired to prepare the tax provision.

[67] These observations are not intended to describe the situation at every company, but the reality is that few outside of those who prepare and review tax provisions truly grasp how challenging they can be to complete accurately and on time. As a result, the Tax Group's work may not be fully recognized, valued, or appreciated. By the same token, it's important for tax professionals to appreciate the contributions of Controllers, CAOs, CFOs and others who are in the details of preparing financial statements, recognizing that the tax provision is just one part of a much larger process. In summary, successful financial statement preparation is challenging, and it requires great accounting and tax teams that cohesively work together (as well as with their auditors).

As you audit, do you need to maintain objectivity and independence of thought, even in the face of heavily desired outcomes pressing on you one way or the other? Do you sometimes have to be firm? Will you sometimes need to have hard conversations and relay things to a client that they don't want to hear? The answer is yes to all of these things. But again, this is all done in the spirit of professionalism and trying to get to the right answer, NOT with a "gotcha" mentality or setting out to prove a client is wrong.[68]

In summary, you would be fortunate if you went your entire career working with clients who were successful, committed to doing things the right way, and who never made any serious mistakes. But, as an auditor, if the time comes that you've got a bad client outcome, you need to be sufficiently independent, objective, principled and strong to make decisions based on correct standards. I'm not pretending that's an easy thing to do, but that's the standard and expectation.

First ask the Assurance/Audit Team, and then follow up with the client

In terms of communication, it's important to understand as an auditor that one of the biggest sins (yes, *sins*) you can commit is to ask a client a question that you should already know, or that you could find out on your own. Here are the types of offending questions in the order of their degree of severity (adding a little satire to make some points).

1) You ask the client a question that you have *personally* asked them before – Asking a repeat question is the most serious client question sin of them all, and it's especially bad if the client already provided the answer in writing (such as in an email).[69]
2) You ask a question that a member of the Assurance Team already knows – It's considered bad form to ask the client's Tax Group a question when you can obtain the information from your own audit team.
3) You ask a client about information they've already provided to "the Firm" – As a member of "the Firm," you're expected to know (or to be able to find out) "anything" the client has "ever" told "anyone" in the firm.[70]

---

[68] One way to avoid a battle of wills, egos and opinions with a client is to adopt a mentality of getting to and settling on *what* is right vs. *who* is right.

[69] This applies even if you asked the question, say, five years ago. While you may get a degree of leniency for something that goes that far back, expect clients to cut you less slack in finding information due to the fact that you are juggling 10+ clients. At the rates they pay your firm, they expect to you know them and treat them like they're your *only* client.

[70] Here it's worth mentioning to Tax Groups that it's understandable that you don't want to take time from your busy schedules to answer questions that you've already responded to, or where the answers could be obtained by the auditors on their own time with a reasonable degree of effort. However, for the sake of professionalism and positive relations, it's important not to hold auditors to an unrealistic standard. Can you always find every email you need that you've sent in the last five years? Can you remember all

Are these standards realistic, reasonable, or even a little ridiculous? Perhaps. But if you audit tax provisions, whether you agree that the above standards are fair or not, it's important to understand that they are embedded into the culture of numerous firms.

Carefully manage how you handle client questions

As noted above, before asking a client a question, you're expected to see if you already have the information on file. As a second line of defense, you should ask a member of your audit team. We'll now assume you've done those things, and you now need to follow-up with the client.

- In a perfect world, it would be best if you formulated *all* of your client questions ahead of time, asked them *once* and were done.
- Realistically, however, this will rarely be possible. For deeper or more complex issues, the ideal is to ask a question (or set of questions) to surface the right issue(s), and then ask a single follow-up question (or set of questions) that will give you the "final" answer(s) you need.

The exception to the above is if you feel your client is stonewalling or otherwise dragging their feet in providing important information. In such cases, you may need to be more persistent and demanding. However, before escalating things with the client, you should talk with the audit team, providing them with specifics on the issue, why you feel it's important and how material it may be. They can then provide guidance on whether more follow-up is necessary and, if so, the best way to approach it.

In summary, as an auditor, you have a job to do, and that job often involves following up with the client. However, an important part of being a good auditor is to focus on relevant and material issues, make efficient use of the client's time, and not to subject them to "death by a thousand questions."

Invest time and effort to improve audit efficiency

While the above process can be painful and time-consuming, it's important to invest the time and effort into doing the heavy lifting in the early years of an audit relationship. Thus, if you do good, thorough work, document it well, and continually strengthen and improve your processes, you will create a strong foundation that will enable future audits to be smoother, more efficient, and more accurate to a greater level of detail.

---

of your company's nuances and fact patterns off the top of your head? If not, is it really fair to expect an auditor to remember similar items without first getting refreshed on the facts? In summary, you'll likely have a much better relationship with your auditors if you incorporate some balance and reasonableness into your approach.

7.5   Audit terminology related to tax provisions

There's a lot of audit jargon and terminology. This section is not meant to cover all of it, but to focus on important and commonly used terms.

"Material" and "materiality"

The audit partner determines materiality for a company based on quantitative (e.g. metrics) and qualitative (e.g. judgmental) factors. An item is material if it rises to a level that would be considered meaningful to investors or other users of financial statements. To summarize by way of an example, if a company reports revenue of X and it should have been Y, the question is whether the difference between X and Y is large enough to be considered material by users of the financial statements.

Ultimately, materiality is either directly or indirectly a financial concept. In the example above, the question of materiality centered on whether the numeric difference between what sales were vs. what was reported in the financial statements was sufficiently large enough to matter to financial statement readers. However, events can also be material. For example, if the IRS informs a company that it will be audited, that could be deemed a "material event." While there is no immediate "cost" to an impending audit, the information is likely to be important to investors because it could change their view of the company's risk profile, and it alerts them to the potential of a (possible) material tax assessment. Based on this reasoning, a company is expected to disclose all "material events."[71]

"De minimis"

"De minimis" is a materiality concept. The idea is that if an amount is below the de minimis threshold then it's small enough that, as an auditor, it doesn't matter to you if the company ever corrects it. The rule of thumb is that the de minimis amount is 10% of materiality. But again, that is only a rough estimate. As with materiality, the de minimis threshold is set by the audit partner.

If an audit finding exceeds the de minimis threshold of materiality, but it's still *not* material, then it's added to the auditors' "SUM," or the "Summary of Uncorrected Misstatements."[72] If the company's management chooses to record the items on the SUM prior to the issuance of the financial statements, the SUM is cleared by the auditors, and the financial statements will be issued with what is intended to be a higher degree of accuracy. If the company chooses *not* to book the items on the SUM, or they elect to do

---

[71] If something is not "material," it is said to be "immaterial." If something is immaterial it doesn't mean it is not true or accurate. Rather, something that's immaterial is simply considered not large enough or important enough to "matter" as far as financial statement readers are concerned.

[72] Firms may have different names for this. For example, I've also heard the term "SUD" in practice, meaning the "Summary of Unadjusted Differences."

so in a later accounting period, *the financial statements can still be issued with a clean opinion*. However, the auditors will report the items on the SUM to the Audit Committee of the company's Board of Directors.[73]

Company approaches to recording audit findings that are above de minims but below the materiality threshold

Which approach should a company's management take, to record or not record the items on the SUM? It's faster, easier, less expensive, and more efficient for everyone involved if management does NOT immediately record SUM items found during the audit. In such cases management effectively says to the auditor, "The issue is noted, we don't disagree with your findings, and we will book those items in the next accounting period (or not at all)." With this kind of approach, both the company and the auditors can keep progressing towards the issuance of the financial statements without having to rework financial accounts, workpapers and related support.

Some companies take a different approach, adopting a "zero tolerance" policy towards SUM items. While this may be done with the well-intentioned desire to have high-quality financial reporting, it puts a substantial amount of pressure on the company's tax and accounting teams, as well as the auditors. Why? Because, for purposes of financial statement reporting *the de minimis materiality threshold effectively becomes the de factor materiality threshold*.

Illustrating the considerations for making a late adjustment for an immaterial amount

To illustrate this concept, assume a company's de minimis and overall materiality thresholds are 10 and 100, respectively. During the audit, an error is found that should increase the company's tax expense by 15. What happens? Senior management could say the tax provision workpapers and the GAAP books will stay as they are because the error is immaterial, and no adjusting entry will be booked. However, the issue will be reported to the Board's Audit Committee, and it can be corrected (or "trued up") in the next accounting period.

On the other hand, if the company's management requires all items above the de minimis threshold to be booked before the issuance of the financial statements, it means the following:

---

[73] As background, a company's shareholders elect the members of the Board of Directors (the "Board"). Thus, the Board represents the collective shareholder interests of the company. Among other things, the Board is responsible for appointing the Chief Executive Officer of the company. Thus, the CEO is accountable to the Board. Boards often divide themselves into subcommittees to better manage their responsibilities according to the members' expertise. The Audit Committee of the Board is responsible for overseeing the company's financial reporting (and public companies must have an Audit Committee).

1) The tax provision will need to be recalculated, and the workpapers, memos and other items that have been impacted will all need to be updated as well.[74]
2) The tax provision will need to be *carefully reviewed* to ensure there are no unexpected changes or additional errors caused by the update.[75]
3) After the tax provision is updated and reviewed, the GL will need to be opened, and a tax adjusting entry will need to be booked.[76]
4) The financial statements will need to be updated, including all figures and footnote disclosures that may have been impacted by the change.
5) The audit team will need to re-examine all of the above to ensure that the revised tax provision and financial statements are correct.
6) Each of these steps is likely to take place late in the year-end close process when the pressure is high, and everyone is feeling the strain from working long hours and the stress to get things right.[77]

In my view, while high quality financial reporting is the standard, care should be exercised between living with materially correct but imperfect financials vs. the time, cost, and risk of making late changes to draw closer to "perfection."

Restatements and material weaknesses from an auditor's point of view

Restatements are not only bad from a company's perspective (management, the Board, etc.), but from the auditor's viewpoint as well. A restatement is essentially a public announcement that the auditors failed to detect a material misstatement as part of their examination procedures, and they also failed to uncover the ineffective internal controls that allowed it to happen. As a result, auditors are highly sensitive to restatements.

---

[74] It may be tempting to do a quick "topside adjustment" to make a late correction. This means booking an entry at the consolidated level rather than at the entity level where the change occurred. This avoids the time and headache of a reconsolidation, but it's *very hazardous* due to the possibility of making (another) error, to the point that some companies do not allow topside adjustments as a matter of policy.

[75] This can be tricky, because tax calculations have many moving parts. Thus, what may seem like a simple adjustment could lead to unanticipated changes due to certain tax-related limitations or thresholds being breeched, which change could cause a tax calculation to be computed by Method A instead of Method B, and so on.

[76] In practice, it's possible to correct the tax provision workpapers and the financial statements right away and book the correcting entry after the audit is complete. However, it's not advisable.

[77] This is the irony of requiring de minimis items to be booked in the pursuit of high-quality financial reporting. When late adjustments are made under time pressure to a highly complex calculation such as the tax provision, it can actually increase the probability of an error.

An auditor's finding of a material weakness *without* a restatement is certainly a negative from management's perspective, but not necessarily from the auditor's point of view.[78] In other words, if materially correct financial statements are issued with the finding of a material weakness then auditor is effectively saying, "We audited the financial statements and they are now materially correct, but only after we helped management by uncovering a significant error due to their ineffective internal controls." Alternatively, if the auditor's issue a material weakness finding even though the actual numbers reported were okay, it's like saying, "The financial statements are materially correct but, because of weak controls implemented and overseen by management, they *could have been* materially misstated had certain circumstances come about."

---

[78] This statement doesn't take into account the strain an auditor's finding of a material weakness may have on the relationship with management, especially in cases where they (management) do not fully agree with the likelihood or magnitude of the internal controls failure.

8 An Introduction to Book/Tax Differences

Up to this point, we've covered basic tax accounting concepts, the relationship between the tax provision and the tax return, how to prepare a basic tax provision, and what auditors are looking for when reviewing the tax provision. With this foundational understanding, you're now prepared to learn more in-depth tax accounting concepts, rules, and mechanics, starting with book/tax differences.

8.1   Learning objectives
- Learn why there are differences between pretax book income for GAAP and taxable income for compliance purposes.
- Be able to recognize terminology used in practice that relates to book/tax differences.
- Understand why GAAP is the starting point for calculating taxable income and review the process for doing so.
- Name the four sources for identifying and calculating book/tax differences.
- Get introduced to the relationship between book/tax differences and permanent differences.

8.2   Book/ tax differences exist because of different rules and objectives for financial and tax reporting

In Example #1, there was no difference between book (or "GAAP") income and taxable income. This is almost never the case for a company of any size and complexity. Therefore, it's important to understand why there are differences between a company's book income and taxable income, even though both figures are derived from the same underlying economic activities.

Book/tax differences exist primarily because GAAP and the Internal Revenue Code have different objectives. GAAP is designed to comprehensively capture a company's income and expenses within a specific time period to provide as complete and accurate a picture as possible of its financial condition. One could endlessly debate whether the GAAP rules do that effectively, but that's the intention.

The Internal Revenue Code ("IRC"), on the other hand, is designed to achieve different objectives. The purpose of the IRC is to generate taxes to finance the activities of the U.S. government, as well as to implement, promote, or support tax reporting, enforcement, economic, political, and social policies and objectives by providing rules, incentives, and penalties for various activities.

As an example, Congress has passed laws allowing companies to elect accelerated depreciation for the purchase of certain assets to promote spending that's intended to boost economic activity. Thus, while a $10,000 asset may be depreciated evenly over its estimated economic life for book purposes, the company may be able to deduct half or more of the cost in Year 1 for tax purposes.[79] This asymmetry between GAAP and the IRC on the treatment of the same asset purchase is what drives the book/tax difference in depreciation.

As another example, assume a company spends $40,000 on entertainment for sales and marketing purposes. This is a real economic cost to the company, meaning that it has $40,000 less cash in the bank because of expenses it incurred on activities that have a bona fide business purpose. However, based at least partially on perceived abuses, Congress has passed laws that altogether prohibit expenses for entertainment, meaning a company would get no tax deduction for these activities.

8.3 Book/tax terminology – "Schedule M's" and "M-1's"

If you have an accounting rather than a tax background, it's important to be aware of how tax professionals refer to book/tax differences. Here are some of the terms you will likely hear.

- "Schedule M's" – Book/tax differences are referred to this way because large companies report them on Schedule M-3 of the corporate tax return.
- "M-1's" – It's becoming rarer as time goes on, but you will sometimes hear book/tax differences referred to as M-1's. It's because that was the name of the schedule that book/tax differences were reported on before Schedule M-3 was created by the IRS.[80]

To see how this sounds in a real situation…

- If a book expense was $30,000,
- $10,000 was disallowed for tax and
- The net tax deduction reported on the corporate return was $20,000 then
- The "Schedule M" (or "M-1") for this item would be $10,000.

---

[79] Examples of accelerated depreciation for tax purposes include MACRS depreciation, bonus depreciation, and IRC 179.
[80] Schedule M-1 still exists, but large corporations don't use it because Schedule M-3 is required when total assets equal or exceed $10M at the end of the tax year.

8.4 GAAP financial data is the starting point for determining taxable income

Book (or GAAP) financial data is the starting point for calculating taxable income. In doing so, you follow these steps.

1) Start with the assumption (which you will almost certainly prove wrong) that taxable income is equal to pretax book income (not net income).
2) Examine all GAAP income, expense, and balance sheet items.
3) Modify or adjust these items (or accounts) for tax reporting (or "compliance") purposes as required by the Internal Revenue Code and its accompanying rules and regulations[81]; these are your book/tax differences
4) Taxable income is computed by summing GAAP income plus the net book/tax differences determined in step #3.

8.5 Income (and not book/tax differences) gives rise to income taxes

"Income" gives rise to "income taxes"

It should be noted that book/tax differences by themselves do *not* give rise to income taxes. Rather, "income" is what gives rise to "taxable income," and taxable income is what gives rise to income taxes.

To illustrate this point, recall that in Example #1 the company had no book/tax differences, and yet its tax expense was $31,250. In the example, the company's pretax book income was $125,000, there were no adjustments, and so taxable income was $125,000. In summary, despite the fact that there were no book/tax differences, the company in Example #1 owed income tax (on its *income*) of $31,250 at a 25% rate.

Book/tax differences can be favorable or unfavorable

It should also be noted that book/tax differences are not always *unfavorable*. In fact, favorable book/tax differences can shield a company from tax. For example, assume that a company has pretax book income of $100,000. Absent any other considerations, at a tax rate of 25%, it would owe income tax of $25,000. However, if this company had a *favorable* book/tax difference of $125,000, it would have a taxable loss of $25,000 ($100,000 minus $125,000) and owe zero in income tax.

---

[81] This is an important point; book equals tax unless there are tax rules that require an adjustment. Also, it's sound policy for taxable income to be derived from book income. The alternative is the same economic activities of a company would need to be recorded in two entirely different sets of books, one for GAAP and the other for taxable income per the IRC.

Again, don't think of book/tax differences as causing or not causing a company to have taxable income. Rather, think of book/tax differences as *modifying* (up or down) the income tax a company will owe on its GAAP-basis book income.

8.6 The sources for identifying and calculating book/tax differences

This book is focused on tax accounting and tax provision concepts, not tax compliance and the broad range of rules pertaining to the Internal Revenue Code. For this reason, we will not go into great detail about how to calculate numerous Schedule M's. However, it's helpful for tax provision purposes to understand the four different sources of book/tax differences.

Source #1 - Unmodified (or "pure") trail balance amounts

Some book/tax differences are calculated from figures that come straight from the trial balance without any modification. Here are some examples:

- Club dues – These amounts are non-deductible. Therefore, if there's a specific GL account where club membership costs are recorded, the entire amount will be treated as an unfavorable book/tax difference.
- Municipal interest income – This type of interest income is tax-exempt. Therefore, if it's recorded in a separate account on the GL, the entire amount will be treated as a favorable book/tax difference.
- Accrued expenses – Many accrued expenses for book purposes are not deductible for tax until they're actually paid. To determine the book/tax difference for certain accrued expenses you can "flux" the balance sheet account. For example, if the company accrues a loss contingency of $500,000 for GAAP (a non-cash book expense), the unfavorable Schedule M (or tax addback) of $500,000 is calculated as follows:

Beginning balance sheet balance for loss contingencies:	$0
Plus: Accrued loss contingencies for the period:	$500,000
Less: Cash settlements:	$0
Equals: Schedule M (unfavorable)	$500,000[82]

There are many other examples, but the point I'm trying to make is that each of the above book/tax differences was calculated from *unmodified* figures that came straight from the trial balance. These are the easiest kinds of book/tax differences to identify and to compute.

---

[82] This is a $500,000 unfavorable addition to taxable income.

Source #2 - Modified trial balance (or GL) amounts

The second type of book/tax difference is one that's derived from GL account data, but it takes some work to get to the answer. To illustrate, assume that $100,000 of food and beverage-related expenses are booked to a GL account labelled "Meals." First, you cannot say that the unmodified amount of $100,000 for meals is a book/tax difference. At a minimum, you would need to make the following adjustment:

Total meal expenses per the GL	$100,000
Times: Tax limitation percentage	50%
Equals: Schedule M for meals	$50,000[83]

To further complicate matters, not all "meal expenses" are disallowed at 50%. For example, after examining the GL detail in the meals account, you determine that it breaks down as follows:

Sales and marketing meals	$50,000 (50% deductible)
Meals billed to clients and reimbursed	$40,000 (100% deductible)
Entertainment booked to the meals account	$10,000 (100% nondeductible)

Based on this more detailed analysis, you determine the deduction for meals should be $65,000 rather than $50,000. And setting aside what changes may happen with the deductibility of meals over time, the main point is there are book/tax difference that you can't simply pull straight from the trial balance; determining some Schedule M's requires analysis and modification of GL data. This example also provides some valuable insights on ways to increase the speed and accuracy of tax provision calculations.

1) Create separate GL accounts for "tax sensitive" items – Ideally, you should work with the Accounting Group to create separate GL accounts for book/tax differences, thus turning "modified" book/tax calculations into ones that are "unmodified." Following the example above, you could ask the Accounting Group to book meals to three accounts so you can quickly calculate and support the related Schedule M:[84]

---

[83] To be clear, this means the total book expense for meals is $100,000 and the unfavorable book/tax difference is $50,000, meaning the allowable tax deduction is $50,000. Also note that this percentage changes over time based on laws passed by Congress. For example, as part of pandemic relief, the meals deduction is slated to go up to 100% for a few years to help the restaurant industry, and it's anyone's guess what Congress will do after that.

[84] This is not necessarily something the Accounting Group will know to do without your prompting and initiative. Remember, their job is to keep the books according to GAAP, and meals are NOT treated differently for book purposes than any other standard operating expense. Also, it's not enough just to have the Accounting Group create the tax-related GL accounts that you request. As a tax professional (if that's your role), you need to provide training and guidance on what kinds of expenses should be booked to

        a. Meals – Sales and Marketing
        b. Meals – Billable
        c. Entertainment – Booked to an "Entertainment" account.[85]

2) <u>Independently</u> obtain and analyze GL detail – If you cannot get separate accounts created for tax-related items, second prize is to get the training and systems access necessary to obtain GL account details (e.g. for "Meals") *on your own*. That way, you can independently slice and dice the data (food pun intended) how you need to calculate book/tax differences.

3) Gather information from the Accounting Group – What if you don't have access to the GL? And even if you do, what if you run a report to obtain information on an account only to find the output is in a format that you cannot interpret or understand, or the information isn't sufficiently broken out for your purposes?[86] Here are three possible scenarios:

    a. You have cultivated a good relationship with the Accounting Group by communicating well, and you have a history of coming through for each other. As a result, when you make your request, they're responsive and provide accurate, timely, and organized information.
    b. The Accounting Group is slow to get back to you and, based on time pressure and the necessity of keeping the tax provision moving, you make assumptions based on the information you do have. In our "Meals" example, you might feel the need to be conservative and assume that all meal-related expenses ($100,000) are limited.[87]

---

each account and why. While this takes some effort, it will increase the speed and enhance the accuracy of tax-related calculations for years to come.

[85] At some companies, creating an account is no big deal; they have hundreds of them. Other companies take a leaner approach in developing their chart of accounts. In those cases, they will likely be more resistant to breaking one meal account (efficient for GAAP) into three separate accounts (inefficient for GAAP). However, if you explain the "why" behind your request, it will more likely be approved.

[86] In a perfect world, the "tax patient" is put in front of you in a timely fashion, and you have all the facts, data, software, and other tools you need to successfully complete the "tax surgery." In practice, however, you may have limited facts on the "tax patient," and you may need to run around the "hospital" (the company) yourself to get the information and systems access you need. Then, under pressure, you will need to use the imperfect tools and systems you have available at the time to do the "surgery." In short, working on tax provisions can look and feel more like battlefield surgery than what happens in a state-of-the-art hospital!

[87] While a quick estimate will, of course, save you time on the front end, there are potential consequences. For example, by not doing a full analysis of the "Meals" account in our example you may conclude that the deductible expense is $50,000 ($100,000 x

c. You go back and forth following up with the Accounting Group and finally get the information and clarifications you need to do a full account analysis, but the consequence is that it will strain your ability to meet your tax provision time budget or deadline.[88]

In summary, segregate tax-related accounts on the GL to the extent possible so that tax provision calculations are quick and easily supportable.[89] However, this may not always be possible. As a result, to calculate some book/tax differences, it will be necessary to analyze GL account data. Ideally, you want to be able to do this independently by obtaining your own reports and doing your own analysis. However, if you cannot do so, you will need to work with the Accounting Group (and potentially others) to obtain the data and information you need to support various tax provision calculations.

Source #3 - Special tax calculations

Up to now, we've said that some GL accounts have a direct impact on taxable income ("unmodified"), and others contain data that can be used to compute an adjustment ("modified").

However, there are certain tax calculations that are not associated with any one GL account, meaning they require information and figures that come from multiple accounts or sources. As an example, consider the deduction for interest expense. There is no single expense line item in the GL that you can use or modify to compute this tax benefit.

50%), leaving a deduction of $15,000 on the table. If this $15,000 difference were to ever surface then it could be characterized as an error on the part of the Tax Group, and that has financial statement (i.e. restatement) and SOX controls implications based on the level of materiality.

[88] In other words, the "ideal" solution of "Do a complete analysis on everything" when you're under intense time pressure and working with disorganized, voluminous, and potentially incomplete information, is easier said than done.

[89] Cal Ripken was a Hall of Fame shortstop that played for the Baltimore Orioles. Despite his stellar achievements, there were some who criticized his defense, complaining that he rarely made "spectacular plays" like other shortstops of his day. However, the genius of Cal Ripken was that he was so fundamentally sound and so smart about where he positioned himself on the field, he rarely needed to make a "spectacular play" (even though he demonstrated on numerous occasions that he was capable of doing so if necessary). In like fashion, you should work smartly and continuously on the tax provision on the *front end* of the process to maximize efficiency and minimize complexity where possible, thus enhancing the speed and accuracy of your work. Conversely, it's highly inadvisable and risky to solely rely on a "spectacular play" mentality in tax provision work. This means that you're counting on technical brilliance, your ability to manage chaos, and/or adopting an up-all-night approach to save the day on the back end. This is not to say that you should expect tax provision work to be easy but, taking a page from Cal Ripken's playbook, you should work to make it *"look"* as easy as possible.

Instead, additional calculations using separate data must be done to determine what portion of a company's interest expense is allowable and what portion may be limited.

Depreciation, something we covered earlier, is another example of a special tax calculation. If you recall, the depreciation *expense* for book purposes and the depreciation *deduction* for tax purposes are rarely the same. Also, it's not enough to simply "modify" the book depreciation account to arrive at taxable income; the rules for book and tax depreciation are so different that they must be calculated separately. For depreciation, the adjustment to change book income to taxable income works like this:

Pretax book income	$100,000 – This ties to the financial statements
Reverse book depreciation	$15,000 – This is the GL amount
Deduct tax depreciation	($20,000) – This is reported on IRS Form 4562
Taxable Income	$95,000 – This ties to the tax return

For these figures, the Accounting Group is responsible for calculating and supporting book depreciation ($15,000) according to GAAP and the Tax Group is responsible for computing tax depreciation ($20,000) based on the rules of the IRC. Thus, arriving at the correct deduction requires more than just analyzing and modifying the GL account(s) for depreciation; more reports and information are required.

Source #4 - Tax credits

Tax credits are difficult to classify, but they can be categorized as a type of book/tax difference. As with the "special tax calculations" category above, tax credit computations frequently require data and information from both the GL and other sources. However, unlike the special tax calculations above, tax credits affect a company's *tax expense* rather than its taxable income.

Consider the R&D tax credit as an example. Computing the credit requires information from multiple GL accounts, wage data from the Payroll Group, and survey information from R&D personnel. Assuming our company in Example #1 calculated a $10,000 R&D credit based on this data, we would calculate its tax liability as shown in the illustration.

The Impact of Tax Credits

Pretax Book Income	$125,000
Schedule M Book/Tax Differences	$0
Subtotal: Taxable Income	$125,000
Times: Tax Rate	25%
Subtotal: Income Tax Before Credits	$31,250
Less: R&D Tax Credit	($10,000)
Equals: Net Income Tax After Credits	$21,250

8.7 The relationship between book/tax differences and temporary and permanent differences

In the previous section, we discussed the four different approaches to identify and compute book/tax differences:

1) Unmodified trial balance amounts
2) Modified trial balance amounts
3) Special tax calculations
4) Tax credits

Regardless of the source, *all* book/tax differences fall into one of two categories for tax provision (and tax compliance) purposes:

1) Permanent differences
2) Temporary differences

It's important to understand that a book/tax difference from any of the four sources cited above can be characterized as a permanent difference *or* a temporary difference. For example, certain Schedule M's that come from unmodified trial balance amounts are permanent in nature, and others are temporary. It is the *nature* of an item that determines whether it is permanent or temporary, not the *source* of the data needed to calculate it. Permanent and temporary differences will be the subject of the next two chapters.

9 Permanent Differences and Tax Provision Example #2

9.1 Learning objectives
- Understand the meaning behind the term "permeant difference," and how it relates to book (GAAP) and taxable income.
- Recognize the difference between favorable and unfavorable differences.
- Follow an example of how to incorporate a permanent difference into a tax provision workbook.
- Gain insight into how permanent differences impact the effective tax rate, and how to compute the impact.

9.2 Permanent differences defined

Permanent differences between book and tax are those that will *never* reverse with time. Recall from our earlier discussion that amounts spent on entertainment (assume $40,000 as an example) are fully expensed for GAAP purposes. However, entertainment expenses are 100% disallowed as tax deductions. Thus, if this were the only book/tax difference in the history of the company, taxable income would *permanently* be higher than book income by $40,000 (meaning the difference would never reverse).

9.3 Favorable vs. unfavorable permanent differences

Permanent differences can be favorable or unfavorable. For example, entertainment expenses are an *unfavorable* permanent difference because they make taxable income higher than book income. Said another way, it means the income on which the company pays tax is higher than its economic (or GAAP) income. On the other hand, municipal interest income is a *favorable* permanent difference, because it represents book income that will never be subject to tax.

9.4 Tax Provision Example #2 – Permanent Differences

Now that you understand the basic principles of permanent differences, we'll look at an example to see how they impact the tax provision.

Updated background and assumptions

Tax Provision Example #2 has the same background and assumptions as Example #1, with the following addition:

- As part of its Year 1 business operations the company spent $20,000 on meals.
- Assume in Year 1 that the Internal Revenue Code applied a 50% limitation to meal expenses. This means the company will only get a tax deduction of $10,000 for the $20,000 that was spent on meals.

Selected observations on these updates are noted in the comments that follow, and you can refer to the complete set of Example #2 workpapers in the back of the material to see all figures, calculations, explanations, and references.

The trial balance (1600)

The trial balance at workpaper 1600 has been updated with the $20,000 spent on meals (see the illustration – "Expense – Permanent Item").

Revenue - Standard	($340,000)
Revenue - Permanent Item	$0
Expense - Standard	$215,000
Expense - Permanent Item	$20,000

Compared to Example #1, this has reduced pretax book income from $125,000 to $105,000 (see the illustration below)

Pretax Book Income Calculation

	From Unadjusted Opening Trial Balance	From Closing (or "Final") Trial Balance
Option 1 - Revenue & Expense Excluding Income Taxes		
Pretax Book Income/(Loss)	$105,000	$105,000
Option 2 - Net Income with Taxes Added Back		
Current Year Net Income/(Loss)	$105,000	$76,250
Add: Current Tax Expense/(Benefit) - Federal	$0	$28,750
Add: Deferred Expense/(Benefit) - Federal	$0	$0
Equals: Pretax Book Income/(Loss)	$105,000	$105,000

[This space was intentionally left blank].

The tax provision (1000)

- Pretax book income of $105,000 carried over from workpaper 1600 to workpaper 1000, and it's the new starting point for the tax provision calculation.
- Unlike Example #1, there is now a permanent difference between PTBI ($105,000) and taxable income ($115,000). The $10,000 difference is driven by the book/tax difference for meals.
- The current tax expense of the company is $28,750 (which is expected to tie to the tax return when it is filed later in the year).
- Like Example #1, there are no deferred taxes, so the total tax expense of the company is $28,750 ($28,750 current tax plus $0 of deferred tax).

	Tax Provision Current Year
Pretax Book Income	$105,000
Permanent Differences	
Permanent Difference - GL-related Items - Revenue	$0
Permanent Difference - GL-related Items - Expenses	$10,000
Permanent Difference - Special Tax Calculation	$0
Temporary Differences	
Temporary Difference - GL-related Items	$0
Temporary Difference - Depreciation	$0
Tax Return Calculations	
Subtotal: Pre-NOL Federal Taxable Income	$115,000
Times: Federal Tax Rate	25.00%
Subtotal: Federal Tax Before Credits	$28,750
Less: Federal Tax Credits	$0
Subtotal: Fed Tax Return Prov. - Current Tax Exp/(Ben)	$28,750

M-1 calculation summary (1200)

This workpaper calculates the $10,000 book tax difference for meals that ties to the tax provision (see the following illustration).

Permanent Differences - GL-related - Expenses	
Expense - Permanent Item	$20,000
Times: M-1 Statutory Disallowance %	50%
Perm. Difference - GL-related Item - (Fav)/Unfav. Sch M	$10,000

Financial statements (5)

- Pretax book income of $105,000 ties to the proof of pretax book income on workpaper 1600 (see Options 1 and 2), as well as the tax provision at workpaper 1000.
- The total tax expense of $28,750 also ties to the tax provision workpaper at 1000.

Consolidated Statement of Comprehensive Income/(Loss)

Revenue	$340,000
Expenses (Pretax)	($235,000)
Income/(Loss) Before Income Tax Provision	$105,000
Income Tax (Provision)/Benefit	($28,750)
Net Income	$76,250
	In Balance
Other Comprehensive Income	$0
Comprehensive Income/(Loss)	$76,250

The effective tax rate ("ETR") reconciliation (5)

The updated ETR reconciliation is in the illustration that follows. Note that the expected tax based on pretax book income is $26,250 ($105,000 PTBI x 25%), whereas the total tax expense is $28,750. The $2,500 difference is attributable to the $10,000 Schedule M for meals, and it's calculated by multiplying this $10,000 book/tax difference times the statutory tax rate of 25% ($10,000 x 25% = $2,500).

[This space was intentionally left blank].

Effective Tax Rate Reconciliation

The differences between the effective tax rate reflected in the tax provision and the federal statutory rates are as follows:

Description	Dollar	Rate	
Expected Tax Provision/(Benefit) at the Statutory Tax Rate	$26,250	25.00%	From 1000
Nondeductible Meals	$2,500	2.38%	
Income Tax Provision/(Benefit)	$28,750	27.38%	

In the "Rate" column, we see the statutory (or expected) tax rate of the company is 25%. This differs from the effective tax rate of the company, which is 27.38%. The ETR (27.38%) is calculated by dividing the total tax expense ($28,750) by pretax book income ($105,000). In this example, the company paid tax at a rate that's 2.38% higher than the statutory rate based on its level of pretax book income. This 2.38% difference is solely attributable to the book/tax difference for meals, and it's calculated by dividing the tax-effected book/tax difference of $2,500 by pretax book income of $105,000.

Permanent differences DO impact the effective tax rate

I want to draw attention to the fact that *permanent book/tax differences impact the effective tax rate.*

- Unfavorable permanent tax differences have a negative (or "bad") effect on the ETR.

- Favorable permanent tax differences have a positive (or "good") effect on the ETR.

A fundamental element of tax planning is to identify your existing "inventory" of permanent differences and to:

- Reduce or eliminate *current* unfavorable permanent differences.
- Avoid *new* unfavorable permanent differences.
- Increase *current* favorable permanent differences.
- Create *new* favorable permanent differences.

There are a few things to keep in mind that I've learned about tax planning over the course of my career. Here are a few.

- It's an income tax, so if you have income then you will pay tax. The goal then is not to eliminate your company's (or client's) tax burden, but to *optimize* it to the extent realistically possible based on their business operations.
- "The tax tail shouldn't wag the business dog."[90] What that means is a company doesn't make money by saving tax, it makes money by effectively executing on its business plan to sell goods, services, software, or whatever. That means, in my view, that the business should lead, and the goal of the tax function is to make business operations as cost-efficient as possible.

---

[90] I don't know who to credit for coming up with this saying, but it's a good one!

10 Temporary Differences and an Introduction to Deferred Taxes

Temporary differences are the second category of book/tax differences, and they're the subject of this chapter.

10.1 Learning objectives

- Define temporary differences, and how they tie into book/tax differences.
- Gain an understanding of the relationship between temporary differences and deferred taxes.
- Review the ASC 740 language on deferred taxes and learn how to more intuitively understand and apply this tax accounting concept.
- Learn the fundamentals of developing journal entries for deferred taxes.
- List the three sources that give rise to temporary differences.
- Learn how to recognize and interpret temporary differences from a "basis difference" (or balance sheet) point of view.
- Learn about tax basis balance sheets, how they are developed, and how they can be used to identity and prove out deferred taxes.

10.2 Temporary differences defined

As a review from the last chapter, permanent differences between book and tax are those that will *never* reverse with time. Temporary differences between book and tax are those that *will* reverse at some point in the future. Depreciation is a classic example. Say that a company purchases equipment for $50,000 In Year 1. For book purposes, assume that it will depreciate the equipment on a straight-line basis over five years (or $10,000 per year). For tax purposes, assume the company can claim a deduction for the entire purchase in Year 1. The book/tax differences for the company by year and in total are shown in the illustration and take note of the following:

- There is book/tax difference *each individual year*.
- There is a *favorable* book/tax difference of $40,000 in Year 1, and there are *unfavorable* differences of $10,000 in Years 2-5.
- Despite the *annual difference* in book vs. tax depreciation, over a five-

	Book/GAAP Expense	Tax Deduction	Book/Tax Difference
Year 1	$10,000	$50,000	($40,000)
Year 2	$10,000	$0	$10,000
Year 3	$10,000	$0	$10,000
Year 4	$10,000	$0	$10,000
Year 5	$10,000	$0	$10,000
Totals	$50,000	$50,000	$0

year period the *total* depreciation expense for book and the total depreciation deduction is the *same* ($50,000)

The third bullet point is the key; temporary differences are those where there may be a book/tax differences in any given year, but those differences even out as they reverse over time. In other words, given that depreciation is a temporary difference, book and tax depreciation end up being the same on a *cumulative* basis.[91]

10.3 An illustration of temporary differences reversing over time

The illustration below builds on the previous example by showing the tax impact by year of a temporary difference in depreciation.

	Book/GAAP Expense	Tax Deduction	Book/Tax Difference	Tax Rate	Tax Impact	Cumulative Tax Savings
Year 1	$10,000	$50,000	($40,000)	25%	($10,000)	($10,000)
Year 2	$10,000	$0	$10,000	25%	$2,500	($7,500)
Year 3	$10,000	$0	$10,000	25%	$2,500	($5,000)
Year 4	$10,000	$0	$10,000	25%	$2,500	($2,500)
Year 5	$10,000	$0	$10,000	25%	$2,500	$0
Totals	$50,000	$50,000	$0		$0	

Note the following from the illustration:

- In Year 1, tax depreciation exceeds book depreciation by $40,000, which results in an after-tax benefit that's $10,000 higher than a deduction based the book depreciation expense of $10,000.
- The "temporary" $10,000 depreciation benefit the company received in Year 1 does not last; in years 2-5 the company is unable to claim any depreciation deduction (it was all used up in Year 1), so tax is higher by $2,500 a year.
- At the end of Year 5, we see that the benefits of accelerated depreciation in Year 1 were ultimately offset by higher taxes in years 2-5. Thus, tax vs. book depreciation is a *temporary difference*.

---

[91] Based on ASC 740-10-25-20, a temporary difference is defined as, "…a difference between the tax and GAAP basis of an asset or liability that will result in taxable or deductible amounts in future years when the reported amount of the financial statement asset or liability is recovered or settled, respectively." This definition can be confusing, which is why we started our discussion of temporary differences with a more "Plain English" explanation. However, the meaning of this definition, and its references to tax and GAAP basis, will become clearer as we progress through the material.

These concepts are further clarified in the illustration that follows.

	Year 1	Year 2	Year 3	Year 4	Year 5	Tax Totals	Book Totals
Pretax Book Income	$100,000	$100,000	$100,000	$100,000	$100,000	$500,000	$500,000
Reverse Book Depreciation	$10,000	$10,000	$10,000	$10,000	$10,000	$50,000	N/A
Deduct Tax Depreciation	($50,000)	$0	$0	$0	$0	($50,000)	N/A
Taxable Income	$60,000	$110,000	$110,000	$110,000	$110,000	$500,000	$500,000
Times: Tax Rate	25%	25%	25%	25%	25%	25%	25%
Subtotal: Current "Cash" Tax	$15,000	$27,500	$27,500	$27,500	$27,500	$125,000	$125,000
Add: Deferred (Future) Tax	$10,000	($2,500)	($2,500)	($2,500)	($2,500)	$0	N/A
Equals: Total Tax Expense	$25,000	$25,000	$25,000	$25,000	$25,000	$125,000	$125,000
Effective Tax Rate	25%	25%	25%	25%	25%	25%	25%

- In this example, we assume the company has pretax book income of $100,000 in years 1-5, and from there we layer in the impact of the temporary difference in depreciation on a year-by-year basis.
- In Year 1, taxable income is only $60,000 compared to pretax book income of $100,000. This $40,000 favorable difference is because tax depreciation ($50,000) is $40,000 higher than book depreciation ($10,000)
- In Years 2-5 notice that taxable income ($110,000) is higher than pretax book income ($100,000) by $10,000. This is because book depreciation is reversed out in computing taxable income (because book depreciation is a GAAP and not a tax concept), but there is no corresponding tax depreciation deduction because it was all used up in Year 1.
- Because of accelerated depreciation, the company's tax is only $15,000 in Year 1, or $10,000 less than expected based on pretax book income of $100,000.
- The annual amount of tax increases to $27,500 in years 2-5 because tax depreciation is no longer available after Year 1. Thus, tax is $2,500 a year higher than expected based on pretax book income of $100,000 (i.e. tax is $27,500 vs. $25,000).

Now, referring to the shaded "Tax Totals" and "Books Totals" columns in the illustration, here are the *crucial* points to understand about temporary differences:

- Even though there was a difference in pretax book income and taxable book income *every year*, at the end of Year 5 the total amount of taxable income ($500,000) was equal to the amount of pretax book income ($500,000) over the same period.
- Likewise, the yearly tax expense was never what was expected based on pretax book income, which was $25,000 ($100,000 of pretax book income x the 25% tax rate). However, at the end of Year 5, the total amount of tax paid ($125,000) based on taxable income is equal to the tax that would have been paid if pretax book income was taxed at the same rate ($125,000)

In summary, over time, we see that temporary differences do not affect the total amount of tax ($125,000), and the tax liability is driven (in the context of temporary differences) by the level of pretax book income ($500,000).

10.4 Temporary differences give rise to deferred taxes

GAAP is an accrual-based (vs. a cash basis) concept

It's vital to remember that accrual basis accounting (*not* cash basis accounting) is one of the pillars of GAAP.[92] For example, assume a company signs a legally binding $100,000 services agreement, all services are performed, and the company makes a $25,000 cash payment for the services by the end of the year. What's the GAAP expense for services? Would you simply measure it by the cash that's been paid ($25,000) at the time the books were closed? No! Based on accrual accounting the services expense would be $100,000, and the journal entry would look like this:

Services Expense	$100,000	
Cash		$25,000
Accrued Liability – Services		$75,000

This simple example shows that GAAP is designed to *comprehensively* measure a company's economic performance (income statement) and financial position (balance sheet). If we only paid attention to cash in the example above, we would miss the fact that the company is legally obligated to pay a $75,000 liability as of the end of the reporting period (because the agreement has been signed and the work has already been performed).

Following this same example in the illustration below, note how cash basis accounting skews the financial performance of a company. In Year 1, the company incurred a liability of $100,000, yet on a cash basis they showed income of $75,000. However, in Year 2, despite the fact the company engaged in no activities, they "lost" $75,000.

	Cash Basis		Accrual Basis	
	Year 1	Year 2	Year 1	Year 2
Revenue	$100,000	$0	$100,000	$0
Less: Services Expense	($25,000)	($75,000)	($100,000)	$0
Equals: Income	$75,000	($75,000)	$0	$0

---

[92] If that were not the case, we could do away with the income statement and put more focus on the statement of cash flows.

In contrast, referring to the right-hand side of the illustration, accrual-basis accounting assigns (or "matches") expenses to the period in which they are incurred. This provides a more accurate view of the financial condition of a company, more closely aligning it with the economic activities of the enterprise vs. its cash receipts and spending patterns.

Finally, consider this example through the lens of an investor. Would you prefer to see financial statements on a cash or accrual basis? If all you had were the Year 1 cash basis financials to evaluate your investment decisions, you would likely overestimate the value of the company, and the $75,000 loss in Year 2 would come as an unexpected surprise (especially since the company did not engage in any activities in Year 2!). However, if you evaluate the company based on the Year 1 accrual basis financials, you will have a much clearer picture of its operations, and the fact there's no income in Year 2 would be in line with your expectations as opposed to being a surprise.

Tax accounting is an accrual-basis (vs. a cash basis) GAAP concept

Think of tax compliance, the process of completing a tax return and determining how much tax you owe in a given year, as a *cash basis* concept. However, tax accounting, which is governed by the rules of ASC 740, is an *accrual basis* GAAP concept. Now, referring to the illustration below from our depreciation example as an investor, assume you're evaluating the performance of this particular company with only Year 1 cash basis financial statements.

Again, focusing for now on Year 1, you might immediately be drawn to the fact that the company only has a 15% effective tax rate ($15,000 divided by pretax book income of $100,000), which is a full 10% below the 25% you would normally expect! Based on this analysis, what if you proceeded with an investment or acquisition decision with the expectation that company operations would stay the same and the 15% effective rate would carry into the future? You would be in for a rude surprise in Year 2 because the ETR would not only increase dramatically, but it would be 3% higher than the statutory rate (28% less 25%), and it would *stay there* all the way through Year 5 (ouch!).

The ETR Calculation on a Cash Basis

	Year 1	Year 2
Pretax Book Income	$100,000	$100,000
Reverse Book Depreciation	$10,000	$10,000
Deduct Tax Depreciation	($50,000)	$0
Taxable Income	$60,000	$110,000
Times: Tax Rate	25%	25%
Equals: Tax	$15,000	$27,500
Effective Tax Rate	15%	28%

The point is – and this is crucial – that from a tax accounting perspective GAAP is not only designed to inform investors and other readers of financial statements of what *cash taxes* a company is expected to owe for the current year's activities (i.e. Year 1), but what taxes will be owed in *future* years (i.e. Years 2+) based on the current period's (Year 1) activities.

10.5 Deferred taxes – An introduction

An example of deferred taxes

Now that we know that temporary differences give rise to deferred taxes, we will explore this concept further by building on the depreciation example we have been using. First, here are important reminders from the example that relate to the illustration that follows:

- The book expense and the tax deduction for depreciation are the *same* ($50,000) over the five-year life of the asset.
- In Year 1, the "current tax" savings of $10,000 from accelerated depreciation ($40,000 tax depreciation greater than book times 25%) is equally offset by a "deferred tax liability" (see the next point) that will occur in the future when there is no tax depreciation left to offset the company's income.
- This "deferred tax liability" will be settled in the form of higher tax over years 2-5 at the rate of $2,500 a year.

If we incorporate these principles into the company's tax calculations, it will look like this (paying particular attention to the addition of the "Deferred (Future) Tax" line item):

	Year 1	Year 2	Year 3	Year 4	Year 5	Tax Totals	Book Totals
Pretax Book Income	$100,000	$100,000	$100,000	$100,000	$100,000	$500,000	$500,000
Reverse Book Depreciation	$10,000	$10,000	$10,000	$10,000	$10,000	$50,000	N/A
Deduct Tax Depreciation	($50,000)	$0	$0	$0	$0	($50,000)	N/A
Taxable Income	$60,000	$110,000	$110,000	$110,000	$110,000	$500,000	$500,000
Times: Tax Rate	25%	25%	25%	25%	25%	25%	25%
Subtotal: Current "Cash" Tax	$15,000	$27,500	$27,500	$27,500	$27,500	$125,000	$125,000
Add: Deferred (Future) Tax	$10,000	($2,500)	($2,500)	($2,500)	($2,500)	$0	N/A
Equals: Total Tax Expense	$25,000	$25,000	$25,000	$25,000	$25,000	$125,000	$125,000
Effective Tax Rate	25%	25%	25%	25%	25%	25%	25%

Take note of the following observations.

- While the current (cash) tax in Year 1 is only $15,000, there's also a $10,000 deferred tax expense to account for the taxes that will be due in the future when the benefit of accelerated depreciation reverses. Thus, the company's total tax expense (or provision) for Year 1 is $25,000 (current tax expense of $15,000 plus a deferred tax of $10,000).
- Conversely, in years 2-5 the current (cash) tax of $27,500 is *higher* than the $25,000 that would be expected based on pretax book income ($100,000 x 25%). However, there is an offsetting deferred tax *benefit* (or negative expense) of $2,500 because the corresponding deferred tax liability decreases by that amount each year. Thus, the company's total tax expense in years 2-5 is also $25,000.

- While the temporary depreciation differences had an impact on the *current* (cash) tax each year relative to what was expected based on pretax book income each year, the total tax expense was the same every year ($25,000). Thus, we see that *temporary differences do NOT impact the total tax expense of a company ($25,000), nor do they impact the ETR (25%)*.

Year 1 journal entries and observations

The journal entry to record the company's expected Year 1 cash (or current) tax due with the tax return looks like this:

Current Tax Expense[93]	$15,000	
Taxes Payable		$15,000

The journal entry to record the deferred (or future) taxes that will be due in years 2-5 looks like this:

Deferred Tax Expense (I/S)	$10,000	
Deferred Tax Liability (B/S)		$10,000

For a more intuitive understanding, consider deferred taxes within the context of the expected tax vs. the actual tax of a company based on pretax book income. If we applied this reasoning to Year 1, pretax book income would be $100,000 and, absent any book/tax differences, we would expect the Year 1 tax to be $25,000 ($100,000 PTBI x the 25% statutory rate). However, the current (or cash) tax expense of the company was only $15,000, fully $10,000 less than we expected ($25,000). Why?

The reason for the difference is because the company reduced its taxes $10,000 in Year 1 by taking advantage of accelerated depreciation. However, that benefit is "temporary," because it will be offset by $10,000 in future taxes in years 2-5. Thus, from an accrual basis GAAP point of view, the company incurred a $25,000 tax liability in Year 1; $15,000 of it was due with the Year 1 tax return ("current"), and the remaining $10,000 was "deferred" to the tax returns of Years 2-5.

Year 2-5 journal entries and observations

Here we examine Year 2 journal entries, but the same entries and concepts also apply to years 3-5:

Current Tax Expense	$27,500	
Tax Payable		$27,500

---

[93] As stated earlier in the material, the current tax expense of a company is the sum of its cash tax plus other items. However, for purposes of our present discussion, we will continue to assume that the current tax expense of the company is the amount the company expects to report on its tax return.

"The Missing Tax Accounting Guide – A Plain English Guide to ASC 740 Tax Provisions"
@ 2022 Tax Director Services, Inc.
All rights reserved

The following entry is also made:

Deferred Tax Liability (B/S)	$2,500	
Deferred Tax Expense (Benefit) (I/S)		$2,500[94]

Recall that at the end of Year 1, we recorded a $10,000 deferred tax liability to offset the "temporary" tax benefit the company received in the form of lower current (cash) taxes. This $10,000 deferred tax liability is "repaid" in the future in the form of higher taxes. The first "installment" of this deferred tax is paid in Year 2, because the current tax expense is $2,500 higher than expected based on pretax book income ($27,500 vs. $25,000). Because of this higher current tax, we reduce the deferred tax liability by $2,500, with the offset being to a "negative" deferred tax expense (referred to as a "deferred tax benefit"). See the illustration for how the Year 1 deferred tax liability is "repaid" over time.

	Deferred Tax Liability	Excess Tax Paid on PTBI
Year 1	$10,000	
Year 2	$7,500	$2,500
Year 3	$5,000	$2,500
Year 4	$2,500	$2,500
Year 5	$0	$2,500

Other helpful ways to think about deferred tax expenses and liabilities

Here are some other observations and helpful ways to think about deferred taxes to better understand them.

- Deferred tax journal entries do *not* involve current taxes, cash, or taxes payable. Those are "what relates to the current period" concepts; deferred taxes relate to *future* events.
- In theory, *today's deferred tax liability will become tomorrow's tax payable.*
- A deferred tax liability signals that, as of the current reporting period, the company's tax return liability has been *lower* than expected based on pretax book income due to *favorable* temporary differences (e.g. accelerated depreciation).

---

[94] The "deferred tax expense" side of an accounting entry can be difficult to conceptualize. First, because there is a credit to deferred tax expense in years 2-5 in the example above, one might think of it as tax-related "income" of some kind. Instead, it can be more helpful to think a credit to the deferred tax expense account as *a reduction of a liability*. In other words, if you had a liability of $2,500 today which was forgiven, you would think of yourself as $2,500 richer. That's not to say that you got $2,500 of cash in your pocket. Rather, you fully expected to *pay* $2,500, you no longer owe that money, and so you're economically $2,500 better off than you were. Likewise, by paying $2,500 extra in cash taxes in Year 2 relative to pretax book income, we've reduced our outstanding deferred tax liability from $10,000 to $7,500. The reduction of this deferred tax liability is treated as a "negative tax expense," which is the equivalent of income.

- Related to the previous point, a deferred tax liability signals that a company's cash tax liability in the future will be *higher* than expected based on future pretax book income due to the reversal of temporary differences (i.e. future temporary differences will be *unfavorable*).
- Somewhat counter-intuitively, deferred tax liabilities are "good" from a tax planning perspective. While liabilities are generally thought of as "bad," in this case a deferred tax liability means that a company has paid less tax today by pushing payment to the future (both a cash flow and time value of money benefit).
- A deferred tax expense is *still* an expense, meaning the tax due hasn't magically disappeared. Deferred taxes are simply income taxes where you have delayed (cash) settlement to a future period.[95]

10.6 Favorable vs. unfavorable temporary differences

So far, we've talked about temporary differences as if they are always favorable differences (e.g. accelerated depreciation) that give rise to deferred tax expenses on the income statement and deferred tax liabilities on the balance sheet. This is because thinking about deferred taxes as "income taxes due in the future" provides a more intuitive understanding of these concepts. However, as with permanent differences, temporary differences can be favorable *or* unfavorable.

Taxable temporary differences (deferred tax expenses and liabilities)

Items that give rise to *higher* taxable income in future periods are referred to in the accounting standards (ASC 740) as "taxable temporary differences."[96] Accelerated depreciation is an example. While there is a tax benefit for claiming accelerated depreciation in the current year, the reversal of that favorable temporary benefit will result in *higher* taxable income in the future. Taxable temporary differences, therefore, give rise to deferred tax expenses (income statement) and deferred tax liabilities (balance sheet).

---

[95] This recalls the "Services Expense" example on page 100 under the heading, "GAAP is an accrual-based (vs. a cash basis) concept." There it was illustrated that for GAAP you cannot put off accruing an additional expense of $75,000 by measuring only the cash that was paid ($25,000). The services liability of $75,000 was recorded as part of the expense because it's due and payable. Likewise, taxes that will be payable in *future* periods based on the *current* period's activities must be booked as deferred expenses.

[96] See ASC 740-10-25-23. The terminology can be counter-intuitive because a *favorable* difference that lowers current tax (e.g., accelerated depreciation) is referred to in the accounting guidance as a "*taxable* temporary difference." As noted above, this is because the *future* reversals of the temporary difference will be *taxable*. Despite the confusion of the wording, it's very important to understand this terminology because if you don't then you will struggle to make sense of the ASC 740 tax accounting standards as they are written.

Deductible temporary differences (deferred tax benefits and assets)

Items that result in *lower* taxable income in future periods are referred to in the accounting standards as "deductible temporary differences."[97] An accrued warranty reserve is an example. While a company cannot claim a tax deduction in the current year for a non-cash GAAP warranty expense, it will be deductible in the future when the warranty is paid. Thus, the reversal of the unfavorable temporary expense will result in a *deduction* from taxable income in the future. Therefore, deductible temporary differences give rise to deferred tax benefits (income statement) and deferred tax assets (balance sheet).

Deferred tax benefits and deferred tax assets will be discussed in more detail in the next chapter.

10.7 Sources of temporary differences

There are three sources of temporary differences that give rise to deferred taxes.

Timing differences

Timing differences are those that result from the standard operating activities of a company where there are differences between the book and tax treatment of an activity or transaction, and these differences reverse in a measurable pattern over time. Timing differences are the most common category of temporary differences, and examples of timing differences related to depreciation have been the focus of this chapter.

Business combinations

As part of an acquisition, the purchase accounting rules of ASC 805 may require the acquiring company to book deferred tax assets or liabilities to account for the future tax impact of a target company's temporary differences. This is an advanced topic that will not be covered in this chapter.

Indefinite differences

Indefinite differences are *not* permanent differences. Permanent differences are those where the book and tax treatment of a transaction are different, and those differences will *never* reverse.[98] Indefinite differences are temporary differences between book and tax,

---

[97] See ASC 740-10-25-23. Again, the terminology can be counter-intuitive because an *unfavorable* difference that increases current tax (e.g., a warranty reserve) is referred to in the accounting guidance as a "*deductible* temporary difference." As noted above, this is because the *future* reversals of the temporary difference will be *deductible*.

[98] Previously we discussed meals and entertainment being a permanent book/tax difference. Normally a company will expense the full economic outlay spent on meals and entertainment ($40,000, for example). However, for tax, only 50% of this amount ($20,000) would be deductible ($40,000 x the 50% limitation). This difference will never reverse, so it is permanent in nature.

but there is no set, measurable, predictable point in time when the differences will reverse. In other words, indefinite differences are expected to reverse "at some point in the future."

ASC 740 generally requires recognition of deferred taxes for indefinite differences. A key exception is ABP 23, or the "indefinite reinvestment assertion" for foreign subsidiaries.[99] This relates to the (deferred) tax a U.S. company would owe on the receipt of a taxable distribution (such as a dividend) of the excess earnings of a foreign subsidiary. In brief, if a U.S. parent has the ability and intent to defer the distribution of its foreign earnings and it has sufficient evidence to support such a position, it can elect not to record a deferred tax liability on those earnings. As with business combinations, this is an advanced topic that's beyond the scope of this book.

10.8 Temporary differences are measured by book vs. tax basis differences

ASC 740 refers to temporary differences as a balance sheet concept

Up to this point, we have mostly examined temporary differences as an income statement concept, or that the temporary differences between book (GAAP) and income tax expenses will reverse over time. However, it's important to note that the ASC 740 guidance refers to temporary differences as a *balance sheet* concept:

"[Temporary] differences between taxable income and pretax financial income also create differences…between the *tax basis* of an asset or liability and its reported amount in the financial statements (emphasis added)."[100]

Basis and adjusted basis

The concept of basis is easiest to understand in the context of assets (as opposed to liabilities). The "basis" of an asset is equal to its cost or value. The "adjusted basis" of an asset is equal to its *net* value, or the original basis plus or minus applicable adjustments. For example, the basis of equipment is equal to its cost ($50,000). The adjusted basis of equipment ($30,000) is equal to its original cost ($50,000) less depreciation to date ($20,000).

In the practice of tax accounting, when people refer to the "basis" of an asset (or liability), they are usually referring to the *net or adjusted basis* ($30,000) rather than the original cost basis (or purchase price).

---

[99] The formal reference for this exception is ASC 740-30-25-18(a).
[100] From ASC 740-10-25-21.

Tax vs. book basis – Assets – Accelerated tax expenses

Parsing the tax accounting guidance, we get the following concept, "An assumption inherent in a company's [financial statements] is the reported amount of assets will be recovered [or sold] at their net book value. Based on that assumption, a difference between the tax basis of an asset…and its [GAAP basis per the financial statements] will result in taxable or deductible amounts in some future year(s) when the reported amount of the assets are recovered [or sold]."[101]

We'll now look at how to interpret and apply this language in the context of an example. Referring to the illustration, at the end of Year 1, GAAP is saying that if the asset is "recovered" via a hypothetical sale, the company expects to receive $40,000, or the $50,000 purchase price less $10,000 of accumulated depreciation (i.e. the adjusted book basis amount).

Fixed Assets - Book/GAAP

Year	Original Book Basis	Book Depreciation	Accumulated Depreciation	Adjusted Book Basis
Year 1	$50,000	($10,000)	($10,000)	$40,000
Year 2	$50,000	($10,000)	($20,000)	$30,000
Year 3	$50,000	($10,000)	($30,000)	$20,000
Year 4	$50,000	($10,000)	($40,000)	$10,000
Year 5	$50,000	($10,000)	($50,000)	$0

Fixed Assets - Tax

Year	Original Tax Basis	Tax Depreciation	Accumulated Depreciation	Adjusted Tax Basis
Year 1	$50,000	($50,000)	($50,000)	$0
Year 2	$50,000	$0	($50,000)	$0
Year 3	$50,000	$0	($50,000)	$0
Year 4	$50,000	$0	($50,000)	$0
Year 5	$50,000	$0	($50,000)	$0

If this hypothetical sale (or settlement) occurs, the journal entry to record the receipt of the cash and to remove the asset (and its associated accumulated depreciation) from the books looks like this:

Cash	$40,000	
Accumulated Depreciation (Book)	$10,000	
Asset – Equipment		$50,000

Another way to look at this calculation from a book perspective is as follows.

Gross Proceeds	$40,000
Less: Adjusted GAAP Basis – Equipment	$(40,000)
Equals: Book Gain on Sale – Equipment	Zero

---

[101] From ASC 740-10-25-20). Note that I have simplified and clarified the wording by using ellipses and the wording in brackets. This kind of "thick" technical language reminds me of a (modified) quote from, "The Pirates of the Caribbean:" "There are a lot of long words in there, [FASB Standard Setters]; we're naught but humble [accountants]."

A critical thing to note from the above example is that prior to an actual sale, it's assumed that an asset will be settled (or sold) at its adjusted basis ($40,000) and *there is no gain or loss for book purposes*. However, the taxable gain on the hypothetical sale of the *same asset* at the end of Year 1 would be $40,000, which is equal to the net proceeds ($40,000) less the adjusted *tax basis* of the asset ($0). This is illustrated as follows:.

Gross Proceed	$40,000
Less: Adjusted Tax Basis – Equipment	$(0)
Equals: Taxable Gain on Sale – Equipment	$40,000

Thus, a temporary difference in the book and tax basis of the asset resulted in a difference between the book ($0) and taxable ($40,000) gain of a hypothetical sale (or "recovery") of its net book value ($40,000) at the end of Year 1. The results of a hypothetical asset sale at net book value for all years is shown in the following table.

Book/Tax Basis Difference

Year	Book Basis	Tax Basis	Book Over Tax Basis	Tax Rate	Deferred Tax Liability	Deferred Tax Exp/(Ben.)
Year 1	$40,000	$0	$40,000	25%	$10,000	$10,000
Year 2	$30,000	$0	$30,000	25%	$7,500	($2,500)
Year 3	$20,000	$0	$20,000	25%	$5,000	($2,500)
Year 4	$10,000	$0	$10,000	25%	$2,500	($2,500)
Year 5	$0	$0	$0	25%	$0	($2,500)

From a tax accounting perspective, basis of an asset is an amount that offsets a *gain*. Thus, if the book basis of an asset exceeds its tax basis (as is the case in our example), it means the book gain of a sale will be *less* than the taxable gain. Applying this concept to the figures in the illustration, since the book basis exceeds the tax basis in Year 1 by $40,000, there would be a potential $10,000 tax over book liability if the asset were sold (the $40,000 book/tax basis difference x the 25% tax rate). This results in the following Year 1 journal entry (which you have seen before), which is based on the last two columns in the preceding illustration.

Deferred Tax Expense	$10,000	
Deferred Tax Liability		$10,000

In Year 2, the potential tax over book liability drops by $2,500, from $10,000 to $7,500, which would result in the following entry.

Deferred Tax Liability	$2,500	
Deferred Tax Expense (Benefit)		$2,500[102]

---

[102] If the equipment were held to the end of Year 5, this same tax accounting entry would be made in years 2-5, which would ultimately reduce the book/tax difference to zero.

To summarize, temporary differences for assets are measured by the difference between the book and tax *basis* differences for those assets in any given period. The corresponding deferred tax liability (and deferred tax expense) is calculated by multiplying the difference between the book over tax basis times the tax rate.[103]

10.9 Tax basis balance sheets

Some companies use a tax basis balance sheet to calculate and support their deferred tax liabilities. A book balance sheet is one that is prepared according to the rules of GAAP (which is the responsibility of the Accounting Group). A tax basis balance sheet is prepared according to tax rules. Book/tax differences are then compared by measuring the difference between the book and tax basis balance sheet amounts.

Based on the facts and figures in Year 1 of the accelerated depreciation example, following is an illustration of a book (GAAP) and tax income statements as well as the resulting book vs. tax basis balance sheets.

Book vs. Tax Income Statement	Book	Tax	Difference
Revenue	$110,000	N/A	
Less: Depreciation	($10,000)	N/A	
Subtotal: Pretax Book Income	$100,000	$100,000	
Tax Adj. - Add Book Depreciation	N/A	$10,000	
Tax Adj. - Deduct Tax Depreciation	N/A	($50,000)	
Equals: Pretax/Taxable Income/(Loss)	$100,000	$60,000	$40,000
Times: Tax Rate	N/A	25%	
Less: Current (Cash) Tax Expense	($15,000)	($15,000)	$0
Less: Deferred Tax Expense	($10,000)	N/A	($10,000)
Equals: Net (After-tax) Income	$75,000	$45,000	$30,000

[This space was intentionally left blank].

---

[103] The opposite treatment applies if the tax basis of an asset exceeds its book basis. In those cases, a deferred tax asset (a balance sheet concept) is created with a corresponding deferred tax benefit (an income statement concept). Deferred tax assets are covered in more detail in a separate chapter starting on page 115.

Book vs. Tax Basis Balance Sheet

	Book Basis Balance Sheet	Tax Basis Balance Sheet	Difference
Cash	$60,000	$60,000	$0
Asset - Equipment	$50,000	$50,000	$0
Asset - Accumulated Depreciation	($10,000)	($50,000)	$40,000
Net Property, Plant and Equipment	$40,000	$0	$40,000
Total Assets	$100,000	$60,000	
Tax Payable	$15,000	$15,000	$0
Deferred Tax Liability	$10,000	N/A	$10,000
Common Stock/APIC	$0	$0	
Retained (Earnings)/Loss (Pretax)	$75,000	$45,000	$30,000
Net Equity (Pretax)	$75,000	$45,000	
Total Liabilities & Equity	$100,000	$60,000	

Book (GAAP) journal entries

Following is a summary of the GAAP entries used to create the *book* (GAAP) income statement and balance sheet in the example above.

The company generated $110,000 of revenue from operations.[104]

| Revenue | $110,000 | |
| Cash (or A/R) | | $100,000 |

The company purchased equipment for $50,000.

| Asset – Equipment | $50,000 | |
| Cash | | $50,000 |

The company depreciated the equipment on a straight-line basis assuming a 5-year life.

| Depreciation Expense | $10,000 | |
| Accumulated Depreciation | | $10,000 |

The company projected a current (cash) tax with its return of $15,000.

| Current Tax Expense | $15,000 | |

---

[104] As a simplification, we will assume there was no opening contribution to common stock or additional paid-in capital.

Tax Payable		$15,000

The company recorded a deferred tax liability to offset the current year benefit of accelerated depreciation.

Deferred Tax Expense	$10,000	
Deferred Tax Liability		$10,000

Tax journal entries

Following is a summary of the tax journal entries used to create the tax income statement and the tax basis balance sheet. Note that *these entries are not booked in the GAAP general ledger!* They are "tax entries" kept in the "tax books" only, and they're used by the Tax Group to create a tax basis balance sheet for the purpose of calculating and proving out deferred tax-related amounts. The entries are as follows.

The company generated $110,000 of revenue from operations.

Revenue	$110,000	
Cash (or A/R)		$100,000

The company purchased equipment for $50,000.

Asset – Equipment	$50,000	
Cash		$50,000

Up to this point the book and tax journal entries for GAAP and tax have been the same. The first difference is when the company elects to fully depreciate the asset for tax purposes, which results in the following entry.

Depreciation Expense (Tax)	$50,000	
Accumulated Depreciation		$50,000

Finally, for the tax income statement and balance sheet, the company only takes current (cash) taxes into account (deferred taxes are a GAAP-only concept).

Current Tax Expense	$15,000	
Tax Payable		$15,000

Observations on the book vs. tax income statements

Referring to the prior illustrations and journal entries, note the following:

- The book income statement computes GAAP pretax book income ($100,000) and net income ($60,000), but the tax income statement computes taxable income ($60,000) and net after-tax income ($45,000).

- GAAP pretax book income ($100,000) ties to the financial statements and taxable income ($60,000) ties to the tax return.
- Book depreciation ($10,000) and deferred taxes (also $10,000) are GAAP-only concepts, and these are part of the computation of net income ($60,000).
- Net income per book ($60,000) ties to the Year 1 ending retained earnings on the book balance sheet.
- Tax ($50,000) rather than book ($10,000) depreciation is used to compute taxable income.
- Deferred tax expense is not a tax concept, so it's not shown on the tax income statement or the tax basis balance sheet.

Observations on the book vs. tax basis balance sheets

Also note the following:

- The book and tax basis for cash is always the same ($60,000), and there should never be a difference ($0).
- The original book and tax basis in the equipment is the same ($50,000); the $40,000 book/tax difference is driven by the difference in GAAP accumulated depreciation vs. accelerated tax depreciation.
- The tax payable ($15,000) is a book *and* tax concept, so there is no basis difference.
- Deferred tax liabilities ($10,000) only appear on the GAAP balance sheet because deferred taxes are not a tax concept.
- The Year 1 ending book and tax retained earnings tie to the book and tax income statements, respectively ($75,000 and $45,000)

In summary, a tax basis balance sheet offers a comprehensive way to calculate and support all book/tax differences. While the use of a tax basis balance sheet is theoretically the best method for identifying, computing and proving out book/tax differences, they're not easy to develop and maintain.[105] As a result, in practice, account-by-account methodologies may instead be employed to calculate and support book/tax differences as opposed to developing a comprehensive tax basis balance sheet.[106]

---

[105] This is especially true for a company that has been in existence for years where a tax basis balance sheet has not historically been maintained.

[106] An account-by-account methodology is one where each temporary difference giving rise to a deferred tax amount is separately tracked and calculated (depreciation, accrued expenses, etc.) without any kind of proof or tie-out to a company-wide tax basis balance sheet.

11 Deferred Tax Liabilities/Expenses and Deferred Tax Assets/Benefits

As previously noted, to this point we've mostly focused on deferred tax liabilities and deferred tax expenses. Now our discussion will also incorporate deferred tax assets (a balance sheet concept) and deferred tax benefits (an income statement concept).

11.1 Learning objectives

- Review additional principles, examples and journal entries related to deferred tax assets and liabilities to reinforce your understanding.
- Review different scenarios on book/tax basis differences and whether those difference result in deferred tax assets (and income statement benefits) or deferred tax liabilities (and income statement expenses).
- Get introduced to valuation allowances, why they exist and their impact on deferred taxes.

11.2 Current tax expense/payable vs. current tax benefit/receivable

Before we cover deferred tax concepts in more detail, it's helpful to revisit some concepts related to current taxes.

Current tax expense and taxes payable

As previously noted, there are multiple components that make up current taxes but, as we did earlier, we'll continue to assume that current taxes are only comprised of a company's cash tax liability, or the amount it expects to owe with its tax return. The current tax expense in the income statement is associated with taxes payable on the balance sheet. For a company that has $100,000 of income (assuming no book/tax differences) and a 25% tax rate, the journal entry to book for the provision is as follows:

Current Tax Expense	$25,000	
Taxes Payable		$25,000

The accounting entry to record tax payments to satisfy the liability for taxes payable looks like this.

Taxes Payable	$25,000	
Cash		$25,000

Based on these facts, there is no tax expense adjustment necessary when the tax return is filed; the $25,000 current tax expense was booked earlier in the year, and the $25,000 is due with the tax return (unless it was prepaid in quarterly estimated tax installments of $6,250 over four quarters).

Current tax benefits and taxes receivable

A current tax benefit is the opposite of a current tax expense. A current tax benefit is associated with taxes *receivable* on the balance sheet. And how does a company get a "benefit" for income taxes? As a simplified example, assume that a company has a loss of $100,000 in its first year of operations. Therefore, instead of paying tax with the tax return, a refund of $25,000 is expected. Here is the journal entry.

Taxes Receivable	$25,000	
Current Tax Benefit		$25,000[107]

This result would be unusual because governments (including the U.S.) don't normally allow loss companies that have never paid tax to obtain cash refunds. Instead, net operating loss ("NOL") rules typically allow companies to carry losses forward ("NOL carryforwards") to offset future taxable income.

Another example of a current tax benefit is when the tax provision expense is overestimated. For example, assume the tax provision was initially booked as a current tax expense (with no deferred tax expense) of $100,000, but later in the year it needs to be trued up to $90,000. The entry would be as follows.

Taxes Payable	$10,000	
Current Tax Expense		$10,000

Here, note that a credit to the current tax expense is actually a "benefit." Following the same logic, there is a reduction (debit) to the taxes payable.

11.3 Deferred tax expenses/liabilities vs. deferred tax benefits/assets

Deferred tax expenses and deferred tax liabilities

A deferred tax expense recognizes for financial statement purposes a tax liability that will be due in the future based on the current period's activities. The accelerated depreciation example in the prior chapter is a good illustration. Without fully reviewing that analysis again here, recall that <u>deferred tax expenses (income statement) and deferred tax</u>

---

[107] This can also be recorded as a credit entry to the "Current Tax Expense" account, making it a "negative expense" (which is income).

liabilities (balance sheet) result when tax deductions are initially faster than their corresponding book expenses.

Similarly, when taxable revenues are initially slower than book revenues, this also gives rise to deferred tax expenses and deferred tax liabilities. For example, assume a company that has elected the installment method for tax earns $100,000 of book revenue in Year 1 but taxable income is zero (because no cash was received)[108]. There would be no current tax entry because no cash tax is due. However, a journal entry for deferred taxes would be recorded as follows.[109]

Deferred Tax Expense	$25,000[110]	
Deferred Tax Liability		$25,000

Assume in Year 2 the company collects $60,000 in cash and recognizes an equal amount of taxable income. That means the company will owe cash tax with its return of $15,000 ($60,000 x 25%), and the journal entry will look like this.

Current Tax Expense	$15,000	
Tax Payable		$15,000

This $15,000 current tax payment by the company can be viewed as a repayment of the deferred tax liability of $25,000 it booked in Year 1. In other words, in Year 1 the company effectively said with its journal entry, "While no current tax is due, eventually the company will owe $25,000 in tax on its $100,000 sale." Because the company paid $15,000 of this tax in Year 2 in the form of current taxes, the deferred tax liability is now reduced by the same amount.

Deferred Tax Liability	$15,000	
Deferred Tax Expense (or Benefit)		$15,000

Following the comments above, note that the total tax expense of the company is Year 2 is *zero* ($15,000 of current tax offset by a $15,000 deferred tax benefit). Why does that make sense? Because tax accounting is a GAAP concept, the company booked the full tax impact of the $100,000 of book earnings in Year 1 when it recorded the $25,000 deferred tax expense and the corresponding deferred tax liability. Finally, note that the company's remaining deferred tax liability is $10,000 (it was originally $25,000, but was reduced $15,000 by the journal entry above). Does that make sense? Yes, because the

---

[108] In brief, when electing the installment method, taxable income is not recognized until cash is received, i.e. it is a cash basis concept.

[109] Installment sale treatment is a temporary difference that results in deferred taxes because, over time, the amount of book and tax income from the sale will be the same.

[110] The deferred tax expense is equal to the $100,000 of taxable income over book income that will be due in the future times the 25% tax rate.

company is still owed $40,000 on its $100,000 installment sale, and the future tax due on that income will be $10,000 ($40,000 x 25% tax rate).

Deferred tax benefits and deferred tax assets

We'll now return to the $100,000 loss company example in the "Current Tax Benefit" example on page 116. Let's assume the company cannot obtain a cash refund for its loss upon filing its tax return, nor can it carry the loss back. Again, because there is no avenue for the company to obtain a refund, there is no *current* (cash) tax benefit.

Tax Receivable	No entry	
Current Tax Benefit		No entry

However, this company does expect to be able to obtain a $25,000 tax benefit at some point by using its $100,000 net operating loss to offset future taxable ($100,000 NOL deduction x 25% tax rate). The journal entry to record the future tax benefit associated with the NOL carryforward looks like this.

Deferred Tax Asset	$25,000	
Deferred Tax Benefit		$25,000

Now assume in Year 2 that the company generates $130,000 of income (with no difference between book and tax). The company will owe $7,500 of current tax as shown in the illustration.

Income	$130,000
Less: NOL Carryforward	($100,000)
Taxable Income	$30,000
Times: Tax Rate	25%
Equals: Current Tax	$7,500

The first Year 2 journal entry records the current tax impact of the company's operations.

Current Tax Expense	$7,500	
Tax Payable		$7,500

Also, since the company fully utilized its NOL carryforward, the corresponding deferred tax asset created in Year 1 must be written off as follows.

Deferred Tax Expense	$25,000	
Deferred Tax Asset		$25,000

The chart that follows summarizes the income-tax related activities for all years.

	Year 1	Year 2	All Years
Current Tax Expense	Zero	$7,500	$7,500
Deferred Tax Expense/(Benefit)	($25,000)	$25,000	Zero
Total Tax Expense/(Benefit)	($25,000)	$32,500	$7,500
Pretax Book Income/(Loss)	($100,000)	$130,000	$30,000
Effective Tax Rate	25%	25%	25%

Note the following with respect to the illustration above that summarizes the previous NOL example.

- At first, the tax benefit in Year 1 ($25,000) may seem "overly generous" given that the company lost money.
- It's also interesting to note that the company's ETR is a *positive* 25% even though it has a pretax book loss (negative $25,000 divided by negative $100,000 equals positive 25%).
- Because the company has a loss in Year 1, the way to interpret the ETR is to say that the company expects to receive a future tax benefit (in the form of an NOL deduction) equal to 25% of its pretax book loss.
- For Year 2, unlike the first bullet, the deferred tax expense ($25,000) may seem "overly harsh" given the level of the company's taxable income (only $30,000). However, the presence of the deferred tax expense brings the company's ETR (25%) in line with what we would expect based on the company's pretax book income ($125,000).
- This example illustrates that deferred tax accounting has a *smoothing effect* on the ETR because tax expenses and benefits are *matched* to the periods when income and losses are generated.

11.4 Tax vs. book basis differences with assets and liabilities

There is a deferred tax impact to the extent that income or expenses for book and tax are recognized in different periods. However, as we covered earlier, the ASC 740 tax accounting guidance talks of temporary differences in the context of *basis* (not income) differences between book and tax. Therefore, it's important to have an intuitive sense of what book and tax basis differences mean in various contexts to interpret the tax accounting guidance, as well as to more effectively prepare, understand, and review tax provision workpapers.

Assets – Book basis exceeds tax basis = Deferred tax liability (and expense)

Basis is interpreted differently depending on whether you are evaluating the asset or liability side of the balance sheet. Basis concepts are more intuitive with assets, so we'll start there. It was previously stated that, from a tax accounting perspective, *basis for an asset is an amount that offsets a gain*. Thus, basis is "bad news" from a book perspective because it reduces net income. However, basis is "good news" from a tax perspective because it reduces taxable income. To summarize, *when the book basis ("bad news") exceeds the tax basis ("good news") for an asset, it will give rise to a deferred tax liability* (and a corresponding expense).

To understand why this is the case, let's review the accelerated depreciation example from earlier in the book (see the footnote for the reference).[111] At the end of Year 1, the net book basis in the equipment was $40,000 (the $50,000 purchase price less $10,000 of book depreciation). Thus, based on the assumptions of GAAP, if this equipment were sold for its carrying value of $40,000, the gain would be zero ($40,000 proceeds less the adjusted book basis of $40,000). However, because the tax basis was zero at the end of Year 1 (the $50,000 purchase price less $50,000 of tax depreciation), the sale of the asset at its carrying value of $40,000 would result in a taxable gain of $40,000. This would result in the need to book a deferred tax expense and a deferred tax liability of $10,000 (the $40,000 basis difference times the 25% tax rate).

The installment sale method example in the "Deferred tax expenses and deferred tax liability" section starting on page 116 is an example of how to view basis for an item of income. There, the company recognized $100,000 for book purposes in Year 1, and the entry looked like this:

Accounts Receivable	$100,000	
Revenue		$100,000

Because there was no cash received in Year 1, there was no taxable income and thus no tax basis balance sheet entry. Thus, because the book basis ("bad news") in accounts receivable ($100,000) exceeds the tax basis ("good news") of accounts receivable ($0), there was a deferred tax expense/liability of $25,000 ($100,000 x 25%).

Another way to think about this is when cash is received for book purposes then the cash account on the GL will be debited and the credit will go to accounts receivable (which has a balance of $100,000). However, for tax purposes, no accounts receivable is reflected on the tax basis balance sheet. As a result, when cash is debited in future periods as it's collected, the credit has nowhere else to go but to income. That, conceptually, is why an installment sale gives rise to a deferred tax expense/liability.

Assets – Tax basis exceeds book basis = Deferred tax asset (and benefit)

While not as common, there will be instances when the tax basis for assets exceeds the book basis. In such cases, it means that any potential gain on assets sold (or "recovered"

---

[111] See page 108 starting under the heading, "Tax vs. book basis – Assets – Accelerated tax expenses."

per the ASC language) would result in a *lower* taxable than book gain. When this is the case, it results in deferred tax assets and deferred tax benefits.

Assume, for example, that the book and tax basis of an intangible asset (aside from goodwill) is $70,000 and it needs to be written off for GAAP purposes. If there were no book and tax basis differences for the asset, the write-off entry would look like this:

Impairment Expense	$70,000	
Intangible Asset		$70,000

Since a deduction is not allowed for tax until a future sale of the intangible asset (or the company itself), the follow-on tax accounting entry would be this:

Deferred Tax Asset	$17,500	
Deferred Tax Benefit		$17,500

The deferred tax benefit of $17,500 is recorded because, even though the asset has been written off for book purposes, the company still has a tax basis of $70,000 in the intangible asset. That means selling it in the future will reduce any taxable gain relative to book income by $70,000 ($70,000 x 25% = $17,500 deferred tax asset/benefit).

Liabilities – Book basis exceeds tax basis = Deferred tax asset (and benefit)

Analyzing the tax accounting guidance for liabilities we get the following concept, "An assumption inherent in a company's [financial statements] is the reported amount of liabilities will be settled at their net book value. Based on that assumption, a difference between the tax basis of a liability…and its [GAAP basis per the financial statements] will result in taxable or deductible amounts in some future year(s) when the reported amount of the liabilities are settled."[112]

First, recall that basis is "good news" from a tax perspective when it comes to assets. For example, if an asset is sold then the gain can be reduced by any applicable tax basis, thus reducing taxable income and tax. The *opposite* is true of basis when evaluating book/tax basis differences on the liability side of the balance sheet. In those cases, basis is "bad news" because it increases taxable income, typically in the form of a delayed deduction. For example, for GAAP purposes, a company may create a reserve with the following entry:

Contingency (Expense)	$100,000	
Reserve Liability		$100,000

---

[112] Adapted from ASC 740-10-25-20, with the language being simplified and clarified by ellipses and the wording in brackets.

While a reserve results in an expense for book purposes, it's not deductible for tax purposes until its paid. Hence, reserves are not recorded on a tax basis balance sheet. In this example, it means the book basis in the reserve ($100,000) will exceed its tax basis ($0), thus resulting in a deferred tax asset of $25,000 ($100,000 x 25%). This is recorded in the books as follows:

Deferred Tax Asset	$25,000	
Deferred Tax Benefit		$25,000[113]

When the reserve is paid it will result in a current tax benefit.

Tax Payable	$25,000 (a reduction of taxes payable)	
Current Tax Expense		$25,000 (a reduction of tax expense)

With the reserve fully settled, the corresponding deferred tax asset would need to be written off as follows:

Deferred Tax Expense (Benefit)	$25,000	
Deferred Tax Asset		$25,000

In the example above, deferred tax assets and deferred tax benefits resulted from a <u>tax deduction that was delayed relative to the book expense</u>. Deferred tax assets and benefits can also be generated when <u>taxable income is recognized faster than book income</u>. Consider an example where a company received a $300,000 cash advance for three years of rental income. For book purposes, $100,000 of revenue is recognized each year, but for tax purposes it's all recognized in Year 1 (when the cash is received). The Year 1 book journal entry looks like this:

Cash	$300,000	
Deferred Rental Income		$200,000 (classified as a liability)
Revenue		$100,000

In constructing a tax basis balance sheet, the tax entry would be as follows:

Cash	$300,000	
Revenue		300,000

Note that deferred rental income (a liability) has a basis of $200,000 for book purposes but a zero basis for tax purposes. As a result, the following GAAP/tax accounting entries would be necessary in Year 1.

Current Tax Expense	$75,000 ($300,000 cash received x 25%)

---

[113] This could also be a credit to a Deferred Tax Expense income statement account.

Tax Payable $75,000

However, despite a high cash tax in Year 1, the company will have lower taxable income than book income in the future, resulting in the following entry:

Deferred Tax Asset $50,000 ($200,000 book over tax basis x 25%)
  Deferred Tax Benefit $50,000

To summarize, <u>when the book basis in liabilities exceeds the tax basis it results in the creation of deferred tax assets and benefits</u>. Another parting thought to help make book/tax basis difference for liabilities more intuitive is this: when a payment is made there is a credit to cash for both book and tax purposes (i.e. the book/tax basis for cash is always the same). The issue is what will be debited. If a liability has basis because there has been an expense accrual, the liability will be debited and there will be no expense (which is most common for GAAP). On the other hand, if there is no tax basis in the liability (which is most common for tax), there is no liability to debit. This means the debit must go to expense, and this will result in a tax deduction (i.e. a benefit).

Liabilities – Tax basis exceeds book basis = Deferred tax liability (and expense)

If the tax basis of a liability exceeds the book basis, it implies that expenses for tax were allowed faster than they were for book. This is not the case most of the time. It's more common that book and tax expenses are either allowed at the same rate (i.e. no book/tax difference) or that a tax deduction related to an expense is delayed until it's paid. However, there is one common exception which we have already reviewed extensively: accelerated depreciation.

The reason that depreciation is sometimes not thought of as an example where the tax basis exceeds the book basis is because accumulated depreciation (which has a credit balance) is shown on the *asset* side of the balance sheet. In other words, fixed assets are typically viewed on a net basis. However, if the book and tax basis of the asset are the same (e.g. equipment purchased for $50,000) and you only look at the accumulated depreciation, the tax basis of accumulated depreciation in excess of book (due to accelerated depreciation) results in a deferred tax liability and a corresponding deferred tax expense.

11.5 Valuation allowances and deferred tax assets

A fundamental characteristic of an asset for GAAP purposes is that it has future economic value, i.e. there is a reasonable expectation its value will be realized equal to the carrying amount. With that in mind, let's return to the example of the $100,000 loss company we reviewed earlier.[114] Recall that the company booked the following entry to

---

[114] See the section, "Deferred tax benefits and deferred tax assets" starting on page 118.

record the future benefit it expected to receive from offsetting future income with its NOL.

Deferred Tax Asset $25,000 ($100,000 NOL x 25%)
   Deferred Tax Benefit $25,000

If this entry is left to stand on its own, the company is effectively taking the position that it's more likely than not that it will have sufficient taxable income within the carryforward period to fully utilize its net operating losses. If that's NOT a position the company can reasonably support with objective and verifiable evidence, it must create a "valuation allowance" as a contra-asset to offset the benefit created by the deferred tax asset. The entry for this example is as follows:

Deferred Tax Benefit (Expense) $25,000 (reversing the tax benefit above)[115]
   Valuation Allowance $25,000

The booking of a valuation allowance is treated as a *permanent* rather than as a temporary difference. Likewise, the reversal of a valuation allowance after a company shows it will have sufficient taxable income to utilize its NOLs is also treated as a permanent difference.[116]

11.6 Parting thoughts on deferred tax assets and benefits

- Theoretically, today's deferred tax asset will either become tomorrow's tax receivable or, more likely, a reduction in tomorrow's tax payable.
- A deferred tax asset signals that, as of the current reporting period, the company's tax liability has been *higher* than expected based on pretax book income due to *unfavorable* temporary differences (e.g. expenses for book where the deduction has been delayed for tax).
- Related to the previous point, a deferred tax asset signals that a company's tax liability in the future will be *lower* than expected relative to future pretax book income due to the reversal of temporary differences (i.e. future temporary differences will be *favorable*).
- A deferred tax benefit is still a "real" benefit, it will simply take place in the future.
- Somewhat counter-intuitively, deferred tax assets are "bad" from a tax planning perspective. While assets are generally thought of as "good," a deferred tax asset means that you've paid more tax today relative to what one would expect based

---

[115] An expense (or reversal) to a valuation allowance will always be to a deferred tax account; it is a GAAP rather than a tax concept.

[116] This means – and this is an important point – that either creating or reversing a valuation allowance will have an impact on the effective tax rate.

on pretax book income. Therefore, because these tax benefits won't be received until sometime in the future, it's a negative from both a cash flow and a time value of money perspective.

12 Tax Provision Example #3 – Temporary Differences and Deferred Taxes

To apply the deferred tax concepts we've been discussing to an actual tax provision, we'll now walk through the example in the Appendix, "Tax Provision Example #3 – Temporary Differences and Deferred Taxes" (referred to in this chapter as "Example #3").

12.1 Learning objectives

- Learn how to apply the concepts of temporary differences and deferred taxes in the context of a tax provision example.
- Understand the relationship between deferred taxes and a company's effective tax rate ("ETR").

12.2 Updated background and assumptions

Example #3 has the same background and assumptions as Example #1, with the following additions:

- During Year 1, the company booked a $20,000 expense accrual for GAAP that's not deductible for tax until it's paid in cash.
- At the end of the Year 1, no part of this $20,000 accrual had been paid.

Selected observations on how these updates are reflected in the tax provision package are noted in the comments and illustrations that follow.[117]

[This space was intentionally left blank].

---

[117] Refer to the complete set of Example #3 workpapers in the back of the material to see all figures, calculations, explanations, and references.

The trial balance (1600)

The trial balance at workpaper 1600 has been updated for the $20,000 expense accrual, both in the income statement (Expense – Temporary Item) and the balance sheet (Liability – Accrued Expenses).

Compared to Example #1, this expense accrual reduced pretax book income from $125,000 to $105,000 (see the illustration).

Liability - Accrued Expenses	($20,000)
Liability - Tax Payable - Federal	$0
Liability - Deferred Tax Liability - Federal	$0
Liability - Other	$0
Equity - Common Stock & APIC	($1,000,000)
Equity - Retained Earnings (beginning of year)	$0
Revenue - Standard	($340,000)
Revenue - Permanent Item	$0
Expense - Standard	$215,000
Expense - Permanent Item	$0
Expense - Temporary Item	$20,000
Expense - Depreciation - Book	$0

Pretax Book Income Calculation

	From Unadjusted Opening Trial Balance	From Closing (or "Final") Trial Balance
Option 1 - Revenue & Expense Excluding Income Taxes		
Pretax Book Income/(Loss)	$105,000	$105,000
Option 2 - Net Income with Taxes Added Back		
Current Year Net Income/(Loss)	$105,000	$78,750
Add: Current Tax Expense/(Benefit) - Federal	$0	$31,250
Add: Deferred Expense/(Benefit) - Federal	$0	($5,000)
Equals: Pretax Book Income/(Loss)	$105,000	$105,000

12.3 The tax provision (1000)

Pretax book income of $105,000 carried over from workpaper 1600 to workpaper 1000, and it's the new starting point for the tax provision calculation.

[This space was intentionally left blank].

	Tax Provision
	Current Year
Pretax Book Income	$105,000
Permanent Differences	
Permanent Difference - GL-related Items - Revenue	$0
Permanent Difference - GL-related Items - Expenses	$0
Permanent Difference - Special Tax Calculation	$0
Temporary Differences	
Temporary Difference - GL-related Items	$20,000
Temporary Difference - Depreciation	$0
Tax Return Calculations	
Subtotal: Pre-NOL Federal Taxable Income	$125,000
Times: Federal Tax Rate	25.00%
Subtotal: Federal Tax Before Credits	$31,250
Less: Federal Tax Credits	$0
Subtotal: Fed Tax Return Prov. - Current Tax Exp/(Ben)	$31,250

- Unlike Example #1, there is now a temporary difference between PTBI ($105,000) and taxable income ($125,000). The $20,000 difference is caused by the book/tax difference related to the accrued expenses.
- The current tax expense of the company is $31,250 (which is expected to tie to the tax return when it's filed later in the year).
- There's now a deferred tax benefit of $5,000, so the total tax expense of the company is $26,250 ($31,250 of current tax less the deferred tax benefit of $5,000 – see the illustration).

Summary of Current and Deferred Taxes	
Current Tax Expense/(Benefit) - Federal	$31,250
Deferred Tax Expense/(Benefit) - Federal	($5,000)
Total Tax Provision	$26,250

12.4 Schedule M calculation summary (1200)

This workpaper shows the support for the $20,000 book/tax difference for accrued expenses that ties to the tax provision (see the following illustration).[118]

---

[118] Detailed comments on Example #3 workpapers 1300 and 1310 (related to the deferred tax rollforward) are beyond the scope of this discussion. For the present, referring to workpaper 1310, the important conceptual point to understand is that the deferred tax benefit of $5,000 was determined by the net change between deferred tax assets at the beginning ($0) and the end ($5,000) of the period.

Temporary Differences - GL-related	
Liabilities - Accrued Expenses	$20,000
Less: Liabilities - Accrued Expenses - Prior Year	$0
Equals: Unfavorable/(Favorable) Schedule M	$20,000

12.5 Tax payable/receivable (60)

Referring to the illustration that follows:

Current Tax (Expense)/Benefit - Current Period (Q4)	($31,250)
Other Adjustments	$0
Subtotal	($31,250)
Other Adjustments	$0
End of Year ("EOY") Tax Receivable/(Payable)	($31,250)

- The ending tax payable ($31,250) is driven by the amount of current tax the company projects to pay with its Year 1 tax return.
- Deferred taxes ($5,000) do *not* impact the tax payable because they are not cash tax obligations. Rather, deferred taxes are a projection of the company's income tax liability on future tax returns.

12.6 Tax journal entry (50)

This tax entry is more complicated than Example #1 (and Example #2), because now we have deferred taxes to consider.

Account Description	Opening Balance From 1600[1]	Calculated Balance "Plug"[2]	Adjusting (Tax) Journal Entry Carries to 1600[3]
Asset - Deferred Tax Asset - Federal	$0	$5,000	$5,000
Asset - Tax Receivable - Federal	$0	$0	$0
Liability - Deferred Tax Liability - Federal	$0	$0	$0
Liability - Tax Payable - Federal	$0	($31,250)	($31,250)
Expense - Income Tax - Federal - Current Exp./(Ben.)	$0	$31,250	$31,250
Expense - Income Tax - Federal - Deferred Exp./(Ben.)	$0	($5,000)	($5,000)
Totals / Check Figure (should be zero)			$0

"The Missing Tax Accounting Guide – A Plain English Guide to ASC 740 Tax Provisions"
@ 2022 Tax Director Services, Inc.
All rights reserved

- The journal entry foots to zero, i.e., total debits (positive) and total credits (negative) are in balance (see the "Check Figure' line at the bottom).
- The current (cash) tax projection of $31,250 is related to the tax payable of $31,250.
- In the tax entry, notice the relationship of the deferred tax asset of $5,000 on the balance sheet and the accompanying deferred tax benefit of $5,000 in the income statement.
- The source of each of the entries above are referenced in the Example #3 workpapers.
- These journal entries carry to the "Tax Adjusting Entries" column on workpaper 1600 (refer to the full example in the back of the material), which adjusts the opening (unadjusted) trial balance amounts from what they were to what they should be (i.e. to the "closing" or "final" trial balance amounts).

12.7 Financial statements (5)

- Pretax book income of $105,000 ties to workpaper 1600 and to the tax provision at workpaper 1000.
- The total tax expense of $26,250 also ties to the tax provision at workpaper 1000.

Consolidated Statement of Comprehensive Income/(Loss)

Revenue	$340,000
Expenses (Pretax)	($235,000)
Income/(Loss) Before Income Tax Provision	$105,000
Income Tax (Provision)/Benefit	($26,250)
Net Income	$78,750
	In Balance
Other Comprehensive Income	$0
Comprehensive Income/(Loss)	$78,750

12.8 The effective tax rate ("ETR") reconciliation (5)

The updated ETR reconciliation is shown in the illustration that follows. Note that the expected tax based on pretax book income is $26,250 ($105,000 PTBI x 25%), which matches the company's total tax expense of $26,250. In the "Rate" column, we see the statutory tax rate of the company is 25%, which is the *same* as the effective tax rate of the company (this was NOT the case with the permanent difference illustrated in Example #2). The ETR (25%) is calculated by dividing the total tax expense ($26,250) by pretax book income ($105,000).

Effective Tax Rate Reconciliation

The differences between the effective tax rate reflected in the tax provision and the federal statutory rates are as follows:

Description	Dollar	Rate	
Expected Tax Provision/(Benefit) at the Statutory Tax Rate	$26,250	25.00%	From 1000
Nondeductible Meals	$0	0.00%	
Income Tax Provision/(Benefit)	$26,250	25.00%	

12.9 Deferred taxes related to timing "normalize" the effective tax rate

Sometimes in practice you'll hear the phrase, "Deferred taxes don't impact the rate," referring to the company's effective tax rate (25%) relative to the statutory tax rate (also 25% in our example). *This is a a very misleading statement!*

Notes to Consolidated Financial Statements ("The Footnotes")

Income Taxes

The income tax provision/(benefit) for the year consisted of the following:

Current Taxes	$31,250	From 1000
Deferred Taxes	($5,000)	
Total Tax Provision or Expense/(Benefit)	$26,250	
	In Balance	

Here, further comments and insights would be made on the income tax expense of the company, such as how it compared against the prior period, whether there were important trends, risks, etc.

Referring to the illustration, you will see that in the *absence* of the deferred taxes the total tax expense of the company would be $31,250, or $5,000 higher than the expected tax of $26,250 (PTBI of $105,000 x 25%). It is only *after* taking into account the $5,000 deferred tax benefit that the tax expense of the company "normalizes" to the expected total of $26,250. Thus, *deferred taxes DO impact both the total tax expense and the effective tax rate by <u>removing</u> the effects of temporary differences related to <u>timing</u>*.[119] Therefore, instead of saying, "Deferred taxes don't impact the rate," it is more accurate to say, "Deferred taxes relating to timing 'normalize' the effective tax rate."

---

[119] I want to emphasize that deferred taxes related to *timing differences* don't impact the ETR. However, deferred taxes that relate to indefinite differences, such as those that result from an APB 23 permanent reinvestment assertion, CAN impact the effective tax rate. Also, a valuation allowance expense is considered a deferred tax expense, and it also impacts the rate. Thus, it's inaccurate to say that deferred taxes NEVER affect the ETR. Refer to page 106 under the heading "Sources of temporary differences" for the discussion on timing differences, business combinations, and indefinite differences.

12.10 Tax Provision Example #4 – Comprehensive Example (Permanent and Temporary Differences

Refer to the Appendix for Example #4 on page 207 to see how temporary and permanent differences and current and deferred taxes interact with each other when they're both present in the same tax provision workpaper package.

13 An Introduction to State Income Taxes

Understanding how state income taxes are accounted for in a tax provision can be very tricky, particularly because related figures don't appear to consistently tie out in the workpapers and in the financial statements. The purpose of this chapter is to review state income taxes in a provision where there are no permanent or temporary differences. This will make it easier to see how state income tax figures are calculated, accounted for, and presented in the financial statements. The next chapter will then layer in the state tax-related impact of permanent and temporary differences.

13.1 First complete the state tax provision (1100)

It may seem natural to complete the federal tax provision prior to the state tax provision for a number of reasons. First, federal income taxes are almost always more material than state income taxes. Second, if you have experience with state tax compliance, you know that federal taxable income (or some derivation of it) is the starting point for many state income tax returns, meaning the federal income tax return is prepared prior to the state tax returns.

However, it's important to remember that ASC 740 is an *accounting* concept and not a tax compliance concept. The tax rules allow companies to deduct state income taxes from their federal taxable income.[120] Thus, the state tax provision must be computed *first* to estimate this deduction on the federal tax provision.

What follows is an example of how this works in the form of an abbreviated or simplified state tax provision. As noted at the beginning of the chapter, there are no temporary or permanent differences in this example. Thus, the provision for state income taxes ($6,250) is simply pretax book income ($125,000) multiplied by the state tax rate (5%).

[This space was intentionally left blank].

---

[120] See Internal Revenue Code Section 164.

1100 - State Tax Provision Summary

State Tax Provision Calculation	Tax Provision Current Year	Notes/Explanations
Pretax Book Income	$125,000	From 1600
Permanent Differences		
Permanent Difference - GL-related Items - Revenue	$0	From 1200 - Sch M Summary workpaper
Permanent Difference - GL-related Items - Expenses	$0	
Permanent Difference - Special Tax Calculation	$0	
Temporary Differences		
Temporary Difference - GL-related Items	$0	
Temporary Difference - Depreciation	$0	
Tax Return Calculations		
Subtotal: Pre-NOL State Taxable Income	$125,000	
Times: State Tax Rate	5.00%	From 80 - Tax Rates Summary
Subtotal: State Tax Before Credits	$6,250	
Less: State Tax Credits	$0	From 1200 - Sch M Summary workpaper
Subtotal: State Tax Return Prov. - Current Tax Exp/(Ben)	$6,250	Tax expense/(benefit) on a tax return (cash) basis
Other Adjustments & True-ups	$0	
Subtotal: Other Adjustments & True-ups	$0	
Equals: Total State Taxes - Current	$6,250	Carries to the summary below

13.2 The next step is to complete the federal tax provision (1000)

Having estimated state income taxes ($6,250) as part of preparing the state tax provision, you're now prepared to compute the federal tax provision. Like the state tax provision, there are no temporary or permanent differences in the calculation. A key item to note in the example that follows is that while the pretax book income ($125,000) *starting point* for the state and federal tax provisions is the same, federal taxable income ($118,750) is $6,250 *less* than state taxable income ($125,000) because of the deduction for state income taxes.

[This space was intentionally left blank].

1000 - Federal-only Tax Provision*

See workpaper 1100 for the state tax provision.

Calculation of Current Federal Taxes

	Tax Provision	Dollar Amt.	ETR	
	Current Year	Current Year	Current Year	Notes/Explanations
Pretax Book Income	$125,000	$26,250	21.00%	From 1600	The expected tax expense/rate of PTBI at the statutory tax rate
State Taxes				
(Deduction)/Benefit for State Taxes - Current Exp/(Ben)	($6,250)	($1,313)	-1.05%	From 1100 - State Tax Provision
Tax Return Calculations				
Subtotal: Pre-NOL Federal Taxable Income	$118,750			
Times: Federal Tax Rate	21.00%			From 80 - Tax Rates Summary
Subtotal: Federal Tax Before Credits	$24,938			
Less: Federal Tax Credits	$0	$0	0.00%	From 1200 - Sch M Summary workpaper
Subtotal: Fed Tax Return Prov. - Current Tax Exp/(Ben)	$24,938	$24,938	19.95%	Tax expense/(benefit) on a tax return (cash) basis
Other Adjustments & True-ups	$0			
Subtotal: Other Adjustments & True-ups	$0			
Total Current Taxes - Federal-only //Federal ETR	$24,938	$24,938	19.95%	Carries to the "Summary of Current and Deferred Taxes" below

Summary of Current and Deferred Federal Taxes

Current Tax Expense/(Benefit) - Federal	$24,938			Carries to 5 - Financial Statements
Deferred Tax Expense/(Benefit) - Federal	$0			From 1310 - USP Deferreds - Fed; carries to 50 - Tax JE
Total Tax Provision - Federal	$24,938			

"The Missing Tax Accounting Guide – A Plain English Guide to ASC 740 Tax Provisions"
@ 2022 Tax Director Services, Inc.
All rights reserved

13.3 State income taxes in the financial statement footnotes (5)

The following table shows how state (and federal) income taxes are presented in the financial statement footnotes.

Notes to Consolidated Financial Statements ("The Footnotes")

Income Taxes
The income tax provision/(benefit) for the year consisted of the following:

Current Income Taxes
Current Taxes - Federal	$24,938	From 1000 - Federal Tax Provision
Current Taxes - State	$6,250	From 1100 - State Tax Provision

Deferred Income Taxes
Deferred Taxes - Federal	$0	From 1000 - Federal Tax Provision
Deferred Taxes - State	$0	From 1100 - State Tax Provision
Total Tax Provision or Expense/(Benefit)	$31,188	

As one would intuitively expect, current income taxes as presented above for both federal and state purposes tie directly to their respective tax provision calculations. And, as previously noted, we are not presently considering the impact of deferred taxes.

13.4 State income taxes in the effective tax rate reconciliation (5)

The presentation of income taxes in the ETR reconciliation

Up to this point, I believe it can be said that accounting for state income taxes and presenting them in the financial statements has followed a logical progression. However, things take a turn when it comes to the effective tax rate ("ETR") reconciliation.

Effective Tax Rate Reconciliation
The differences between the effective tax rate reflected in the tax provision and the federal statutory rates are as follows:

Description	Dollar	Rate
Expected Tax Provision/(Benefit) at the Statutory Tax Rate	$26,250	21.00%
State Taxes Net of Federal Benefit	$4,938	3.95%
Other Adjustments	$0	0.00%
Income Tax Provision/(Benefit) / Effective Tax Rate (ETR)	$31,188	24.95%

Note that neither federal nor state income taxes in the above reconciliation tie to any of the figures we have reviewed so far. How can that be? Up to this point in this book, the first line of the ETR has been calculated using the simplified method of multiplying pretax book income times a *blended* federal and state tax rate. But in practice, meaning in the actual financial statements of a company, the first line of the ETR reconciliation ($26,250) is computed by multiplying pretax book income ($125,000) times the *federal* tax rate (21%).

Thus, one of the main purposes of the ETR reconciliation, and what makes it so valuable and insightful for financial statement readers, is that it answers this question: how much income tax ($26,250) would the company owe if pretax book income ($125,000) was taxed at the *federal statutory tax rate* (21%)? From that point, the ETR reconciliation compares the "expected tax" ($26,250) with actual income taxes per the tax provision ($31,188) and shows all reconciling items in between (such as state taxes of $4,938).

Understanding the difference between income taxes in the ETR reconciliation and elsewhere in the financial statements

So, let's come back to our original question, why do federal and state taxes presented in the ETR reconciliation not tie to income taxes as presented in the financial statement footnotes? As noted above, the first line of the ETR reconciliation is NOT federal income taxes per the federal tax provision ($24,938), but the EXPECTED tax of the company ($26,250) if pretax book income ($125,000) was taxed at the federal statutory rate (21%). The difference between these figures, what they represent, and where they're located in the federal tax provision workpapers is shown in the following illustration.

Calculation of Current Federal Taxes	Tax Provision Current Year	Dollar Amt. Current Year	ETR Current Year
Pretax Book Income	$125,000	$26,250	21.00%
State Taxes			
(Deduction)/Benefit for State Taxes - Current Exp/(Ben)	($6,250)	($1,313)	-1.05%
Tax Return Calculations			
Subtotal: Pre-NOL Federal Taxable Income	$118,750		
Times: Federal Tax Rate	21.00%		
Subtotal: Federal Tax Before Credits	$24,938		
Less: Federal Tax Credits	$0	$0	0.00%
Subtotal: Fed Tax Return Prov. - Current Tax Exp/(Ben)	$24,938	$24,938	19.95%
Other Adjustments & True-ups	$0		
Subtotal: Other Adjustments & True-ups	$0		
Total Current Taxes - Federal-only / /Federal ETR	$24,938	$24,938	19.95%

A second item to note is that, while the *individual* federal and state figures in the "Income Taxes" footnote are different than the ETR reconciliation amounts, the *combined* tax provision in both tables is the same ($31,188). Thus, by definition, if federal taxes in the ETR reconciliation are $26,250 then, mathematically, state taxes MUST be $4,938 for the total to come to $31,188. The question is how is that $4,938 computed, and what's the reasoning behind it? The answer is that in the ETR reconciliation, state taxes are reported "net of the federal benefit" (sometimes abbreviated "NOFB"). The illustration that follows shows how state taxes NOFB is calculated in our example.

State Taxes Net of the Federal Benefit

Calculation of State Taxes "NOFB"

Total Provision for State Taxes	$6,250	From the summary abvoe
Less: Federal Benefit of State Taxes	($1,313)	Calculated below
Equals: State Taxes Net of the Federal Benefit	$4,938	Ties to 10 - Financial Statement Tie-out

Federal Benefit of State Taxes

The Federal Deduction for State Taxes	($6,250)	From 1000 - Federal Tax Provision
Time: Federal Tax Rate	21.00%	From 80 - Tax Rates Summary
Equals: The Federal Benefit of State Taxes	($1,313)	Carries 10 - Financial Statement Tie-out

Summary of Current and Deferred State Taxes

Current Tax Expense/(Benefit) - State	$6,250	From above - Carries to 1000 - Federal Tax Provision
Deferred Tax Expense/(Benefit) - State	$0	There are no state deferred taxes in this example
Total Provision for State Taxes	$6,250	Carries to 1000 - Federal Tax Provision

"State taxes net of the federal benefit"

What exactly are "state taxes net of the federal benefit?" Conceptually, they represent "gross" state taxes ($6,250) less the benefit (or subsidy) received by the company ($1,313) for state taxes deducted on the federal tax return. Thus, state taxes "NOFB" are a "net" ($4,938) vs. a "gross" concept. In summary, state taxes are reported as a "gross" concept in the financial statements and footnotes EXCEPT as part of the ETR reconciliation where they're reported on a "net" concept.

13.5 State taxes and the taxes payable on the balance sheet (5 and 60)

According to the balance sheet on the face of the financial statements, the taxes payable of the company is $31,188 (see the illustration that follows).

[This space was intentionally left blank].

Consolidated Balance Sheet	Amounts
Other Assets (this includes all non-tax-related assets)	$1,125,000
Deferred Tax Asset - Federal or State	$0
Total Assets	**$1,125,000**
Liability - Taxes Payable	$31,188

Because this example is based on simplified assumptions, it's easy to think the support for the $31,188 payable is from the tax provision calculation we have been reviewing so far. It is not. Below, we see that the $31,188 is the sum of the federal ($24,938) and state ($6,250) taxes payable as shown on workpaper 60 (the "Tax Payable Rollforward").

Taxes (Payable)/Rec. Rollforward	Federal	State	Totals
Beginning of Year ("BOY") Tax Receivable/(Payable)	$0	$0	$0
Tax (Expense)/Benefit - Q1 through Q3	$0	$0	$0
Subtotal - Tax Expense/(Benefit) through Q1 - Q3	$0	$0	$0
Summary of Cash Taxes Paid/(Received)			
Tax Payments/(Refunds) - Q1 Estimated Tax	$0	$0	$0
Tax Payments/(Refunds) - Q2 Estimated Tax	$0	$0	$0
Tax Payments/(Refunds) - Q3 Estimated Tax	$0	$0	$0
Subtotal - Tax Payments/(Refunds) - Q1 - Q3	$0	$0	$0
Subtotal: Net Receivable/(Payable) - Q1 - Q3	$0	$0	$0
Current Tax (Expense)/Benefit - Current Period (Q4)	($24,938)	($6,250)	($31,188)
Other Adjustments	$0	$0	$0
End of Year ("EOY") Tax Receivable/(Payable)	($24,938)	($6,250)	($31,188)

13.6 The use of blended tax rates

In general

The company in our simplified example operates in a single state. In practice, even a modest-sized company can be required to file tax returns in multiple states. By default, ASC 740 guidelines require a company to prepare a separate tax provision calculation for each jurisdiction (i.e., each state in this case) in which it has a filing requirement. However, the ASC 740 rules are also sufficiently pragmatic to allow a combined state tax calculation through the use of a blended tax rate.[121]

It should be noted, however, that the use of a combined or blended state tax rate should *not* be taken for granted. Regardless of the approach, a company is expected to be materially correct in its separate computations of federal *and* state income taxes. Therefore, if a you desire to use a blended state tax rate in the preparation of the provision, you need to prepare a sufficient amount of analysis and support to show that it will result in a state tax expense that's reasonably close to what it would be if state taxes were computed separately for each jurisdiction.

Balancing volume, the related complexity, and materiality

An individual state tax provision isn't typically very difficult to understand, compute, and track. However, if a company files in all fifty states then, even if the income tax in any given state isn't material (except for, perhaps, one or two states), the volume of tax provision workpapers can quickly explode. That kind of volume adds complexity, and complexity increases the risk of a material tax-related misstatement.

It's for this reason that many companies combine, or "blend," their state tax provision calculations in some form or another, computing state taxes in the aggregate rather than on a state by state basis. It's also possible for companies to take a hybrid approach. For example, assume that a company files in ten states. Nine of those states have a similar approach for taxing the income of a corporation, but one has a very different approach. It should be acceptable to develop a methodology for applying a blended approach to the nine states and preparing a separate state tax provision for the "outlier" state (for a total of two state tax provisions).

---

[121] See ASC 740-10-55-25.

14 State Taxes – Permanent and Temporary Differences

In the previous chapter you gained an understanding of how state income taxes are calculated for tax provision purposes, as well as the difference for how they are presented in the effective tax rate reconciliation and income tax table sections of the financial statement footnotes. In this chapter, we will layer in permanent and temporary differences and evaluate not only how they impact state income taxes, but other aspects of the tax provision calculation, as well as the financial statements and accompanying footnote disclosures.

14.1 An example of a permanent difference and state taxes

Current tax provision – State taxes (1100)

Permanent Differences - GL-related - Expenses	
Expense - Permanent Item	$20,000
Times: Sch M Statutory Disallowance %	50%
Perm. Difference - GL-related Item - (Fav)/Unfav. Sch M	$10,000

In this first example, there is a GAAP expense of $20,000 that is only 50% deductible for tax purposes, meaning the tax deduction is $10,000 (see the illustration above).

State Tax Provision Calculation	Tax Provision Current Year
Pretax Book Income	$105,000
Permanent Differences	
Permanent Difference - GL-related Items - Revenue	$0
Permanent Difference - GL-related Items - Expenses	$10,000
Permanent Difference - Special Tax Calculation	$0
Temporary Differences	
Temporary Difference - GL-related Items	$0
Temporary Difference - Depreciation	$0
Tax Return Calculations	
Subtotal: Pre-NOL State Taxable Income	$115,000
Times: State Tax Rate	5.00%
Subtotal: State Tax Before Credits	$5,750
Less: State Tax Credits	$0
Subtotal: State Tax Return Prov. - Current Tax Exp/(Ben)	$5,750
Other Adjustments & True-ups	$0
Subtotal: Other Adjustments & True-ups	$0
Equals: Total State Taxes - Current	$5,750

As explained in the previous chapter, you complete the state tax provision prior to the federal tax provision. A screenshot of workpaper 1100 ("State Tax Provision") with the permanent difference of $10,000 is shown to the left.

A key observation – and this is something that can even be missed by experienced tax professionals – is that part of the impact of permanent items is *embedded* in the state tax expense (this will be covered in more detail later in the chapter).

Current tax provision – Federal taxes (1000)

With the state tax provision completed, you now know the amount of state income taxes ($5,750) that can be deducted in the federal tax provision. Taking that into account, along with the permanent difference ($10,000), the federal tax provision computation looks like this:

Calculation of Current Federal Taxes	Current Year
Pretax Book Income	$105,000
State Taxes	
(Deduction)/Benefit for State Taxes - Current Exp/(Ben)	($5,750)
Permanent Differences	
Permanent Difference - GL-related Items - Revenue	$0
Permanent Difference - GL-related Items - Expenses	$10,000
Permanent Difference - Special Tax Calculation	$0
Temporary Differences	
Temporary Difference - GL-related Items	$0
Temporary Difference - Depreciation	$0
Tax Return Calculations	
Subtotal: Pre-NOL Federal Taxable Income	$109,250
Times: Federal Tax Rate	21.00%
Subtotal: Federal Tax Before Credits	$22,943
Less: Federal Tax Credits	$0
Subtotal: Fed Tax Return Prov. - Current Tax Exp/(Ben)	$22,943
Other Adjustments & True-ups	$0
Subtotal: Other Adjustments & True-ups	$0
Total Current Taxes - Federal-only / /Federal ETR	$22,943

So far in this book we have assumed that the current tax expense is an estimate at the time the provision is prepared (e.g., January and February) of the taxes that will be due when the tax returns are filed (e.g., September or October). Ignoring the impact of extension and estimated tax payments, this means we expect we will owe $5,750 with our state income tax return and $22,943 with our federal income tax return.

Taxes payable rollforward (60)

With current tax concepts in mind, it's helpful to look at the taxes payable rollforward (workpaper 60):

Taxes (Payable)/Rec. Rollforward	Federal	State	Totals
Beginning of Year ("BOY") Tax Receivable/(Payable)	$0	$0	$0
Tax (Expense)/Benefit - Q1 through Q3	$0	$0	$0
Subtotal - Tax Expense/(Benefit) through Q1 - Q3	$0	$0	$0
Summary of Cash Taxes Paid/(Received)			
Tax Payments/(Refunds) - Q1 Estimated Tax	$0	$0	$0
Tax Payments/(Refunds) - Q2 Estimated Tax	$0	$0	$0
Tax Payments/(Refunds) - Q3 Estimated Tax	$0	$0	$0
Subtotal - Tax Payments/(Refunds) - Q1 - Q3	$0	$0	$0
Subtotal: Net Receivable/(Payable) - Q1 - Q3	$0	$0	$0
Current Tax (Expense)/Benefit - Current Period (Q4)	($22,943)	($5,750)	($28,693)
Other Adjustments	$0	$0	$0
End of Year ("EOY") Tax Receivable/(Payable)	($22,943)	($5,750)	($28,693)

Notice here that the payable balances for federal ($22,943) and state ($5,750) taxes correspond to the current federal and state tax provision calculations, respectively. Thus, in the context of this example, the taxes payable rollforward is equal to actual (or cash) taxes that are expected to be payable to tax authorities based on the tax returns that will be filed.

The financial statement balance sheet (5)

The taxes payable on the balance sheet ($28,693) ties back to the combined amount in the taxes payable rollforward (see the illustration in the previous subsection above).

Consolidated Balance Sheet	Amounts
Other Assets (this includes all non-tax-related assets)	$1,105,000
Deferred Tax Asset - Federal & State	$0
Total Assets	$1,105,000
Liability - Taxes Payable	$28,693
Deferred Tax Liability - Federal or State	$0
Other Liabilities (this includes all non-tax-related liabilities)	$0
Equity - Common Stock & APIC	$1,000,000
Equity - Retained Earnings	$76,308
Total Liabilities & Stockholders' Equity	$1,105,000

"The Missing Tax Accounting Guide – A Plain English Guide to ASC 740 Tax Provisions"
@ 2022 Tax Director Services, Inc.
All rights reserved

The income tax table in the financial statement footnotes (5)

The table for income taxes in the financial statement footnotes is presented as follows:

Income Taxes		
The income tax provision/(benefit) for the year consisted of the following:		
Current Income Taxes		
Current Taxes - Federal	$22,943	From 1000 - Federal Tax Provision
Current Taxes - State	$5,750	From 1100 - State Tax Provision
Deferred Income Taxes		
Deferred Taxes - Federal	$0	From 1000 and 1310 - Federal Tax Prov. and Fed. Tax Deferred RF
Deferred Taxes - State	$0	From 1100 and 1320 - State Tax Prov. and State Tax Deferred RF
Total Tax Provision or Expense/(Benefit)	$28,693	Ties to the income statement on page 1 of 2

Important observations are as follows:

- The "Current Income Taxes" section of the footnote ties to the federal and state tax provision calculations, respectively.
    - It's possible to look at the total tax provision amount of $28,693 and conclude that it relates to the taxes payable rollforward since the totals are the same.
    - While that's the case in this example, it's only because of simplified assumptions (it's year 1 and there were no extension or estimated tax payments).
    - In summary, while there is a *relationship* between current taxes (an income statement concept) and taxes payable (a balance sheet concept), the totals for each are rarely the same in an actual tax provision.
- There are no temporary differences in this example, and thus no deferred taxes.

14.2 State taxes and the effective tax rate reconciliation

The ETR reconciliation – In general (5)

Thus far, state income taxes in the tax provision have followed a logical pattern in the sense that each computation is what we would (theoretically) expect to tie to a past or future tax return. However, as explained in the previous chapter, the presentation of the effective tax rate ("ETR") reconciliation follows a different approach.

Effective Tax Rate Reconciliation
The differences between the effective tax rate reflected in the tax provision and the federal statutory rates are as follows:

Description	Dollar	Rate	
Expected Tax Provision/(Benefit) at the Statutory Tax Rate	$22,050	21.00%	From 1000 - Federal Tax Provision
State Taxes Net of Federal Benefit	$4,543	4.33%	From 1100 - State Tax Provision
Nondeductible Expenses	$2,100	2.00%	From 1000 - Federal Tax Provision
Income Tax Provision/(Benefit) / Effective Tax Rate (ETR)	$28,693	27.33%	Ties to the financial statements and the footnote above

The following observations are similarities and differences between the income tax table (pictured at the top of the previous page) and the ETR reconciliation.

- The total taxes in both tables are the same ($28,693).
- The first line of the ETR reconciliation, or the "expected tax" of the company ($22,050), is equal to pretax book income ($105,000) times the federal statutory tax rate (21%).
    - By definition, this means the federal taxes per the income tax table ($22,943) will *rarely* (if ever) tie to the expected federal taxes per the ETR ($22,050).
- Related to the previous point, it's important to recognize that, from a theoretical perspective, the company should "only" have federal income taxes equal to $22,050. If the actual income tax provision is a different amount ($28,693), such differences are itemized in the ETR reconciliation.

There are other important observations to make, but these will be pointed out separately in the following subsection on state taxes and the ETR reconciliation.

State taxes and the effective tax rate reconciliation

You'll notice from the ETR table on the previous page that one of the key reconciling differences between the expected tax at the federal statutory tax rate ($22,050) and the total income tax provision ($28,693) is state taxes ($4,543).[122] However, recall from the state tax provision calculation, the total states taxes were calculated to be $5,750 (see the illustration to the right).

State Tax Provision Calculation	Tax Provision Current Year
Pretax Book Income	$105,000
Permanent Differences	
Permanent Difference - GL-related Items - Revenue	$0
Permanent Difference - GL-related Items - Expenses	$10,000
Permanent Difference - Special Tax Calculation	$0
Temporary Differences	
Temporary Difference - GL-related Items	$0
Temporary Difference - Depreciation	$0
Tax Return Calculations	
Subtotal: Pre-NOL State Taxable Income	$115,000
Times: State Tax Rate	5.00%
Subtotal: State Tax Before Credits	$5,750
Less: State Tax Credits	$0
Subtotal: State Tax Return Prov. - Current Tax Exp/(Ben)	$5,750
Other Adjustments & True-ups	$0
Subtotal: Other Adjustments & True-ups	$0
Equals: Total State Taxes - Current	$5,750

What accounts for the $1,208 difference between the current tax provision amount of $5,750 and the state taxes per the ETR reconciliation of $4,543? The answer is that state taxes in the ETR reconciliation are shown *net* of the federal benefit (or "NOFB"), and the impact of

---

[122] The other difference in this example is a permanent difference of $2,100, which we will address shortly.

permanent differences explains the rest. These concepts are illustrated in the calculations that follow, with a focus on the reconciliation bracketed in red.

State Taxes Net of the Federal Benefit	PTBI	Perm	Totals
Taxable Income	$105,000	$10,000	$115,000
Times: Rate	5.00%	5.00%	5.00%
State Taxes	$5,250	$500	$5,750
Less: Fed. Benefit of State Taxes	($1,103)	($105)	($1,208)
Equals: State Taxes Net of Fed. Benefit	$4,148	$395	$4,543

Federal Benefit of State Taxes			
State Taxes	($5,250)	($500)	($5,750)
Times: Federal Rate	21.00%	21.00%	21.00%
Equals: Fed. Benefit of State Taxes	($1,103)	($105)	($1,208)

Total Permanent Differences	
Federal Tax Rate	21.00%
Add: State Tax Rate Net of Fed. Benefit	3.95%
Subtotal: Total Blended Tax Rate	24.95%
Times: Total Permanent Differences	$10,000
Equals: Total Blended Tax on Perms	$2,495

Permanent Item Impact on State Taxes	
Total Blended Tax on Perms	$2,495
State Tax NOFB from the Financial Stmt. Rate Reconciliation	($2,100)
Equals: Perm. Item Impact on State Taxes	$395

- As previously noted, state taxes in the ETR reconciliation are presented net of the federal benefit for the deduction of state taxes.
- Focusing solely on the PTBI amount that's driving taxable income, $105,000 times 5% equals state taxes of $5,250, and the federal deduction for this amount is $1,103 (see the calculations above).
- There is a permanent difference impact on state taxes NOFB as well ($105), as shown in the "Perm" column of the calculation in the top section.
- Some have the erroneous understanding that the state tax expense is *only* comprised of "state taxes." However, the calculations above clearly show that a portion of the company's overall permanent differences are embedded in both current state taxes ($5,750) and state taxes NOFB ($4,543).
    - See the calculations with the headings "Total Permanent Differences" and "Permanent Item Impact on State Taxes" to further illustrate this point.
    - Based on a blended federal and state tax rate concept (24.95%), we would expect the total impact of the permanent difference of $10,000 to equal $2,495.

- However, when referring to the ETR reconciliation, the tax impact of permanent differences is only $2,100. Thus, the separate line item for permanent differences only shows the *federal* impact ($10,000 times 21%).
  - The $395 state impact of the permanent difference of $10,000 is embedded in the calculation of current state taxes. It's equal to $10,000 times the state tax rate of 5% ($500) less the $105 federal benefit of state taxes (state taxes of $500 times the 21% federal tax rate).

In summary, state taxes are computed at "gross" amounts throughout the tax provision calculation, and conceptually these gross amounts can be thought of as tax return concepts. However, for purposes of the ETR:

- State taxes are reported <u>net</u> of the federal benefit (NOFB) of the state tax deduction on the federal return and
- Permanent difference in the ETR reconciliation ($2,100 in the ETR table) only include the federal tax impact (or the $10,000 permanent difference times 21%).

The rationale for the presentation of state taxes in the financial statements

So, why have all of the complexity in the presentation of state taxes in the financial statements? Why isn't there consistency between state income taxes in the income tax table ($5,750) and the ETR reconciliation ($4,543)? While I confess not to know the full history of how this standard evolved as part of SEC reporting, I will attempt an educated guess.

I believe it mostly comes down to making the financial statements useful to those who read and analyze them. Even sophisticated and experienced finance and accounting (and tax!) professionals can have difficulty following and understanding all the income tax-related aspects of the financial statements. And some even bypass an in-depth analysis of income taxes altogether, focusing instead on metrics such as pretax book income, EBITDA, various non-GAAP figures and summaries, and other measures that exclude income taxes.

Still, taxes are a significant and material item for many companies, and it's important for "non-tax" financial statement readers to have a straightforward way to assess a company's tax profile. That's where the ETR reconciliation comes in. The first line of the ETR reconciliation is intuitive and answers the question, "What's the expected federal tax of the company solely based on pretax book income?" It also answers the questions:

- "If the company's actual income tax provision isn't that number, why not?" and
- "What factors are driving the differences between the expected tax based on pretax book income and actual taxes per the total income tax provision?"

However, in order to have simplicity in this one area (i.e., the ETR reconciliation), the computational mechanics are such that it creates complexity with rationalizing and reconciling the figures in the ETR reconciliation with other aspects of the tax provision. That said, I personally believe that after understanding the reasoning behind these differences, the tradeoff of complexity for additional insight provided by the ETR reconciliation is worth it.

14.3 A simple example of a temporary difference and deferred taxes that includes state taxes

A progressive introduction to temporary differences and state taxes

In this section, we'll walk through a simple example that involves accounting for temporary differences and the related deferred taxes that includes state income taxes. What makes this example "simple?"

- There are no permanent differences.
- There is a single unfavorable temporary difference in the form of an accrued expense of $20,000 that's an expense for book but not deductible for tax until it's paid.
- Revenue ($20,000) is set to be an exact offset to accrued expenses (also $20,000), so pretax book income is equal to zero ($0).

These simplifications should enable you to more easily isolate and see the state-related impacts caused by temporary differences. In the next section, we'll layer in additional revenue and expenses so that pretax book income is positive, but there will still be no permanent differences in the tax provision calculation.

Finally, while I have separated the presentation and analysis of the state tax impacts of permanent and temporary differences in this chapter, Appendix 5 is a comprehensive example that *combines* permanent differences, temporary differences, deferred taxes, and state income taxes in a single tax provision calculation so you can see how all of these concepts come together.

Pretax book income (5 and 1600)

As noted in the introduction to this section, in this simplified example revenue and expenses offset, meaning pretax book income is zero.

Revenue	$20,000
Expenses (Pretax)	($20,000)
Income/(Loss) Before Income Tax Provision	$0

The current state income tax expense (1100)

Remember, just because pretax book income is zero, it doesn't automatically follow that *taxable* income is zero. In this example, the accrued expenses of $20,000 are a GAAP expense, but they are an unfavorable temporary difference for tax purposes. This is reflected in the computation of the current (as opposed to deferred) state income taxes in the illustration that follows.

State Tax Provision Calculation	Tax Provision Current Year	Notes/Explanations
Pretax Book Income	$0	From 1600
Permanent Differences		
Permanent Difference - GL-related Items - Revenue	$0	From 1200 - Sch M Summary workpaper
Permanent Difference - GL-related Items - Expenses	$0	
Permanent Difference - Special Tax Calculation	$0	
Temporary Differences		
Temporary Difference - GL-related Items	$20,000	
Temporary Difference - Depreciation	$0	
Tax Return Calculations		
Subtotal: Pre-NOL State Taxable Income	$20,000	
Times: State Tax Rate	5.00%	From 80 - Tax Rates Summary
Subtotal: State Tax Before Credits	$1,000	
Less: State Tax Credits	$0	From 1200 - Sch M Summary workpaper
Subtotal: State Tax Return Prov. - Current Tax Exp/(Ben)	$1,000	Tax expense/(benefit) on a tax return (cash) basis
Other Adjustments & True-ups	$0	
Subtotal: Other Adjustments & True-ups	$0	
Equals: Total State Taxes - Current	$1,000	Carries to the summary below

This example is interesting in the sense that the company is projected to have a current state (cash) tax liability when it files its tax return even though its pretax book income is zero. However, the total tax provision (meaning the sum of current and deferred taxes) of the company in this example of the company will also be zero. Why and how that's the case is addressed in the subsection that follows.

The deferred tax calculations for state income taxes (1320)

Recall from previous chapters that temporary differences between book (GAAP) and tax are by their very nature *temporary*. In other words, they will reverse over time. In our example, this means the $20,000 unfavorable temporary difference that's increasing taxable income in the current year will, in theory, be a $20,000 *deduction* in a future year.[123]

What the combination of the concepts above mean is the <u>net</u> state tax for provision purposes in this example will be zero. One way to see what may seem like a counterintuitive outcome is by reviewing the journal entries to record state taxes. Referring to the state tax provision calculation in the previous subsection, the current state income tax is $1,000, and the journal entry is as follows:

State Income Tax Expense – Current	$1,000	
Taxes Payable – State Income Taxes		$1,000

The entry for the deferred state tax benefit is as follows, with the support in the table that follows (workpaper 1320).[124]

Deferred Tax Asset – State Income Tax	$1,000	
State Income Tax <u>*Benefit*</u> – Deferred[125]		$1,000[126]

[This space was intentionally left blank].

---

[123] There are a lot of assumptions built into this simplified statement. First, the $20,000 deduction may or may not all occur in a single future tax period. Second, the state tax rate applicable to the current year's tax deduction (5% in this example) may increase or decrease in the future. And, finally, the company must have sufficient taxable income in the future to be able to use the deduction. The considerations and analysis related to this last point will fall under the topic of valuation allowances, which I do not address in this book. In summary, for purposes of the present example, we will assume that all deferred tax assets will be realizable in the future and that future taxable income will be taxed at a rate that's the same as Year 1.

[124] If you need a review of temporary differences and deferred taxes then see the applicable chapters from earlier in the material. But, in brief, the table shows that the $20,000 disallowed in the current year will result in a state tax benefit of $1,000 in a future period (the $20,000 deduction times the 5% tax rate). This is recognized in the current year as a deferred tax benefit (a $1,000 credit to tax expense) and as an offsetting deferred tax asset ($1,000).

[125] This line of the journal entry hits the P&L, and it's a tax benefit in the sense that it's a negative tax expense (or a credit to deferred taxes).

[126] Unless you're relying on tax provision software, I recommend separating the journal entries for current and deferred taxes because it makes it far easier to rationalize, document, and support.

Deferred Tax Asset/Liability Computation

Description	Gross Beg. Balance	Adjustments BOY Balance	Adjusted Beg. Balance	Current Activity	Times: State Tax Rate	Unadjusted Deferred Tax Asset/(Liability)	Adjustments	Adjusted Deferred Tax Asset/(Liability)
Accrued Expenses	$0	$0	$0	$20,000	5.00%	$1,000	$0	$1,000
Other Temporary Differences	$0	$0	$0	$0	5.00%	$0	$0	$0
Total Deferred Tax Assets/(Liabilities) - State	$0	$0	$0	$20,000		$1,000	$0	$1,000

From tab 1300 Pretax Deferreds

Deferred Tax Expense/Benefit Calculation

BOY Deferred Tax Assets/(Liabilities) - State	$0
Less: EOY Deferred Tax Assets/(Liabilities) - State	($1,000)
Equals: Deferred Tax Expense/(Benefit)	($1,000)

Notice from the journal entries that the current tax expense is $1,000, but, unlike for a permanent difference, there is an *equal and offsetting* deferred tax benefit (a credit entry) of $1,000. Thus, when you net these two items together, the net income tax expense of the company is zero. This is a concept that we will revisit in more detail shortly, but let's first look at federal income taxes.

The current federal income tax expense (1000)

The current federal income tax expense is calculated as follows:

Calculation of Current Federal Taxes	Tax Provision Current Year
Pretax Book Income	$0
State Taxes	
(Deduction)/Benefit for State Taxes - Current Exp/(Ben)	($1,000)
Permanent Differences	
Permanent Difference - GL-related Items - Revenue	$0
Permanent Difference - GL-related Items - Expenses	$0
Permanent Difference - Special Tax Calculation	$0
Temporary Differences	
Temporary Difference - GL-related Items	$20,000
Temporary Difference - Depreciation	$0
Tax Return Calculations	
Subtotal: Pre-NOL Federal Taxable Income	$19,000
Times: Federal Tax Rate	21.00%
Subtotal: Federal Tax Before Credits	$3,990
Less: Federal Tax Credits	$0
Subtotal: Fed Tax Return Prov. - Current Tax Exp/(Ben)	$3,990
Other Adjustments & True-ups	$0
Subtotal: Other Adjustments & True-ups	$0
Total Current Taxes - Federal-only / /Federal ETR	$3,990

As a review from previous sections, the deduction for state taxes ($1,000) is factored into the computation of federal taxable income ($19,000). Thus, the current federal tax expense of the company is $3,990, and the journal entry to record this result is:

Federal Income Tax Expense – Current	$3,990	
Taxes Payable – Federal Income Taxes		$3,990

The deferred tax calculations for federal income taxes (1310)

The computation of the deferred tax asset and benefit for federal income taxes is computed in a manner that's analogous to state income taxes with one key difference. Like the computation of federal current taxes, the deferred federal tax computation must take the deduction for state taxes income account. Here is the computation of the deferred tax asset in what I'll refer to as "Method #1:"

Deferred Tax Assets/Liabilities - Method #1

Description	Gross Beg. Balance	Current Year Gross Temp. Differences	Adjusted Balance	Fed. Tax Rate Less the Fed. Benefit of State Taxes	Unadjusted Deferred Tax Asset/(Liability)	Other Adjustments	Adjusted Deferred Tax Asset/(Liability)
Accrued Expenses	$0	$20,000	$20,000	19.95%	$3,990	$0	$3,990
Other Temporary Differences	$0	$0	$0	19.95%	$0	$0	$0
Total Deferred Tax Assets/(Liabilities) - Federal	$0	$20,000	$20,000	See the rate calculation	$3,990	$0	$3,990

In the table above, notice that the deferred tax asset of $3,990 (a debit), which is a *balance sheet* representation of the future value of federal tax deductions, is exactly equal to the current federal tax expense for Year 1 (see the previous subsection). Similarly, the computation of the deferred federal tax benefit (a credit), a *P&L* concept, is as follows:

Deferred Tax Expense/Benefit Calculation (Methods #1 and #2)

BOY Deferred Tax Assets/(Liabilities) - Federal	$0
Less: EOY Deferred Tax Assets/(Liabilities) - Federal	($3,990)
Equals: Deferred Tax Expense/(Benefit) (P&L impact)	($3,990)

Thus, the journal entry to record deferred taxes is as follows:

Deferred Tax Asset – Federal Income Tax	$3,990	
Federal Income Tax *Benefit* – Deferred		$3,990

Similar to state taxes, since the *current* federal tax expense (a debit of $3,990) and the *deferred* federal tax benefit (a credit of $3,990) are equal, the *net* federal income tax expense of the company is zero. In other words, because of the nature of temporary differences, the federal tax owed by the company for Year 1 as a current tax expense ($3,990) will be offset by a deferred tax benefit ($3,990) when the temporary difference of $20,000 is deducted in a future federal tax return.

While the concept of future tax benefits offsetting current taxes may seem intuitive, it's not so easy to see where the 19.95% tax rate comes from in the deferred tax asset table that makes the math come out right, or a tax rate that results in a deferred federal tax asset and deferred tax benefit of $3,990. After all, the federal statutory rate is 21%. So, again, where does the 19.95% come from? The answer is this percentage (19.95%) is equal to the federal tax rate (21%) less the rate for the federal benefit of the state tax deduction (1.05%), as illustrated in the calculation to the right.

Federal Statutory Rate - Current Year	21.00%
Less: Federal Benefit of the State Tax Deduction	-1.05%
Equal: Federal Tax Rate for Deferred Taxes	19.95%

This leads to another question: how is the federal benefit of the state tax deduction of 1.05% calculated? The answer is as follows:

The Federal Benefit of the State Tax Deduction Percentage

Gross Blended State Tax Rate	5.00%
Times: Federal Statutory Rate	21.00%
Equals: Federal Benefit of the State Tax Deduction	1.05%

If you find the "Method #1" percentage approach to be a difficult way to visualize the state effects on the federal computation of deferred taxes, consider this "Method #2" approach that, I believe, more clearly illustrates the effect of the state tax deduction:

Deferred Tax Assets/Liabilities - Method #2

Description	Gross Beg. Balance	Adjusted Beg. Balance	Gross Temporary Differences	(Ded.)/Benefit for State Tax Expense[1]	Temp. Diff. Net of State Tax (Ded.)/Ben.	Times: Federal Tax Rate	Deferred Tax Asset/(Liability)
Accrued Expenses	$0	$0	$20,000	($1,000)	$19,000	21.00%	$3,990
Other Temporary Differences	$0	$0	$0			21.00%	$0
Total Deferred Tax Assets/(Liabilities) - Federal	$0	$0	$20,000				$3,990

Observations for this "Method #2" approach are as follows:

- Similar to the current tax provision, the tax benefit of state income taxes ($1,000) is deducted from the gross temporary difference ($20,000), which results in a federal temporary difference of $19,000.
- This federal temporary difference ($19,000) is then multiplied by the federal *statutory* rate of 21% to compute the deferred tax asset ($3,990).
- The deferred tax benefit (a credit of $3,990) associated with the deferred tax asset (a debit of $3,990) is computed as shown in Method #1.

The financial statements and the footnotes (5)

I've repeatedly emphasized that for this example the net income tax expense is zero. Let's see what that looks like in the various elements of the financial statements and the related footnotes. First, the income statement:

Consolidated Statement of Comprehensive Income/(Loss)

Revenue	$20,000
Expenses (Pretax)	($20,000)
Income/(Loss) Before Income Tax Provision	$0
Income Tax (Provision)/Benefit	$0
Net Income	$0

- Revenue ($20,000) is equal to accrued expenses (also $20,000), so pretax book income is zero.
- Also, the income tax provision is equal to zero because the federal and state current tax expenses associated with the unfavorable temporary difference are offset by corresponding deferred tax benefits.

Now, let's look at the rate reconciliation:

Description	Dollar
Expected Tax Provision/(Benefit) at the Statutory Tax Rate	$0
State Taxes Net of Federal Benefit	$0
Nondeductible Expenses	$0
Income Tax Provision/(Benefit) / Effective Tax Rate (ETR)	$0

- The expected tax provision on line one is equal to pretax book income ($0) times the federal statutory rate (21%), which is equal to zero.
- Following this logic, the income tax provision per the ETR table is also equal to zero, and there are no reconciling items between book and tax income.

Finally, let's look at the income tax table in the footnotes, the illustration that provides the most insight for understanding this example.

Income Taxes

The income tax provision/(benefit) for the year consisted of the following:

Current Income Taxes

Current Taxes - Federal	$3,990
Current Taxes - State	$1,000

Deferred Income Taxes

Deferred Taxes - Federal	($3,990)
Deferred Taxes - State	($1,000)
Total Tax Provision or Expense/(Benefit)	$0

- Here we can see the net tax provision is zero, which is consistent with the income statement and the ETR reconciliation analysis above.

- However, with this presentation, it's far easier to see that, despite the fact that the net tax provision is zero, it's only because current year federal and state taxes are offset by deferred federal and state taxes.
    - Restating this point in a slightly different way, the table also shows that, despite owing taxes for the current year, the company expects to receive equal and offsetting tax benefits from future tax deductions based on the eventual reversal of the Year 1 temporary difference.

The mistake of netting the tax rate when computing deferred state income taxes

There may be times in practice where you may see the state tax rate net of the federal benefit used as a "shortcut" or as a "simplification" to compute state deferred taxes. Here is how that "shortcut" rate is computed:

The State Tax Rate Net of the Federal Benefit	
Gross Blended State Tax Rate	5.00%
Less: Fed. Benefit of the State Tax Deduction	-1.05%
Equals: State Tax Rate Net of the Federal Benefit	3.95%

Here is that same tax rate being used in the computation of deferred state taxes:

Description	Gross Beg. Balance	Adjustments BOY Balance	Adjusted Beg. Balance	Current Activity	Times: State Tax Rate	Deferred Tax Asset/(Liability)
Accrued Expenses	$0	$0	$0	$20,000	3.95%	$790
Other Temporary Differences	$0	$0	$0	$0	3.95%	$0
Total Deferred Tax Assets/(Liabilities) - State	$0	$0	$0	$20,000		$790

From tab 1300
Pretax Deferreds

Deferred Tax Expense/Benefit Calculation
BOY Deferred Tax Assets/(Liabilities) - State	$0
Less: EOY Deferred Tax Assets/(Liabilities) - State	($790)
Equals: Deferred Tax Expense/(Benefit)	($790)

Following this logic, the federal *statutory rate* is used to compute federal deferred taxes:

Description	Gross Beg. Balance	Gross Temp. Differences	Adjusted Balance	Benefit of State Taxes	Deferred Tax Asset/(Liability)
Accrued Expenses	$0	$20,000	$20,000	21.00%	$4,200
Other Temporary Differences	$0	$0	$0	21.00%	$0
				See the rate	
Total Deferred Tax Assets/(Liabilities) - Federal	$0	$20,000	$20,000	calculation	$4,200
	From 1300	From 1200		below	

Deferred Tax Expense/Benefit Calculation (Methods #1 and #2)
BOY Deferred Tax Assets/(Liabilities) - Federal	$0
Less: EOY Deferred Tax Assets/(Liabilities) - Federal	($4,200)
Equals: Deferred Tax Expense/(Benefit) (P&L impact)	($4,200)

"The Missing Tax Accounting Guide – A Plain English Guide to ASC 740 Tax Provisions"
@ 2022 Tax Director Services, Inc.
All rights reserved

However, the problem with this method becomes clearer when we review the income tax table from the financial statement footnotes in the illustration that follows:

Income Taxes

The income tax provision/(benefit) for the year consisted of the following:

Current Income Taxes	
Current Taxes - Federal	$3,990
Current Taxes - State	$1,000
Deferred Income Taxes	
Deferred Taxes - Federal	($4,200)
Deferred Taxes - State	($790)
Total Tax Provision or Expense/(Benefit)	$0

First, it's true that this "net method" gets us to the same place as the "gross method" in the computation of the total tax provision ($0), because *total* federal and state current taxes are fully offset by *total* deferred taxes. But notice that this approach results in a mismatch between the current and deferred federal and state taxes. In other words, in the company's present fact pattern, federal and state taxes *should* individually net to zero. However, the current federal taxes ($3,990) do not fully offset against the federal deferred benefit ($4,200), and state taxes have the same issue (a $1,000 current tax expense vs. a $790 deferred tax benefit).

This example shows that employing a "net method" to state taxes in computing either current or deferred taxes is incorrect. Instead, the "gross method" of using the full state tax rate (5%) should be used in state income tax calculations, and the deduction for state taxes should be reflected in both federal current and deferred calculations. The exception is that a net state income tax concept should be employed in the ETR reconciliation, a concept that we've previously covered in detail.[127]

Finally, what do you do in practice if you encounter a company that employs the "net method" for state tax computations?[128] First, you should recognize that it's not technically correct and inform the appropriate individuals that is the case.[129] However, as a purely practical matter, it's something you *may* be able to note but pass on if the overall impact on the financial statements and the accompanying footnotes is immaterial.[130]

---

[127] For further support, see ASC 740-10-55-20 and ASC 740-10-45-6.

[128] This could happen if you're new to a company or if you're auditing a company's tax provision.

[129] Who those individuals are will vary based on the situation, as well as whether you are working for the company or auditing them.

[130] What if a company is audited and they have consistently used the "net method," but it's not an issue the auditors have ever raised? Does this mean the auditors have signed off on the approach? You should not assume that's the case. The auditors may uncover this and other findings during the course of the audit they don't agree with. However, if

14.4 A more realistic example of a temporary difference and deferred taxes that includes state taxes

The company has pretax book income and a tax expense

Now that we've covered the fundamentals of how state income taxes interact with temporary differences in a tax provision, we'll examine a more realistic example where the company has pretax book income and a tax expense (instead of both being zero), which is summarized in the income statement as follows:

Revenue	$340,000
Expenses (Pretax)	($235,000)
Income/(Loss) Before Income Tax Provision	$105,000
Income Tax (Provision)/Benefit	($26,198)
Net Income	$78,803

The breakdown of the $235,000 pretax expenses (that exclude the tax expense) is as follows:

- $215,000 are "standard" expenses where GAAP (or "book") and tax are the same.
- As with the previous simplified example, there is a $20,000 amount that is an expense for GAAP but is a temporary difference for tax.
    - This $20,000 amount is not deductible in Year 1, but it will be deducible in a future period when the amount is paid or settled.

The current state income tax expense (1100)

The current state tax expense, or the cash tax expense expected upon the filing of the Year 1 tax return, is $6,250.[131] It is computed as follows:

[This space was intentionally left blank].

---

such items are immaterial, they may document them in their audit workpapers without raising them with the client.

[131] We are presently continuing with the assumption that current taxes are a proxy for cash taxes, but there are other factors to consider in practice.

State Tax Provision Calculation	Tax Provision Current Year
Pretax Book Income	$105,000
Permanent Differences	
Permanent Difference - GL-related Items - Revenue	$0
Permanent Difference - GL-related Items - Expenses	$0
Permanent Difference - Special Tax Calculation	$0
Temporary Differences	
Temporary Difference - GL-related Items	$20,000
Temporary Difference - Depreciation	$0
Tax Return Calculations	
Subtotal: Pre-NOL State Taxable Income	$125,000
Times: State Tax Rate	5.00%
Subtotal: State Tax Before Credits	$6,250
Less: State Tax Credits	$0
Subtotal: State Tax Return Prov. - Current Tax Exp/(Ben)	$6,250

It's worth noting in this example that pretax book income ($105,000), not the unfavorable temporary difference ($20,000), is the main driver of the current tax expense ($6,250).

The current federal income tax expense (1000)

The current federal income tax expense is as follows:

Calculation of Current Federal Taxes	Current Year
Pretax Book Income	$105,000
State Taxes	
(Deduction)/Benefit for State Taxes - Current Exp/(Ben)	($6,250)
Permanent Differences	
Permanent Difference - GL-related Items - Revenue	$0
Permanent Difference - GL-related Items - Expenses	$0
Permanent Difference - Special Tax Calculation	$0
Temporary Differences	
Temporary Difference - GL-related Items	$20,000
Temporary Difference - Depreciation	$0
Tax Return Calculations	
Subtotal: Pre-NOL Federal Taxable Income	$118,750
Times: Federal Tax Rate	21.00%
Subtotal: Federal Tax Before Credits	$24,938
Less: Federal Tax Credits	$0
Subtotal: Fed Tax Return Prov. - Current Tax Exp/(Ben)	$24,938

Similar to the previous example, the deduction for state income taxes ($6,250) has an impact on federal taxable income.

The deferred tax calculations for state income taxes (1320)

The computation and related commentary for state deferred tax assets (a debit of $1,000) and the corresponding deferred tax benefit (a credit of $1,000) is the same as in the previous section.

Deferred Tax Asset/Liability Computation

Description	Gross Beg. Balance	Adjustments BOY Balance	Adjusted Beg. Balance	Current Activity	Times: State Tax Rate	Unadjusted Deferred Tax Asset/(Liability)	Adjustments	Adjusted Deferred Tax Asset/(Liability)
Accrued Expenses	$0	$0	$0	$20,000	5.00%	$1,000	$0	$1,000
Other Temporary Differences	$0	$0	$0	$0	5.00%	$0	$0	$0
Total Deferred Tax Assets/(Liabilities) - State	$0	$0	$0	$20,000		$1,000	$0	$1,000

From tab 1300 Pretax Deferreds

Deferred Tax Expense/Benefit Calculation

BOY Deferred Tax Assets/(Liabilities) - State	$0
Less: EOY Deferred Tax Assets/(Liabilities) - State	($1,000)
Equals: Deferred Tax Expense/(Benefit)	($1,000)

The deferred tax calculations for federal income taxes (1310)

The computation and related commentary for federal deferred tax assets (a debit of $3,990) is the same as in the previous section.

Deferred Tax Assets/Liabilities - Method #1

Description	Gross Beg. Balance	Current Year Gross Temp. Differences	Adjusted Balance	Fed. Tax Rate Less the Fed. Benefit of State Taxes	Unadjusted Deferred Tax Asset/(Liability)	Other Adjustments	Adjusted Deferred Tax Asset/(Liability)
Accrued Expenses	$0	$20,000	$20,000	19.95%	$3,990	$0	$3,990
Other Temporary Differences	$0	$0	$0	19.95%	$0	$0	$0
Total Deferred Tax Assets/(Liabilities) - Federal	$0	$20,000	$20,000	See the rate calculation	$3,990	$0	$3,990

Similarly, the computation of the deferred federal tax benefit (a credit of $3,990) is the same as well:

Deferred Tax Expense/Benefit Calculation (Methods #1 and #2)

BOY Deferred Tax Assets/(Liabilities) - Federal	$0
Less: EOY Deferred Tax Assets/(Liabilities) - Federal	($3,990)
Equals: Deferred Tax Expense/(Benefit) (P&L impact)	($3,990)

The income tax table in the financial statements (5)

The presentation of the income tax table in the financial statements is insightful, especially when comparing it to the previous example where pretax book income was zero.

Income Taxes

The income tax provision/(benefit) for the year consisted of the following:

Current Income Taxes	
Current Taxes - Federal	$24,938
Current Taxes - State	$6,250
Deferred Income Taxes	
Deferred Taxes - Federal	($3,990)
Deferred Taxes - State	($1,000)
Total Tax Provision or Expense/(Benefit)	$26,198

- Deferred taxes (benefits of $3,990 and $1,000) are exactly the same as in the previous example, because both examples reflect the impact of a $20,000 unfavorable temporary differences (that will be a deductible tax benefit in the future).
- The current taxes section is different. This is because the federal and state current tax expenses include the impact of unfavorable temporary differences ($20,000) *and* pretax book income ($105,000).
    - These amounts tie back to the federal and state current tax provision calculations, respectively.

The taxes payable rollforward (60)

The taxes payable/receivable rollforward is as follows:

Taxes (Payable)/Rec. Rollforward	Federal	State	Totals
Beginning of Year ("BOY") Tax Receivable/(Payable)	$0	$0	$0
Tax (Expense)/Benefit - Q1 through Q3	$0	$0	$0
Subtotal - Tax Expense/(Benefit) through Q1 - Q3	$0	$0	$0
Summary of Cash Taxes Paid/(Received)			
Tax Payments/(Refunds) - Q1 Estimated Tax	$0	$0	$0
Tax Payments/(Refunds) - Q2 Estimated Tax	$0	$0	$0
Tax Payments/(Refunds) - Q3 Estimated Tax	$0	$0	$0
Subtotal - Tax Payments/(Refunds) - Q1 - Q3	$0	$0	$0
Subtotal: Net Receivable/(Payable) - Q1 - Q3	$0	$0	$0
Current Tax (Expense)/Benefit - Current Period (Q4)	($24,938)	($6,250)	($31,188)
Other Adjustments	$0	$0	$0
End of Year ("EOY") Tax Receivable/(Payable)	($24,938)	($6,250)	($31,188)

- There was no need to show this table in the previous example because federal and state taxes were zero.
- Federal ($24,398) and state ($6,250) taxes payable correspond to the (cash) tax liability expected to be payable when federal and state tax returns are filed based on their respective current tax calculations.

The tax adjusting journal entry ("tax AJE") (50)

Assuming no previous journal entries were made to income tax accounts in Year 1, the tax AJE based on the facts of this example are as follows:

Account Description	Opening Balance From 1600[1]	Calculated Balance "Plug"[2]	Adjusting (Tax) Journal Entry Carries to 1600[3]
Deferred Tax Asset - Federal	$0	$3,990	$3,990
Deferred Tax Asset - State	$0	$1,000	$1,000
Liability - Tax Payable - Federal	$0	($24,938)	($24,938)
Liability - Tax Payable - State	$0	($6,250)	($6,250)
Liability - Deferred Tax Liability - Federal or State	$0	$0	$0
Expense - Income Tax - Federal - Current Exp./(Benefit)	$0	$24,938	$24,938
Expense - Income Tax - State - Current Exp./(Benefit)	$0	$6,250	$6,250
Expense - Income Tax - Federal - Deferred Exp./(Benefit)	$0	($3,990)	($3,990)
Expense - Income Tax - State - Deferred Exp./(Benefit)	$0	($1,000)	($1,000)
Totals / Check Figure (should be zero)			$0

- The sum of all adjusting journal entries foots to zero.
- When there are numerous entries it can be difficult (if not overwhelming) to think of them all together. However, the tax entries are far easier to conceptualize when you break them down into their individual components as follows:

Current – Federal
Federal Tax Expense – Current $24,398
    Taxes Payable – Federal $24,398

Current – State
State Tax Expense – Current $6,250
    Taxes Payable – State $6,250

Deferred – Federal

Deferred Tax Asset – Federal	$3,990	
Deferred Tax Benefit – Federal		$3,990

Deferred - State

Deferred Tax Asset – State	$1,000	
Deferred Tax Benefit – State		$1,000

The effective tax rate reconciliation (5)

Let's now take a look at the ETR reconciliation:

Effective Tax Rate Reconciliation

The differences between the effective tax rate reflected in the tax provision and the federal statutory rates are as follows:

Description	Dollar	Rate
Expected Tax Provision/(Benefit) at the Statutory Tax Rate	$22,050	21.00%
State Taxes Net of Federal Benefit	$4,148	3.95%
Nondeductible Expenses	$0	0.00%
Income Tax Provision/(Benefit) / Effective Tax Rate (ETR)	$26,198	24.95%

The first line of $22,050 is equal to pretax book income ($105,000) times the federal statutory tax rate (21%). Understanding the build-up of the second line, the state income taxes net of the federal benefit of $4,148, is more complex. The first step is to determine the total provision for state income taxes, which is as follows:

Summary of Current and Deferred State Taxes

Current Tax Expense/(Benefit) - State	$6,250
Deferred Tax Expense/(Benefit) - State	($1,000)
Total Provision for State Taxes	$5,250

Now that you have the total provision for state taxes, you can compute state (income) taxes net of the federal benefit ($4,148) as shown in the illustration to the right.

State Taxes Net of the Federal Benefit

Calculation of State Taxes "NOFB"

Total Provision for State Taxes	$5,250
Less: Federal Benefit of State Taxes	($1,103)
Equals: State Taxes Net of the Federal Benefit	$4,148

Federal Benefit of State Taxes

Total Provision for State Taxes	($5,250)
Time: Federal Tax Rate	21.00%
Equals: The Federal Benefit of State Taxes	($1,103)

Referring to the ETR reconciliation on the previous page, notice that the tax rate (3.95%) associated with the state taxes NOFB ($4,148) in the ETR reconciliation table ties to the "Tax Rates Summary" workpaper (see the percentage bracketed in red).

Federal Statutory Rate	Current Year	Notes/Explanation
Federal Statutory Rate - Current Year	21.00%	
State Tax Rate		
Blended State Tax Rate		
Gross Blended State Tax Rate	5.00%	This is the average tax rate for all states in which the company operates
The State Tax Rate Net of the Federal Benefit		
Gross Blended State Tax Rate	5.00%	From above
Less: Fed. Benefit of the State Tax Deduction	-1.05%	Calculated below
Equals: State Tax Rate Net of the Federal Benefit	3.95%	
The % Federal Benefit of the State Tax Deduction		
Gross Blended State Tax Rate	5.00%	From above
Times: Federal Statutory Rate	21.00%	Same
Equals: Federal Benefit of the State Tax Deduction	1.05%	Carries above

Will this always be the case? The answer in no, because when permanent differences come into play the state rate in the ETR reconciliation will differ from that in the "Tax Rates Summary" above. However, because there are no permanent differences in this example, the ETR reconciliation shows that the federal tax rate (21%) and the state tax rate (3.95%) are in line with expectations. And here is one final way to think of these concepts in a way that ties back to the ETR reconciliation:

Pretax Book Income	$105,000
Times: Combined Federal and State Tax Rate	24.95%
Equals: Total Tax Provision or Expense/(Benefit)	$26,198

14.5 Appendix 5 – Combining permanent differences, temporary differences and state taxes

A significant milestone

You've now reached a significant milestone in your knowledge of tax provisions, which is that you now have the capability to combine the following concepts into a single tax provision calculation:

- Federal taxes
- State taxes
- Permanent differences
- Temporary differences

This means you're ready to review the example in Appendix 5 starting on page 221. In addition, you now have the foundational knowledge necessary to understand and apply more advanced tax accounting concepts. I wish you the very best on your continuing professional education journey! I would love to stay connected with you along the way, so feel free to sign on to my mailing list (www.nctaxdirector.com) and to connect with (or follow) me on LinkedIn.

15 Conclusion

15.1 Feedback and corrections

Constructive feedback on the material is greatly appreciated so that future versions of the book can be improved. This includes items related to spelling, grammar, the clarity (or lack of it) of various explanations, figures, descriptions, referencing in the examples, and so on. I can be reached at trent@nctaxdirector.com.

15.2 Receive notifications for future books, CPE seminars and webinars

- Sign on to my mailing list at www.nctaxdirector.com to receive notifications for new tax accounting, federal tax, international tax, Excel, Alteryx, and other material and CPE courses that I produce.
- Any reader of this book is welcome to connect with me on LinkedIn.
- If you have benefitted from this material, please leave a positive rating and comments on Amazon, and recommend it to colleagues.

16 APPENDIX – Example #1 – A Basic Tax Provision Workpaper Package

Note: Some workpapers in Example #1 reference other workpapers that are not included in this example. In those situations, such workpapers were not included to simplify the material being presented and because they contained no data or information necessary to support the overall tax provision calculation.

Example #1 - A Basic Tax Provision Workpaper Package
5 - Financial Statements (1 of 2)

This is a set of abbreviated financial statements and related footnotes that are derived from the final adjusted trial balance (see the third column at 1600) and supported by the tax provision (1000) and other workpapers.

Consolidated Balance Sheet	Amounts	Notes/Explanation/Reference
Other Assets (this includes all non-tax-related assets)	$1,125,000	From 1600 - Closing trial balance (third column on page 1 of 1)
Deferred Tax Asset - Federal	$0	From 1600 - Closing trial balance and 1310 Deferred tax rollforward
Total Assets	$1,125,000	Ties to the company's published financial statements
Liability - Tax Payable - Federal	$31,250	From 1600 (closing trial balance) and 60 (tax payable rollforward)
Other Liabilities (this includes all non-tax-related liabilities)	$0	From 1600 - Closing trial balance (third column on page 1 of 1)
Equity - Common Stock & APIC	$1,000,000	From 1600 - Closing trial balance (third column on page 1 of 1)
Equity - Retained Earnings	$93,750	See the "Retained Earnings Rollforward" on 2 of 2
Total Liabilities & Stockholders' Equity	$1,125,000	Ties to the company's published financial statements
	In Balance	

Consolidated Statement of Comprehensive Income/(Loss)		
Revenue	$340,000	From 1600 - Closing trial balance (third column on page 1 of 1)
Expenses (Pretax)	($215,000)	Same
Income/(Loss) Before Income Tax Provision	$125,000	Ties to pretax book income per 1600 (page 2 of 2)
Income Tax (Provision)/Benefit	($31,250)	See the "Income Taxes" footnote on page 2 of 2
Net Income	$93,750	
	In Balance	"In Balance" - Ties to net income per 1600 (page 2 of 2)
Other Comprehensive Income	$0	
Comprehensive Income/(Loss)	$93,750	Ties to the company's published financial statements

Example #1 - A Basic Tax Provision Workpaper Package
5 - Financial Statements (2 of 2)

Notes to Consolidated Financial Statements ("The Footnotes")

Income Taxes
The income tax provision/(benefit) for the year consisted of the following:

Current Taxes	$31,250	From 1000
Deferred Taxes	$0	
Total Tax Provision or Expense/(Benefit)	$31,250	
	In Balance	

Here, further comments and insights would be made on the income tax expense of the company, such as how it compared against the prior period, whether there were important trends, risks, etc.

Effective Tax Rate Reconciliation
The differences between the effective tax rate reflected in the tax provision and the federal statutory rates are as follows:

Description	Dollar	Rate	
Expected Tax Provision/(Benefit) at the Statutory Tax Rate	$31,250	25.00%	From 1000
Nondeductible Meals	$0	0.00%	
Income Tax Provision/(Benefit)	$31,250	25.00%	
	In Balance	In Balance	

Supporting Calculations (NOT shown in the financial statements)

Retained Earnings Rollforward

Beginning Retained Earnings/(Deficit)	$0	From 1600 (column one)
Add: Net Income/(Loss) for the Period	$93,750	From page 1 of 1
Less: Dividends and Other Distributions	$0	
Equals: Ending Retained Earnings	$93,750	Ties to the balance sheet on page 1 of 1
	In Balance	

Example #1 - A Basic Tax Provision Workpaper Package
50 - Tax Journal Entry Summary

The purpose of this workpaper is to adjust the period's beginning (or opening) balances to the correct ending (or calculated) balances based on tax provision calculations.

Column three below, the adjusting tax journal entry ("tax AJE"), is one of the key products of the Tax Group's work on the tax provision. When this entry is provided to the Accounting Group and booked in the general ledger (column two of 1600) then the company's trial balance should be final (column three of 1600). When that happens, the company can prepare its financial statements and the accompanying footnotes (summarized at workpaper 5).

For consolidated companies with multiple entities, tax adjusting entries should be prepared on a separate company basis (as opposed to a consolidated "top side" adjustment). Also, when applicable, tax adjusting journal entries ("AJE's") should be prepared in the local currency of the entity (USD or otherwise) because that is how they will be entered into the accounting system.

Account Description	Opening Balance From 1600[1]	Calculated Balance "Plug"[2]	Adjusting (Tax) Journal Entry Carries to 1600[3]	Notes/Explanation/Reference
Asset - Deferred Tax Asset - Federal	$0	$0	$0	Calculated at 1310 - Tax-effected deferred tax rollforward
Asset - Tax Receivable - Federal	$0	$0	$0	Calculated at 60 - Tax Payable (or Receivable) Rollforward
Liability - Deferred Tax Liability - Federal	$0	$0	$0	Calculated at 1310 - Tax-effected deferred tax rollforward
Liability - Tax Payable - Federal	$0	($31,250)	($31,250)	Calculated at 60 - Tax Payable Rollforward
Expense - Income Tax - Federal - Current Exp.-/(Ben.)	$0	$31,250	$31,250	Calculated at 1000 - Tax Provision Summary
Expense - Income Tax - Federal - Deferred Exp.-/(Ben.)	$0	$0	$0	From 1000 - Tax Provision Summary
Totals / Check Figure (should be zero)			$0 In Balance	Total debits and credits should net to zero

1 - These balances are from the first column of workpaper 1600.

2 - These amounts are calculated (or proven out) in various tax provision supporting workpapers as referenced in the "Notes" column.

3 - These adjusting entries carry to the middle column of workpaper 1600. As noted above, they adjust the trial balance from what it was (the first column at 1600) to what it should be (the third column at 1600).

"The Missing Tax Accounting Guide – A Plain English Guide to ASC 740 Tax Provisions"
@ 2022 Tax Director Services, Inc.
All rights reserved

Example #1 - A Basic Tax Provision Workpaper Package
60 - Tax Payable Rollforward

The purpose of this workpaper is to roll forward the tax (payable)/receivable accounts to their ending balances. As a proof, these amounts are compared against known tax returns, tax payments, and other verifiable balances. Note that debits are positive and credits are negative unless otherwise noted.

Summary for Financial Statement Footnotes

Ending Tax (Payable)/Receivable	($31,250)	From below
Total Income Tax Cash Payments/(Refunds)	$0	Same

Federal Taxes (Payable)/Rec. Rollforward

	USD	Notes/Explanations
Beginning of Year ("BOY") Tax Receivable/(Payable)	$0	Ties to the prior year ending balance sheet
Tax (Expense)/Benefit - Q1 through Q3	$0	From 1600 - Year to date ("YTD") activity from the TB (column one)
Subtotal - Tax Expense/(Benefit) through Q1 - Q3	$0	
Summary of Cash Taxes Paid/(Received)		
Tax Payments/(Refunds) - Q1 Estimated Tax	$0	Ties to estimated tax payments and AP cash disbursements
Tax Payments/(Refunds) - Q2 Estimated Tax	$0	
Tax Payments/(Refunds) - Q3 Estimated Tax	$0	
Subtotal - Tax Payments/(Refunds) - Q1 - Q3	$0	
Subtotal: Net Receivable/(Payable) - Q1 - Q3	$0	Ties to 1600 - Trial balance ("TB") opening amount (column one)
Current Tax (Expense)/Benefit - Current Period (Q4)	($31,250)	From 50 - Tax journal entry workpaper
Other Adjustments	$0	
Subtotal	($31,250)	
Other Adjustments	$0	
End of Year ("EOY") Tax Receivable/(Payable)	($31,250)	
	In Balance	"In Balance" - Ties to the net balance sheet tax receivable/payable

Ending Tax (Payable)/Receivable Proof

Total Expected Income Tax Payable per the Provision	$31,250	From 1000 - Tax Provision Summary
Less: Estimated Tax Payments to Date	$0	Ties to estimated tax vouchers & AP cash disbursement records
Equals: Expected Payable/(Receivable) Balance	$31,250	Ties to ending payable amount above

Example #1 - A Basic Tax Provision Workpaper Package

80 - Tax Rates Summary

The purpose of this workpaper is to list federal, state, and foreign tax rates that are used for tax provision calculations. Referencing tax rates from one location in the workpapers is efficient, and it also helps to maintain the integrity of internal checks and controls.

Federal Statutory Rate	Current Year	Notes/Explanation
Federal Statutory Rate - Current Year*	25.00%	The PY tax rate will be in the tax provision workpapers of the prior year

* As a simplification for this example, "Federal Statutory Rate" also includes state taxes, for an estimated combined statutory rate of 25%.

Example #1 - A Basic Tax Provision Workpaper Package
1000 - Tax Provision Summary (1 of 2)
US Parent

This workpaper is what is traditionally thought of as "the tax provision." Its purpose is to summarize the total tax provision (federal, state, and foreign income taxes) on an entity by entity basis. Recall that the total tax provision is the sum of current and deferred taxes, both of which are summarized and combined below. Also, the first column is the tax provision calculation. The second and third columns break out the dollar and rate impact on a line by line basis. These columns are the support for the "Effective Tax Rate Reconciliation" in the finanancial statement footnotes on page 2 of workpaper 5.

	Tax Provision	Dollar Amt.	ETR	
	Current Year	Current Year	Current Year	Notes/Explanation
Pretax Book Income	$125,000	$31,250	25.00%	From 1600	The expected tax expense/rate of PTBI at the statutory tax rate
Permanent Differences				
Permanent Difference - GL-related Items - Revenue	$0	$0	0.00%	From 1200 - M-1 Summary workpaper
Permanent Difference - GL-related Items - Expenses	$0	$0	0.00%	
Permanent Difference - Special Tax Calculation	$0	$0	0.00%	
Temporary Differences				
Temporary Difference - GL-related Items	$0	$0	0.00%	
Temporary Difference - Depreciation	$0	$0	0.00%	
Tax Return Calculations				
Subtotal: Pre-NOL Federal Taxable Income	$125,000			
Times: Federal Tax Rate	25.00%			From 80 - Tax Rates Summary
Subtotal: Federal Tax Before Credits	$31,250			
Less: Federal Tax Credits	$0	$0	0.00%	From 1200 - M-1 Summary workpaper
Subtotal: Fed Tax Return Prov. - Current Tax Exp/(Ben)	$31,250			Tax expense/(benefit) on a tax return (cash) basis
Other Adjustments & True-ups	$0			
Subtotal: Other Adjustments & True-ups	$0			
Subtotal: Current Taxes (calculation continues on pg. 2)	$31,250			Carries to the "Summary of Current and Deferred Taxes" on page 2 of 2

Example #1 - A Basic Tax Provision Workpaper Package
1000 - Tax Provision Summary (2 of 2)

Federal Tax-effected Deferred Taxes

			Notes/Explanation
Current Temporary Items - Deferred Tax Exp./(Ben.)	$0	0.00%	From 1310 - Federal Tax-Effected Deferred Rollforward
Credits - Deferred Tax Expense/(Benefit)	$0	0.00%	Same
Subtotal: Deferred Tax Expense/(Benefit)	$0		Carries to the "Summary of Current and Deferred Taxes" on page 2 of 2
	In Balance		
Subtotal: Total Federal Tax Provision	$31,250		
Add: Total State Tax Provision (Current & Deferred)	$0	0.00%	N/A - A blended tax rate is used for this calculation (see workpaper 80)
Equals: Total Tax Provision/Effective Tax Rate	$31,250	25.00%	Ties to the summary below and to the financial statements at workpaper 5
	25.00%	In Balance	In Balance
Calculated Effective Tax Rate ("ETR")		To 5 - Pg. 2	To 5 - Pg. 2

Summary of Current and Deferred Taxes

Current Tax Expense/(Benefit) - Federal	$31,250	To 5 - Financial Statements
Deferred Tax Expense/(Benefit) - Federal	$0	
Total Tax Provision	$31,250	
	In Balance	

Example #1 - A Basic Tax Provision Workpaper Package
1600 - Trial Balance or "TB" (1 of 2)
US Parent

The column on the left is the unadjusted trial balance provided by the Accounting Group to the Tax Group for the purpose of computing the tax provision. The unadjusted trial balance is final (meaning pretax book income is final) except for the tax entries. The middle column contains the adjusting entries for tax (from workpaper 50) based on tax provision calculations. The column on the right is the final (or closing) trial balance.

Shaded cells contain formulas; do not enter data
Debits are (+) and credits are (-) unless otherwise noted

Account Description	Unadjusted Opening Trial Balance	Tax Adjusting Entries	Closing (or "Final") Trial Balance	Notes/Explanation
Asset - Cash (after cash income tax payments)	$1,125,000		$1,125,000	Ties to a reconciliation on page 2 of 2
Asset - Tax Receivable - Federal	$0	$0	$0	From 50 - Tax AJE summary | Ties to 60 - Tax Payable/Receivable Rollforward
Asset - Fixed Assets	$0		$0	From 1700 - Fixed Asset Rollforward
Asset - Accumulated Depreciation	$0		$0	Same
Asset - Deferred Tax Asset - Federal	$0	$0	$0	From 50 - Tax AJE summary | Tie to 1310 - Federal Tax-Effected Deferred Rollforward
Asset - Other	$0		$0	
Liability - Accrued Expenses	$0		$0	Relates to a temporary difference; assumes accrual only, with no cash payments to date
Liability - Tax Payable - Federal	$0	($31,250)	($31,250)	From 50 - Tax AJE summary | Ties to 60 - Tax Payable/Receivable Rollforward
Liability - Deferred Tax Liability - Federal	$0	$0	$0	From 50 - Tax AJE summary | Tie to 1310 - Federal Tax-Effected Deferred Rollforward
Liability - Other	$0		$0	
Equity - Common Stock & APIC	($1,000,000)		($1,000,000)	
Equity - Retained Earnings (beginning of year)	$0		$0	This is beginning of year retained earnings; CY inc. stmt. activity is closed to EOY RE
Revenue - Standard	($340,000)		($340,000)	"Standard" in this context means book revenue equals tax revenue
Expense - Standard	$215,000		$215,000	This book amount is a permanent item for tax
Expense - Permanent Item	$0		$0	"Standard" in this context means book expense equals tax expense
Expense - Temporary Item	$0		$0	This book amount is a permanent item for tax
Expense - Depreciation - Book	$0		$0	This relates to the trial balance line item above "Liabilities - Accrued Expenses"
Expense - Income Tax - Federal - Current Exp./(Ben.)	$0	$31,250	$31,250	From 1700 - Fixed Asset Rollforward
Expense - Income Tax - Federal - Deferred Exp./(Ben.)	$0	$0	$0	From 50 - Tax AJE summary | Ties to 1000 - Tax provision summary (current tax exp.)
				From 50 - Tax AJE summary | Ties to 1000 - Tax provision summary (deferred tax exp.)
Check Figure (should be zero)	$0	$0	$0	Assets (debits), liabilities (credits), income (credits) and exp. (debits) must foot to zero
	In Balance	In Balance	In Balance	
		From 50	Carries to 5	

Example #1 - A Basic Tax Provision Workpaper Package
1600 - Trial Balance or "TB" (2 of 2)

Pretax Book Income Calculation

	From Unadjusted Opening Trial Balance	From Closing (or "Final") Trial Balance	Notes/Explanation
Option 1 - Revenue & Expense Excluding Income Taxes			
Pretax Book Income/(Loss)	$125,000	$125,000	The sum of all current year rev. and exp. items on pg. 1 of 1 except inc. tax accounts
Option 2 - Net Income with Taxes Added Back			
Current Year Net Income/(Loss)	$125,000	$93,750	The sum of all CY revenue and expense items on page 1 of 1
Add: Current Tax Expense/(Benefit) - Federal	$0	$31,250	From page 1 of 1
Add: Deferred Expense/(Benefit) - Federal	$0	$0	Same
Equals: Pretax Book Income/(Loss)	$125,000	$125,000	This amount should tie to the figure above
	In Balance	In Balance	"In Balance" means that Option 1&2 proofs are in balance (equal to one another)
		In Balance	"In Balance" means that tax entries did not impact pretax book income ("PTBI")

Cash Reconciliation

Cash - Beginning Balance	$1,000,000		Original capital provided by investors
Add: Pretax Income/(Loss) for the Period	$125,000		Assumption: All revenue was collected in cash
Add: Accrued Expenses	$0		Assumption: Accrued expenses have not been settled (paid in cash)
Less: Cash Income Tax Payments - Federal	$0		From 60 - Tax Payable/Receivable Rollforward
Cash - Ending Balance	$1,125,000		Ties to page 1 of 1

"The Missing Tax Accounting Guide – A Plain English Guide to ASC 740 Tax Provisions"
@ 2022 Tax Director Services, Inc.
All rights reserved

17 APPENDIX – Example #2 – Permanent Differences

Note: Some workpapers in Example #2 reference other workpapers that are not included in this example. In those situations, such workpapers were not included to simplify the material being presented and because they contained no data or information necessary to support the overall tax provision calculation.

Example #2 - Permanent Differences
5 - Financial Statements (1 of 2)

This is a set of abbreviated financial statements and related footnotes are derived from the final adjusted trial balance (see the third column at 1600) and supported by the tax provision (1000) and

Consolidated Balance Sheet	Amounts	Notes/Explanation/Reference
Other Assets (this includes all non-tax-related assets)	$1,105,000	From 1600 - Closing trial balance (third column on page 1 of 1)
Deferred Tax Asset - Federal	$0	From 1600 - Closing trial balance and 1310 Deferred tax rollforward
Total Assets	$1,105,000	Ties to the company's published financial statements
Liability - Tax Payable - Federal	$28,750	From 1600 (closing trial balance) and 60 (tax payable rollforward)
Other Liabilities (this includes all non-tax-related liabiilities)	$0	From 1600 - Closing trial balance (third column on page 1 of 1)
Equity - Common Stock & APIC	$1,000,000	From 1600 - Closing trial balance (third column on page 1 of 1)
Equity - Retained Earnings	$76,250	See the "Retained Earnings Rollforward" on 2 of 2
Total Liabilities & Stockholders' Equity	$1,105,000	Ties to the company's published financial statements
	In Balance	

Consolidated Statement of Comprehensive Income/(Loss)		
Revenue	$340,000	From 1600 - Closing trial balance (third column on page 1 of 1)
Expenses (Pretax)	($235,000)	Same
Income/(Loss) Before Income Tax Provision	$105,000	Ties to pretax book income per 1600 (page 2 of 2)
Income Tax (Provision)/Benefit	($28,750)	See the "Income Taxes" footnote on page 2 of 2
Net Income	$76,250	
	In Balance	"In Balance" - Ties to net income per 1600 (page 2 of 2)
Other Comprehensive Income	$0	
Comprehensive Income/(Loss)	$76,250	Ties to the company's published financial statements

Example #2 - Permanent Differences
5 - Financial Statements (2 of 2)

Notes to Consolidated Financial Statements ("The Footnotes")

Income Taxes

The income tax provision/(benefit) for the year consisted of the following:

Current Taxes	$28,750	From 1000
Deferred Taxes	$0	
Total Tax Provision or Expense/(Benefit)	$28,750	
	In Balance	

Here, further comments and insights would be made on the income tax expense of the company, such as how it compared against the prior period, whether there were important trends, risks, etc.

Effective Tax Rate Reconciliation

The differences between the effective tax rate reflected in the tax provision and the federal statutory rates are as follows:

Description	Dollar	Rate	
Expected Tax Provision/(Benefit) at the Statutory Tax Rate	$26,250	25.00%	From 1000
Nondeductible Meals	$2,500	2.38%	
Income Tax Provision/(Benefit)	$28,750	27.38%	
	In Balance	In Balance	

Supporting Calculations (NOT shown in the financial statements)

Retained Earnings Rollforward

Beginning Retained Earnings/(Deficit)	$0	From 1600 (column one)
Add: Net Income/(Loss) for the Period	$76,250	From page 1 of 1
Less: Dividends and Other Distributions	$0	
Equals: Ending Retained Earnings	$76,250	Ties to the balance sheet on page 1 of 1
	In Balance	

Example #1 - A Basic Tax Provision Workpaper Package
50 - Tax Journal Entry Summary

The purpose of this workpaper is to adjust the period's beginning (or opening) balances to the correct ending (or calculated) balances based on tax provision calculations.

Column three below, the adjusting tax journal entry ("tax AJE"), is one of the key products of the Tax Group's work on the tax provision. When this entry is provided to the Accounting Group and booked in the general ledger (column two of 1600) then the company's trial balance should be final (column three of 1600). When that happens, the company can prepare its financial statements and the accompanying footnotes (summarized at workpaper 5).

For consolidated companies with multiple entities, tax adjusting entries should be prepared on a separate company basis (as opposed to a consolidated "top side" adjustment). Also, when applicable, tax adjusting journal entries ("AJE's") should be prepared in the local currency of the entity (USD or otherwise) because that is how they will be entered into the accounting system.

Account Description	Opening Balance From 1600[1]	Calculated Balance "Plug"[2]	Adjusting (Tax) Journal Entry Carries to 1600[3]	Notes/Explanation/Reference
Asset - Deferred Tax Asset - Federal	$0	$0	$0	Calculated at 1310 - Tax-effected deferred tax rollforward
Asset - Tax Receivable - Federal	$0	$0	$0	Calculated at 60 - Tax Payable (or Receivable) Rollforward
Liability - Deferred Tax Liability - Federal	$0	$0	$0	Calculated at 1310 - Tax-effected deferred tax rollforward
Liability - Tax Payable - Federal	$0	($28,750)	($28,750)	Calculated at 60 - Tax Payable Rollforward
Expense - Income Tax - Federal - Current Exp./(Ben.)	$0	$28,750	$28,750	Calculated at 1000 - Tax Provision Summary
Expense - Income Tax - Federal - Deferred Exp./(Ben.)	$0	$0	$0	From 1000 - Tax Provision Summary
Totals / Check Figure (should be zero)			$0 In Balance	Total debits and credits should net to zero

1 - These balances are from the first column of workpaper 1600.

2 - These amounts are calculated (or proven out) in various tax provision supporting workpapers as referenced in the "Notes" column.

3 - These adjusting entries carry to the middle column of workpaper 1600. As noted above, they adjust the trial balance from what it was (the first column at 1600) to what it should be (the third column at 1600).

Example #2 - Permanent Differences
60 - Tax Payable Rollforward

The purpose of this workpaper is to roll forward the tax (payable)/receivable accounts to their ending balances. As a proof, these amounts are compared against known tax returns, tax payments, and other verifiable balances. Note that debits are positive and credits are negative unless otherwise noted.

Summary for Financial Statement Footnotes

Ending Tax (Payable)/Receivable	($28,750)	From below
Total Income Tax Cash Payments/(Refunds)	$0	Same

Federal Taxes (Payable)/Rec. Rollforward

	USD	Notes/Explanations
Beginning of Year ("BOY") Tax Receivable/(Payable)	$0	Ties to the prior year ending balance sheet
Tax (Expense)/Benefit - Q1 through Q3	$0	From 1600 - Year to date ("YTD") activity from the TB (column one)
Subtotal - Tax Expense/(Benefit) through Q1 - Q3	$0	
Summary of Cash Taxes Paid/(Received)		
Tax Payments/(Refunds) - Q1 Estimated Tax	$0	Ties to estimated tax payments and AP cash disbursements
Tax Payments/(Refunds) - Q2 Estimated Tax	$0	
Tax Payments/(Refunds) - Q3 Estimated Tax	$0	
Subtotal - Tax Payments/(Refunds) - Q1 - Q3	$0	
Subtotal: Net Receivable/(Payable) - Q1 - Q3	$0	Ties to 1600 - Trial balance ("TB") opening amount (column one)
Current Tax (Expense)/Benefit - Current Period (Q4)	($28,750)	From 50 - Tax journal entry workpaper
Other Adjustments	$0	
Subtotal	($28,750)	
Other Adjustments	$0	
End of Year ("EOY") Tax Receivable/(Payable)	($28,750)	
	In Balance	"In Balance" - Ties to the net balance sheet tax receivable/payable

Ending Tax (Payable)/Receivable Proof

Total Expected Income Tax Payable per the Provision	$28,750	From 1000 - Tax Provision Summary
Less: Estimated Tax Payments to Date	$0	Ties to estimated tax vouchers & AP cash disbursement records
Equals: Expected Payable/(Receivable) Balance	$28,750	Ties to ending payable amount above

"The Missing Tax Accounting Guide – A Plain English Guide to ASC 740 Tax Provisions"
@ 2022 Tax Director Services, Inc.
All rights reserved

Example #2 - Permanent Differences
80 - Tax Rates Summary

The purpose of this workpaper is to list federal, state, and foreign tax rates that are used for tax provision calculations. Referencing tax rates from one location in the workpapers is efficient, and it also helps to maintain the integrity of internal checks and controls.

Federal Statutory Rate

	Current Year	Notes/Explanation
Federal Statutory Rate - Current Year*	25.00%	The PY tax rate will be in the tax provision workpapers of the prior year

* As a simplification for this example, "Federal Statutory Rate" also includes state taxes, for an estimated combined statutory rate of 25%.

Example #2 - Permanent Differences
1000 - Tax Provision Summary (1 of 2)
US Parent

This workpaper is what is traditionally thought of as "the tax provision." Its purpose is to summarize the total tax provision (federal, state, and foreign income taxes) on an entity by entity basis. Recall that the total tax provision is the sum of current and deferred taxes, both of which are summarized and combined below. Also, the first column is the tax provision calculation. The second and third columns break out the dollar and rate impact on a line by line basis. These columns are the support for the "Effective Tax Rate Reconciliation" in the finanancial statement footnotes on page 2 of workpaper 5.

	Tax Provision Current Year	Dollar Amt. Current Year	ETR Current Year	Notes/Explanation
Pretax Book Income	$105,000	$26,250	25.00%	From 1600	The expected tax expense/rate of PTBI at the statutory tax rate
Permanent Differences				
Permanent Difference - GL-related Items - Revenue	$0	$0	0.00%	From 1200 - M-1 Summary workpaper
Permanent Difference - GL-related Items - Expenses	$10,000	$2,500	2.38%	
Permanent Difference - Special Tax Calculation	$0	$0	0.00%	
Temporary Differences				
Temporary Difference - GL-related Items	$0	$0	0.00%	
Temporary Difference - Depreciation	$0	$0	0.00%	
Tax Return Calculations				
Subtotal: Pre-NOL Federal Taxable Income	$115,000			
Times: Federal Tax Rate	25.00%			From 80 - Tax Rates Summary
Subtotal: Federal Tax Before Credits	$28,750			
Less: Federal Tax Credits	$0	$0	0.00%	From 1200 - M-1 Summary workpaper
Subtotal: Fed Tax Return Prov. - Current Tax Exp/(Ben)	$28,750			Tax expense/(benefit) on a tax return (cash) basis
Other Adjustments & True-ups	$0			
Subtotal: Other Adjustments & True-ups	$0			
Subtotal: Current Taxes (calculation continues on pg. 2)	$28,750			Carries to the "Summary of Current and Deferred Taxes" on page 2 of 2

"The Missing Tax Accounting Guide – A Plain English Guide to ASC 740 Tax Provisions"
@ 2022 Tax Director Services, Inc.
All rights reserved

Example #2 - Permanent Differences
1000 - Tax Provision Summary (2 of 2)

Federal Tax-effected Deferred Taxes

			Notes/Explanation
Current Temporary Items - Deferred Tax Exp./(Ben.)	$0	0.00%	From 1310 - Federal Tax-Effected Deferred Rollforward
Credits - Deferred Tax Expense/(Benefit)	$0	0.00%	Same
Subtotal: Deferred Tax Expense/(Benefit)	$0		Carries to the "Summary of Current and Deferred Taxes" on page 2 of 2
	In Balance		
Subtotal: Total Federal Tax Provision	$28,750		
Add: Total State Tax Provision (Current & Deferred)	$0	0.00%	N/A - A blended tax rate is used for this calculation (see workpaper 80)
Equals: Total Tax Provision/Effective Tax Rate	$28,750	27.38%	Ties to the summary below and to the financial statements at workpaper 5
	In Balance	In Balance	
Calculated Effective Tax Rate ("ETR")	27.38%	To 5 - Pg. 2	To 5 - Pg. 2

Summary of Current and Deferred Taxes

Current Tax Expense/(Benefit) - Federal	$28,750	To 5 - Financial Statements
Deferred Tax Expense/(Benefit) - Federal	$0	
Total Tax Provision	$28,750	
	In Balance	

Example #2 - Permanent Differences
1200 - M-1 Calculation Summary
US Parent

The purpose of this workpaper is to centralize and summarize all figures used to compute book/tax differences ("M-1's"). Shaded figures are pulling from other workpapers, and hard coded (unshaded) figures are supported by data and calculations outside of this workpaper (with a reference to the source documents provided).

	Amount	Notes/Explanation
Federal and State Book/Tax Differences		The figures in this section apply to both federal and state tax calculations
Permanent Differences - GL-related - Revenue		
Revenue - Permanent Item	$0	From 1600 - Entity trial balance. (e.g. tax-exempt interest)
Permanent Differences - GL-related - Expenses		
Expense - Permanent Item	$20,000	From 1600 - Entity trial balance
Times: M-1 Statutory Disallowance %	50%	This percentage is an example only (e.g. a meals percentage disallowance)
Perm. Difference - GL-related Item - (Fav)/Unfav. Sch M	$10,000	Amount carries to 1000 & 1100 - Federal and state tax provision summaries
Permanent Differences - Special Tax Calculations		
Perm. Difference - Special Tax Calc. - (Fav)/Unfav. Sch M	$0	Reference separate supporting workpapers here (e.g. IRC 199)
Temporary Differences - GL-related		
Liabilities - Accrued Expenses	$0	From 1600 - Entity trial balance
Less: Liabilities - Accrued Expenses - Prior Year	$0	This figure is from the prior year workpapers (prior year ending balance)
Equals: Unfavorable/(Favorable) M-1	$0	Amount carries to 1000 & 1100 - Federal and state tax provision summaries
		Also carries to 1300 - Pretax Deferred Rollforward
Temporary Differences - Fixed Asset Depreciation		
Book Depreciation	$0	From 1600 & 1700 - Entity trial balance and Fixed Asset Rollforward
Less: Tax Depreciation	$0	From 1700 - Fixed Asset Rollforward
Equals: (Favorable)/Unfavorable M-1	$0	Amount carries to 1000 & 1100 - Federal and state tax provision summaries
Federal-Only Tax Calculations		
Tax Credits - Federal-only		
Tax Credits - Federal-only - (Fav)/Unfav. M-1	$0	From 1800 - Tax credits summary (e.g. the federal R&D credit)

Example #2 - Permanent Differences
1600 - Trial Balance or "TB" (1 of 2)
US Parent

The column on the left is the unadjusted trial balance provided by the Accounting Group to the Tax Group for the purpose of computing the tax provision. The unadjusted trial balance is final (meaning pretax book income is final) except for the tax entries. The middle column contains the adjusting entries for tax (from workpaper 50) based on tax provision calculations. The column on the right is the final (or closing) trial balance.

Shaded cells contain formulas; do not enter data
Debits are (+) and credits are (-) unless otherwise noted

Account Description	Unadjusted Opening Trial Balance	Tax Adjusting Entries	Closing (or "Final") Trial Balance	Notes/Explanation
Asset - Cash (after cash income tax payments)	$1,105,000		$1,105,000	Ties to a reconciliation on page 2 of 2
Asset - Tax Receivable - Federal	$0	$0	$0	From 50 - Tax AJE summary | Ties to 60 - Tax Payable/Receivable Rollforward
Asset - Fixed Assets	$0		$0	From 1700 - Fixed Asset Rollforward
Asset - Accumulated Depreciation	$0		$0	Same
Asset - Deferred Tax Asset - Federal	$0	$0	$0	From 50 - Tax AJE summary | Tie to 1310 - Federal Tax-Effected Deferred Rollforward
Asset - Other	$0		$0	
Liability - Accrued Expenses	$0		$0	Relates to a temporary difference; assumes accrual only, with no cash payments to date
Liability - Tax Payable - Federal	$0	($28,750)	($28,750)	From 50 - Tax AJE summary | Ties to 60 - Tax Payable/Receivable Rollforward
Liability - Deferred Tax Liability - Federal	$0	$0	$0	From 50 - Tax AJE summary | Tie to 1310 - Federal Tax-Effected Deferred Rollforward
Liability - Other	$0		$0	
Equity - Common Stock & APIC	($1,000,000)		($1,000,000)	
Equity - Retained Earnings (beginning of year)	$0		$0	This is beginning of year retained earnings; CY inc. stmt. activity is closed to EOY RE
Revenue - Standard	($340,000)		($340,000)	"Standard" in this context means book revenue equals tax revenue
Revenue - Permanent Item	$0		$0	
Expense - Standard	$215,000		$215,000	This book amount is a permanent item for tax
Expense - Permanent Item	$20,000		$20,000	"Standard" in this context means book expense equals tax expense
Expense - Temporary Item	$0		$0	This book amount is a permanent item for tax
Expense - Depreciation - Book	$0		$0	This relates to the trial balance line item above "Liabilities - Accrued Expenses"
Expense - Income Tax - Federal - Current Exp./(Ben.)	$0	$28,750	$28,750	From 1700 - Fixed Asset Rollforward
Expense - Income Tax - Federal - Deferred Exp./(Ben.)	$0	$0	$0	From 50 - Tax AJE summary | Ties to 1000 - Tax provision summary (current tax exp.)
				From 50 - Tax AJE summary | Ties to 1000 - Tax provision summary (deferred tax exp.)
Check Figure (should be zero)	$0	$0	$0	Assets (debits), liabilities (credits), income (credits) and exp. (debits) must foot to zero
	In Balance	In Balance	In Balance	
		From 50	Carries to 5	

18 APPENDIX – Example #3 – Temporary Differences & Deferred Taxes

Note: Some workpapers in Example #3 reference other workpapers that are not included in this example. In those situations, such workpapers were not included to simplify the material being presented and because they contained no data or information necessary to support the overall tax provision calculation.

Example #3 - Temporary Differences and Deferred Taxes
5 - Financial Statements (1 of 2)

This is a set of abbreviated financial statements and related footnotes that are derived from the final adjusted trial balance (see the third column at 1600) and supported by the tax provision (1000) and other workpapers.

Consolidated Balance Sheet	Amounts	Notes/Explanation/Reference
Other Assets (this includes all non-tax-related assets)	$1,125,000	From 1600 - Closing trial balance (third column on page 1 of 1)
Deferred Tax Asset - Federal	$5,000	From 1600 - Closing trial balance and 1310 Deferred tax rollforward
Total Assets	$1,130,000	Ties to the company's published financial statements
Liability - Tax Payable - Federal	$31,250	From 1600 (closing trial balance) and 60 (tax payable rollforward)
Other Liabilities (this includes all non-tax-related liabilities)	$20,000	From 1600 - Closing trial balance (third column on page 1 of 1)
Equity - Common Stock & APIC	$1,000,000	From 1600 - Closing trial balance (third column on page 1 of 1)
Equity - Retained Earnings	$78,750	See the "Retained Earnings Rollforward" on 2 of 2
Total Liabilities & Stockholders' Equity	$1,130,000	Ties to the company's published financial statements
	In Balance	

Consolidated Statement of Comprehensive Income/(Loss)		
Revenue	$340,000	From 1600 - Closing trial balance (third column on page 1 of 1)
Expenses (Pretax)	($235,000)	Same
Income/(Loss) Before Income Tax Provision	$105,000	Ties to pretax book income per 1600 (page 2 of 2)
Income Tax (Provision)/Benefit	($26,250)	See the "Income Taxes" footnote on page 2 of 2
Net Income	$78,750	
	In Balance	"In Balance" - Ties to net income per 1600 (page 2 of 2)
Other Comprehensive Income	$0	
Comprehensive Income/(Loss)	$78,750	Ties to the company's published financial statements

Example #3 - Temporary Differences and Deferred Taxes
5 - Financial Statements (2 of 2)

Notes to Consolidated Financial Statements ("The Footnotes")

Income Taxes

The income tax provision/(benefit) for the year consisted of the following:

Current Taxes	$31,250	From 1000
Deferred Taxes	($5,000)	
Total Tax Provision or Expense/(Benefit)	$26,250	
	In Balance	

Here, further comments and insights would be made on the income tax expense of the company, such as how it compared against the prior period, whether there were important trends, risks, etc.

Effective Tax Rate Reconciliation

The differences between the effective tax rate reflected in the tax provision and the federal statutory rates are as follows:

Description	Dollar	Rate	
Expected Tax Provision/(Benefit) at the Statutory Tax Rate	$26,250	25.00%	From 1000
Nondeductible Meals	$0	0.00%	
Income Tax Provision/(Benefit)	$26,250	25.00%	
	In Balance	In Balance	

Supporting Calculations (NOT shown in the financial statements)

Retained Earnings Rollforward

Beginning Retained Earnings/(Deficit)	$0	From 1600 (column one)
Add: Net Income/(Loss) for the Period	$78,750	From page 1 of 1
Less: Dividends and Other Distributions	$0	
Equals: Ending Retained Earnings	$78,750	Ties to the balance sheet on page 1 of 1
	In Balance	

Example #1 - A Basic Tax Provision Workpaper Package
50 - Tax Journal Entry Summary

The purpose of this workpaper is to adjust the period's beginning (or opening) balances to the correct ending (or calculated) balances based on tax provision calculations.

Column three below, the adjusting tax journal entry ("tax AJE"), is one of the key products of the Tax Group's work on the tax provision. When this entry is provided to the Accounting Group and booked in the general ledger (column two of 1600) then the company's trial balance should be final (column three of 1600). When that happens, the company can prepare its financial statements and the accompanying footnotes (summarized at workpaper 5).

For consolidated companies with multiple entities, tax adjusting entries should be prepared on a separate company basis (as opposed to a consolidated "top side" adjustment). Also, when applicable, tax adjusting journal entries ("AJE's") should be prepared in the local currency of the entity (USD or otherwise) because that is how they will be entered into the accounting system.

Account Description	Opening Balance From 1600[1]	Calculated Balance "Plug"[2]	Adjusting (Tax) Journal Entry Carries to 1600[3]	Notes/Explanation/Reference
Asset - Deferred Tax Asset - Federal	$0	$5,000	$5,000	Calculated at 1310 - Tax-effected deferred tax rollforward
Asset - Tax Receivable - Federal	$0	$0	$0	Calculated at 60 - Tax Payable (or Receivable) Rollforward
Liability - Deferred Tax Liability - Federal	$0	$0	$0	Calculated at 1310 - Tax-effected deferred tax rollforward
Liability - Tax Payable - Federal	$0	($31,250)	($31,250)	Calculated at 60 - Tax Payable Rollforward
Expense - Income Tax - Federal - Current Exp./(Ben.)	$0	$31,250	$31,250	Calculated at 1000 - Tax Provision Summary
Expense - Income Tax - Federal - Deferred Exp./(Ben.)	$0	($5,000)	($5,000)	From 1000 - Tax Provision Summary
Totals / Check Figure (should be zero)			$0 **In Balance**	Total debits and credits should net to zero

1 - These balances are from the first column of workpaper 1600.

2 - These amounts are calculated (or proven out) in various tax provision supporting workpapers as referenced in the "Notes" column.

3 - These adjusting entries carry to the middle column of workpaper 1600. As noted above, they adjust the trial balance from what it was (the first column at 1600) to what it should be (the third column at 1600).

Example #3 - Temporary Differences and Deferred Taxes
60 - Tax Payable Rollforward

The purpose of this workpaper is to roll forward the tax (payable)/receivable accounts to their ending balances. As a proof, these amounts are compared against known tax returns, tax payments, and other verifiable balances. Note that debits are positive and credits are negative unless otherwise noted.

Summary for Financial Statement Footnotes

Ending Tax (Payable)/Receivable	($31,250)	From below
Total Income Tax Cash Payments/(Refunds)	$0	Same

Federal Taxes (Payable)/Rec. Rollforward

	USD	Notes/Explanations
Beginning of Year ("BOY") Tax Receivable/(Payable)	$0	Ties to the prior year ending balance sheet
Tax (Expense)/Benefit - Q1 through Q3	$0	From 1600 - Year to date ("YTD") activity from the TB (column one)
Subtotal - Tax Expense/(Benefit) through Q1 - Q3	$0	
Summary of Cash Taxes Paid/(Received)		
Tax Payments/(Refunds) - Q1 Estimated Tax	$0	Ties to estimated tax payments and AP cash disbursements
Tax Payments/(Refunds) - Q2 Estimated Tax	$0	
Tax Payments/(Refunds) - Q3 Estimated Tax	$0	
Subtotal - Tax Payments/(Refunds) - Q1 - Q3	$0	
Subtotal: Net Receivable/(Payable) - Q1 - Q3	$0	Ties to 1600 - Trial balance ("TB") opening amount (column one)
Current Tax (Expense)/Benefit - Current Period (Q4)	($31,250)	From 50 - Tax journal entry workpaper
Other Adjustments	$0	
Subtotal	($31,250)	
Other Adjustments	$0	
End of Year ("EOY") Tax Receivable/(Payable)	($31,250)	
	In Balance	"In Balance" - Ties to the net balance sheet tax receivable/payable

Ending Tax (Payable)/Receivable Proof

Total Expected Income Tax Payable per the Provision	$31,250	From 1000 - Tax Provision Summary
Less: Estimated Tax Payments to Date	$0	Ties to estimated tax vouchers & AP cash disbursement records
Equals: Expected Payable/(Receivable) Balance	$31,250	Ties to ending payable amount above

Example #3 - Temporary Differences and Deferred Taxes

80 - Tax Rates Summary

The purpose of this workpaper is to list federal, state, and foreign tax rates that are used for tax provision calculations. Referencing tax rates from one location in the workpapers is efficient, and it also helps to maintain the integrity of internal checks and controls.

Federal Statutory Rate	Current Year	Notes/Explanation
Federal Statutory Rate - Current Year*	25.00%	The PY tax rate will be in the tax provision workpapers of the prior year

* As a simplification for this example, "Federal Statutory Rate" also includes state taxes, for an estimated combined statutory rate of 25%.

Example #3 - Temporary Differences and Deferred Taxes
1000 - Tax Provision Summary (1 of 2)
US Parent

This workpaper is what is traditionally thought of as "the tax provision." Its purpose is to summarize the total tax provision (federal, state, and foreign income taxes) on an entity by entity basis. Recall that the total tax provision is the sum of current and deferred taxes, both of which are summarized and combined below. Also, the first column is the tax provision calculation. The second and third columns break out the dollar and rate impact on a line by line basis. These columns are the support for the "Effective Tax Rate Reconciliation" in the finanancial statement footnotes on page 2 of workpaper 5.

	Tax Provision	Dollar Amt.	ETR	
	Current Year	Current Year	Current Year	Notes/Explanation
Pretax Book Income	$105,000	$26,250	25.00%	From 1600	The expected tax expense/rate of PTBI at the statutory tax rate
Permanent Differences				
Permanent Difference - GL-related Items - Revenue	$0	$0	0.00%	From 1200 - M-1 Summary workpaper
Permanent Difference - GL-related Items - Expenses	$0	$0	0.00%	
Permanent Difference - Special Tax Calculation	$0	$0	0.00%	
Temporary Differences				
Temporary Difference - GL-related Items	$20,000	$5,000	4.76%	
Temporary Difference - Depreciation	$0	$0	0.00%	
Tax Return Calculations				
Subtotal: Pre-NOL Federal Taxable Income	$125,000			
Times: Federal Tax Rate	25.00%			From 80 - Tax Rates Summary
Subtotal: Federal Tax Before Credits	$31,250			
Less: Federal Tax Credits	$0	$0	0.00%	From 1200 - M-1 Summary workpaper
Subtotal: Fed Tax Return Prov. - Current Tax Exp/(Ben)	$31,250			Tax expense/(benefit) on a tax return (cash) basis
Other Adjustments & True-ups	$0			
Subtotal: Other Adjustments & True-ups	$0			
Subtotal: Current Taxes (calculation continues on pg. 2)	$31,250			Carries to the "Summary of Current and Deferred Taxes" on page 2 of 2

Example #3 - Temporary Differences and Deferred Taxes
1000 - Tax Provision Summary (2 of 2)

Federal Tax-effected Deferred Taxes

			Notes/Explanation
Current Temporary Items - Deferred Tax Exp./(Ben.)	($5,000)	-4.76%	From 1310 - Federal Tax-Effected Deferred Rollforward
Credits - Deferred Tax Expense/(Benefit)	$0	0.00%	Same
Subtotal: Deferred Tax Expense/(Benefit)	($5,000)		Carries to the "Summary of Current and Deferred Taxes" on page 2 of 2
	In Balance		
Subtotal: Total Federal Tax Provision	$26,250		
Add: Total State Tax Provision (Current & Deferred)	$0	0.00%	N/A - A blended tax rate is used for this calculation (see workpaper 80)
Equals: Total Tax Provision/Effective Tax Rate	$26,250	25.00%	Ties to the summary below and to the financial statements at workpaper 5
	25.00%	In Balance	
	Calculated Effective Tax Rate ("ETR")	To 5 - Pg. 2 To 5 - Pg. 2	

Summary of Current and Deferred Taxes

Current Tax Expense/(Benefit) - Federal	$31,250	
Deferred Tax Expense/(Benefit) - Federal	($5,000)	To 5 - Financial Statements
Total Tax Provision	$26,250	
	In Balance	

Example #3 - Temporary Differences and Deferred Taxes
1200 - M-1 Calculation Summary
US Parent

The purpose of this workpaper is to centralize and summarize all figures used to compute book/tax differences ("M-1's"). Shaded figures are pulling from other workpapers, and hard coded (unshaded) figures are supported by data and calculations outside of this workpaper (with a reference to the source documents provided).

	Amount	Notes/Explanation
Federal and State Book/Tax Differences		The figures in this section apply to both federal and state tax calculations
Permanent Differences - GL-related - Revenue		
Revenue - Permanent Item	$0	From 1600 - Entity trial balance. (e.g. tax-exempt interest)
Permanent Differences - GL-related - Expenses		
Expense - Permanent Item	$0	From 1600 - Entity trial balance
Times: M-1 Statutory Disallowance %	50%	This percentage is an example only (e.g. a meals percentage disallowance)
Perm. Difference - GL-related Item - (Fav)/Unfav. Sch M	$0	Amount carries to 1000 & 1100 - Federal and state tax provision summaries
Permanent Differences - Special Tax Calculations		
Perm. Difference - Special Tax Calc. - (Fav)/Unfav. Sch M	$0	Reference separate supporting workpapers here (e.g. IRC 199)
Temporary Differences - GL-related		
Liabilities - Accrued Expenses	$20,000	From 1600 - Entity trial balance
Less: Liabilities - Accrued Expenses - Prior Year	$0	This figure is from the prior year workpapers (prior year ending balance)
Equals: Unfavorable/(Favorable) Schedule M	$20,000	Amount carries to 1000 & 1100 - Federal and state tax provision summaries
		Also carries to 1300 - Pretax Deferred Rollforward
Temporary Differences - Fixed Asset Depreciation		
Book Depreciation	$0	From 1600 & 1700 - Entity trial balance and Fixed Asset Rollforward
Less: Tax Depreciation	$0	From 1700 - Fixed Asset Rollforward
Equals: (Favorable)/Unfavorable M-1	$0	Amount carries to 1000 & 1100 - Federal and state tax provision summaries
Federal-Only Tax Calculations		
Tax Credits - Federal-only		
Tax Credits - Federal-only - (Fav)/Unfav. M-1	$0	From 1800 - Tax credits summary (e.g. the federal R&D credit)

Example #3 - Temporary Differences and Deferred Taxes

1300 - Pretax Deferred Rollforward

US Parent

The purpose of this workpaper is to summarize gross (non-tax-effected) basis differences between book (GAAP) and tax. Positive balances give rise to deferred tax assets (and deferred tax benefits on the income statement) and negative balances give rise to deferred tax liabilities (and deferred tax expenses on the income statement). This workpaper serves as the basis for computing deferred tax expenses/benefits (an income statement concept), as well as deferred tax assets and liabilities (a balance sheet concept). See workpaper 1310 for those calculations.

Description	Beg. Balance[1]	Return to Prov. True-up	Other Adjustments	Adjusted Beg. Balance	Current Activity*	Other Adjustments	Ending Balance	Notes/Explanation
Accrued Expenses	$0			$0	$20,000		$20,000	
Fixed Asset Depreciation	$0			$0	$0		$0	
Totals	$0	$0	$0	$0	$20,000	$0	$20,000	

NOTES

1 - The beginning balance of pretax deferreds should tie to the prior year ending balance of this same workpaper.

Example #3 - Temporary Differences and Deferred Taxes
1310 - Federal Tax-Effected Deferred Rollforward
US Parent

The amounts on this worksheet are tax-effected as the federal statutory rate, and they are the source for computing federal deferred tax expenses/benefits (an income statement concept) and federal deferred tax assets and liabilities (a balance sheet concept). Positive balances are deferred tax assets and negative balances are deferred tax liabilities.

Description	Beg. Balance[1]	Tax Rate Changes	Return to Prov. True-up	Other Adj. BOY Balance	Adjusted Beg. Balance	Current Activity	Expiring Tax Benefits	Other Adjustments	Ending Balance	Notes
Accrued Expenses	$0	$0			$0	$5,000			$5,000	From 1300 (tax-effected)
Fixed Asset Depreciation	$0	$0			$0	$0			$0	
Federal Tax Credits	$0	N/A			$0	$0	$0		$0	From 1800
Deferred Tax Asset/(Liability)	$0	$0			$0	$5,000	$0	$0	$5,000	
	See summary below				See summary below				See summary below	

Change in Deferred Taxes Analysis

Net Change in Deferreds
End of Year Deferred Balance	$5,000	From above
Less: Beg. of Year Deferred Balance	$0	From above
Equals: Net Change in Deferred Taxes	$5,000	

Breakout of Net Change in Deferreds
Current Temps - Deferred Tax (Exp)/Ben	$5,000	This relates to current year temporary difference activity
Credits - Deferred Tax (Exp)/Ben	$0	This relates to current year tax credit activity
Subtotal: Current Activity	$5,000	Ties to deferred schedule above
Tax Rate Changes - Tax (Exp.)/Ben.	$0	From the tax-effected rollforward above
Expiring Tax Benefits - (Exp)/Ben	$0	
RTP True-ups	$0	
Other Adjustments to BOY Bal.	$0	
Other Adjustments	$0	
Equals: Net Change in Deferred Taxes	$5,000	Ties to total net change in deferreds above
	In Balance	

Applicable Tax Rate
Current Year Tax Rate	25.00%	From the "Tax Rates" tab
Less: Prior Year Tax Rate	-25.00%	
Equals: Change in Tax Rates	0.00%	Percentage used to calculate the "Rate Change" in the tax-effected rollforward above

NOTES
1 - On this workpaper, the tax-effected beginning balance is calculated, but this amount should also tie to the ending balance of the prior year workpapers.

"The Missing Tax Accounting Guide – A Plain English Guide to ASC 740 Tax Provisions"
@ 2022 Tax Director Services, Inc.
All rights reserved

Example #3 - Temporary Differences and Deferred Taxes
1600 - Trial Balance or "TB" (1 of 2)
US Parent

The column on the left is the unadjusted trial balance provided by the Accounting Group to the Tax Group for the purpose of computing the tax provision. The unadjusted trial balance is final (meaning pretax book income is final) except for the tax entries. The middle column contains the adjusting entries for tax (from workpaper 50) based on tax provision calculations. The column on the right is the final (or closing) trial balance.

Shaded cells contain formulas; do not enter data
Debits are (+) and credits are (-) unless otherwise noted

Account Description	Unadjusted Opening Trial Balance	Tax Adjusting Entries	Closing (or "Final") Trial Balance	Notes/Explanation
Asset - Cash (after cash income tax payments)	$1,125,000		$1,125,000	Ties to a reconciliation on page 2 of 2
Asset - Tax Receivable - Federal	$0	$0	$0	From 50 - Tax AJE summary | Ties to 60 - Tax Payable/Receivable Rollforward
Asset - Fixed Assets	$0		$0	From 1700 - Fixed Asset Rollforward
Asset - Accumulated Depreciation	$0		$0	Same
Asset - Deferred Tax Asset - Federal	$0	$5,000	$5,000	From 50 - Tax AJE summary | Tie to 1310 - Federal Tax-Effected Deferred Rollforward
Asset - Other	$0		$0	
Liability - Accrued Expenses	($20,000)		($20,000)	Relates to a temporary difference; assumes accrual only, with no cash payments to date
Liability - Tax Payable - Federal	$0	($31,250)	($31,250)	From 50 - Tax AJE summary | Ties to 60 - Tax Payable/Receivable Rollforward
Liability - Deferred Tax Liability - Federal	$0	$0	$0	From 50 - Tax AJE summary | Tie to 1310 - Federal Tax-Effected Deferred Rollforward
Liability - Other	$0		$0	
Equity - Common Stock & APIC	($1,000,000)		($1,000,000)	
Equity - Retained Earnings (beginning of year)	$0		$0	This is beginning of year retained earnings; CY inc. stmt. activity is closed to EOY RE
Revenue - Standard	($340,000)		($340,000)	"Standard" in this context means book revenue equals tax revenue
Revenue - Permanent Item	$0		$0	This book amount is a permanent item for tax
Expense - Standard	$215,000		$215,000	"Standard" in this context means book expense equals tax expense
Expense - Permanent Item	$0		$0	This book amount is a permanent item for tax
Expense - Temporary Item	$20,000		$20,000	This relates to the trial balance line item above "Liabilities - Accrued Expenses"
Expense - Depreciation - Book	$0		$0	From 1700 - Fixed Asset Rollforward
Expense - Income Tax - Federal - Current Exp./(Ben.)	$0	$31,250	$31,250	From 50 - Tax AJE summary | Ties to 1000 - Tax provision summary (current tax exp.)
Expense - Income Tax - Federal - Deferred Exp./(Ben.)	$0	($5,000)	($5,000)	From 50 - Tax AJE summary | Ties to 1000 - Tax provision summary (deferred tax exp.)
Check Figure (should be zero)	In Balance	In Balance	In Balance	Assets (debits), liabilities (credits), income (credits) and exp. (debits) must foot to zero
		From 50	Carries to 5	

Example #3 - Temporary Differences and Deferred Taxes
1600 - Trial Balance or "TB" (2 of 2)

Pretax Book Income Calculation

	From Unadjusted Opening Trial Balance	From Closing (or "Final") Trial Balance	Notes/Explanation
Option 1 - Revenue & Expense Excluding Income Taxes			
Pretax Book Income/(Loss)	$105,000	$105,000	The sum of all current year rev. and exp. items on pg. 1 of 1 except inc. tax accounts
Option 2 - Net Income with Taxes Added Back			
Current Year Net Income/(Loss)	$105,000	$78,750	The sum of all CY revenue and expense items on page 1 of 1
Add: Current Tax Expense/(Benefit) - Federal	$0	$31,250	From page 1 of 1
Add: Deferred Expense/(Benefit) - Federal	$0	($5,000)	Same
Equals: Pretax Book Income/(Loss)	$105,000	$105,000	This amount should tie to the figure above
	In Balance	In Balance	"In Balance" means that Option 1&2 proofs are in balance (equal to one another)
		In Balance	"In Balance" means that tax entries did not impact pretax book income ("PTBI")

Cash Reconciliation

Cash - Beginning Balance	$1,000,000	Original capital provided by investors
Add: Pretax Income/(Loss) for the Period	$105,000	Assumption: All revenue was collected in cash
Add: Accrued Expenses	$20,000	Assumption: Accrued expenses have not been settled (paid in cash)
Less: Cash Income Tax Payments - Federal	$0	From 60 - Tax Payable/Receivable Rollforward
Cash - Ending Balance	$1,125,000	Ties to page 1 of 1

19 APPENDIX – Example #4 – Permanent and Temporary Differences

The purpose of this example is to combine permanent differences (from Example #2) and temporary differences (from Example #3) into one tax provision so that you can see what they look like on a combined basis.

Note: Some workpapers in Example #4 reference other workpapers that are not included in this example. In those situations, such workpapers were not included to simplify the material being presented and because they contained no data or information necessary to support the overall tax provision calculation.

Example #4 - Comprehensive Example (Permanent & Temporary Differences)
5 - Financial Statements (1 of 2)

This is a set of abbreviated financial statements and related footnotes that are derived from the final adjusted trial balance (see the third column at 1600) and supported by the tax provision (1000) and other workpapers.

Consolidated Balance Sheet	Amounts	Notes/Explanation/Reference
Other Assets (this includes all non-tax-related assets)	$1,105,000	From 1600 - Closing trial balance (third column on page 1 of 1)
Deferred Tax Asset - Federal	$5,000	From 1600 - Closing trial balance and 1310 Deferred tax rollforward
Total Assets	**$1,110,000**	Ties to the company's published financial statements
Liability - Tax Payable - Federal	$28,750	From 1600 (closing trial balance) and 60 (tax payable rollforward)
Other Liabilities (this includes all non-tax-related liabilities)	$20,000	From 1600 - Closing trial balance (third column on page 1 of 1)
Equity - Common Stock & APIC	$1,000,000	From 1600 - Closing trial balance (third column on page 1 of 1)
Equity - Retained Earnings	$61,250	See the "Retained Earnings Rollforward" on 2 of 2
Total Liabilities & Stockholders' Equity	**$1,110,000** In Balance	Ties to the company's published financial statements

Consolidated Statement of Comprehensive Income/(Loss)		
Revenue	$340,000	From 1600 - Closing trial balance (third column on page 1 of 1)
Expenses (Pretax)	($255,000)	Same
Income/(Loss) Before Income Tax Provision	$85,000	Ties to pretax book income per 1600 (page 2 of 2)
Income Tax (Provision)/Benefit	($23,750)	See the "Income Taxes" footnote on page 2 of 2
Net Income	$61,250 In Balance	"In Balance" - Ties to net income per 1600 (page 2 of 2)
Other Comprehensive Income	$0	
Comprehensive Income/(Loss)	$61,250	Ties to the company's published financial statements

Example #4 - Comprehensive Example (Permanent & Temporary Items)
5 - Financial Statements (2 of 2)

Notes to Consolidated Financial Statements ("The Footnotes")

Income Taxes
The income tax provision/(benefit) for the year consisted of the following:

Current Taxes	$28,750	From 1000
Deferred Taxes	($5,000)	
Total Tax Provision or Expense/(Benefit)	$23,750	
	In Balance	

Here, further comments and insights would be made on the income tax expense of the company, such as how it compared against the prior period, whether there were important trends, risks, etc.

Effective Tax Rate Reconciliation
The differences between the effective tax rate reflected in the tax provision and the federal statutory rates are as follows:

Description	Dollar	Rate	
Expected Tax Provision/(Benefit) at the Statutory Tax Rate	$21,250	25.00%	From 1000
Nondeductible Meals	$2,500	2.94%	
Income Tax Provision/(Benefit)	$23,750	27.94%	
	In Balance	In Balance	

Supporting Calculations (NOT shown in the financial statements)

Retained Earnings Rollforward

Beginning Retained Earnings/(Deficit)	$0	From 1600 (column one)
Add: Net Income/(Loss) for the Period	$61,250	From page 1 of 1
Less: Dividends and Other Distributions	$0	
Equals: Ending Retained Earnings	$61,250	Ties to the balance sheet on page 1 of 1
	In Balance	

Example #1 - A Basic Tax Provision Workpaper Package
50 - Tax Journal Entry Summary

The purpose of this workpaper is to adjust the period's beginning (or opening) balances to the correct ending (or calculated) balances based on tax provision calculations.

Column three below, the adjusting tax journal entry ("tax AJE"), is one of the key products of the Tax Group's work on the tax provision. When this entry is provided to the Accounting Group and booked in the general ledger (column two of 1600) then the company's trial balance should be final (column three of 1600). When that happens, the company can prepare its financial statements and the accompanying footnotes (summarized at workpaper 5).

For consolidated companies with multiple entities, tax adjusting entries should be prepared on a separate company basis (as opposed to a consolidated "top side" adjustment). Also, when applicable, tax adjusting journal entries ("AJE's") should be prepared in the local currency of the entity (USD or otherwise) because that is how they will be entered into the accounting system.

Account Description	Opening Balance From 1600[1]	Calculated Balance "Plug"[2]	Adjusting (Tax) Journal Entry Carries to 1600[3]	Notes/Explanation/Reference
Asset - Deferred Tax Asset - Federal	$0	$5,000	$5,000	Calculated at 1310 - Tax-effected deferred tax rollforward
Asset - Tax Receivable - Federal	$0	$0	$0	Calculated at 60 - Tax Payable (or Receivable) Rollforward
Liability - Deferred Tax Liability - Federal	$0	$0	$0	Calculated at 1310 - Tax-effected deferred tax rollforward
Liability - Tax Payable - Federal	$0	($28,750)	($28,750)	Calculated at 60 - Tax Payable Rollforward
Expense - Income Tax - Federal - Current Exp./(Ben.)	$0	$28,750	$28,750	Calculated at 1000 - Tax Provision Summary
Expense - Income Tax - Federal - Deferred Exp./(Ben.)	$0	($5,000)	($5,000)	From 1000 - Tax Provision Summary
Totals / Check Figure (should be zero)			$0 In Balance	Total debits and credits should net to zero

1 - These balances are from the first column of workpaper 1600.

2 - These amounts are calculated (or proven out) in various tax provision supporting workpapers as referenced in the "Notes" column.

3 - These adjusting entries carry to the middle column of workpaper 1600. As noted above, they adjust the trial balance from what it was (the first column at 1600) to what it should be (the third column at 1600).

Example #4 - Comprehensive Example (Permanent & Temporary Items)
60 - Tax Payable Rollforward

The purpose of this workpaper is to roll forward the tax (payable)/receivable accounts to their ending balances. As a proof, these amounts are compared against known tax returns, tax payments, and other verifiable balances. Note that debits are positive and credits are negative unless otherwise noted.

Summary for Financial Statement Footnotes

Ending Tax (Payable)/Receivable	($28,750)	From below
Total Income Tax Cash Payments/(Refunds)	$0	Same

Federal Taxes (Payable)/Rec. Rollforward

	USD	Notes/Explanations
Beginning of Year ("BOY") Tax Receivable/(Payable)	$0	Ties to the prior year ending balance sheet
Tax (Expense)/Benefit - Q1 through Q3	$0	From 1600 - Year to date ("YTD") activity from the TB (column one)
Subtotal - Tax Expense/(Benefit) through Q1 - Q3	$0	
Summary of Cash Taxes Paid/(Received)		
Tax Payments/(Refunds) - Q1 Estimated Tax	$0	Ties to estimated tax payments and AP cash disbursements
Tax Payments/(Refunds) - Q2 Estimated Tax	$0	
Tax Payments/(Refunds) - Q3 Estimated Tax	$0	
Subtotal - Tax Payments/(Refunds) - Q1 - Q3	$0	
Subtotal: Net Receivable/(Payable) - Q1 - Q3	$0	Ties to 1600 - Trial balance ("TB") opening amount (column one)
Current Tax (Expense)/Benefit - Current Period (Q4)	($28,750)	From 50 - Tax journal entry workpaper
Other Adjustments	$0	
Subtotal	($28,750)	
Other Adjustments	$0	
End of Year ("EOY") Tax Receivable/(Payable)	($28,750)	
	In Balance	"In Balance" - Ties to the net balance sheet tax receivable/payable

Ending Tax (Payable)/Receivable Proof

Total Expected Income Tax Payable per the Provision	$28,750	From 1000 - Tax Provision Summary
Less: Estimated Tax Payments to Date	$0	Ties to estimated tax vouchers & AP cash disbursement records
Equals: Expected Payable/(Receivable) Balance	$28,750	Ties to ending payable amount above

Example #4 - Comprehensive Example (Permanent & Temporary Items)

80 - Tax Rates Summary

The purpose of this workpaper is to list federal, state, and foreign tax rates that are used for tax provision calculations. Referencing tax rates from one location in the workpapers is efficient, and it also helps to maintain the integrity of internal checks and controls.

Federal Statutory Rate

	Current Year	Notes/Explanation
Federal Statutory Rate - Current Year*	25.00%	The PY tax rate will be in the tax provision workpapers of the prior year

* As a simplification for this example, "Federal Statutory Rate" also includes state taxes, for an estimated combined statutory rate of 25%.

Example #4 - Comprehensive Example (Permanent & Temporary Items)

1000 - Tax Provision Summary (1 of 2)

US Parent

This workpaper is what is traditionally thought of as "the tax provision." Its purpose is to summarize the total tax provision (federal, state, and foreign income taxes) on an entity by entity basis. Recall that the total tax provision is the sum of current and deferred taxes, both of which are summarized and combined below. Also, the first column is the tax provision calculation. The second and third columns break out the dollar and rate impact on a line by line basis. These columns are the support for the "Effective Tax Rate Reconciliation" in the finanancial statement footnotes on page 2 of workpaper 5.

	Tax Provision	Dollar Amt.		ETR		Notes/Explanation
	Current Year	Current Year		Current Year		
Pretax Book Income	$85,000	$21,250		25.00%		From 1600	The expected tax expense/rate of PTBI at the statutory tax rate
Permanent Differences						
Permanent Difference - GL-related Items - Revenue	$0	$0		0.00%		From 1200 - M-1 Summary workpaper
Permanent Difference - GL-related Items - Expenses	$10,000	$2,500		2.94%		
Permanent Difference - Special Tax Calculation	$0	$0		0.00%		
Temporary Differences						
Temporary Difference - GL-related Items	$20,000	$5,000		5.88%		
Temporary Difference - Depreciation	$0	$0		0.00%		
Tax Return Calculations						
Subtotal: Pre-NOL Federal Taxable Income	$115,000					
Times: Federal Tax Rate	25.00%					From 80 - Tax Rates Summary
Subtotal: Federal Tax Before Credits	$28,750					
Less: Federal Tax Credits	$0	$0		0.00%		From 1200 - M-1 Summary workpaper
Subtotal: Fed Tax Return Prov. - Current Tax Exp/(Ben)	$28,750					Tax expense/(benefit) on a tax return (cash) basis
Other Adjustments & True-ups	$0					
Subtotal: Other Adjustments & True-ups	$0					
Subtotal: Current Taxes (calculation continues on pg. 2)	$28,750					Carries to the "Summary of Current and Deferred Taxes" on page 2 of 2

Example #4 - Comprehensive Example (Permanent & Temporary Items)

1000 - Tax Provision Summary (2 of 2)

Federal Tax-effected Deferred Taxes				Notes/Explanation
Current Temporary Items - Deferred Tax Exp./(Ben.)	($5,000)		-5.88%	From 1310 - Federal Tax-Effected Deferred Rollforward
Credits - Deferred Tax Expense/(Benefit)	$0		0.00%	Same
Subtotal: Deferred Tax Expense/(Benefit)	($5,000)			Carries to the "Summary of Current and Deferred Taxes" on page 2 of 2
	In Balance			
Subtotal: Total Federal Tax Provision	$23,750			
Add: Total State Tax Provision (Current & Deferred)	$0		0.00%	N/A - A blended tax rate is used for this calculation (see workpaper 80)
Equals: Total Tax Provision/Effective Tax Rate	$23,750		27.94%	Ties to the summary below and to the financial statements at workpaper 5
	In Balance	In Balance		
	To 5 - Pg. 2	To 5 - Pg. 2		
Calculated Effective Tax Rate ("ETR")	27.94%			

Summary of Current and Deferred Taxes

Current Tax Expense/(Benefit) - Federal	$28,750		To 5 - Financial Statements
Deferred Tax Expense/(Benefit) - Federal	($5,000)		
Total Tax Provision	$23,750		
	In Balance		

Example #4 - Comprehensive Example (Permanent & Temporary Differences)
1200 - M-1 Calculation Summary
US Parent

The purpose of this workpaper is to centralize and summarize all figures used to compute book/tax differences ("M-1's"). Shaded figures are pulling from other workpapers, and hard coded (unshaded) figures are supported by data and calculations outside of this workpaper (with a reference to the source documents provided).

	Amount	Notes/Explanation
Federal and State Book/Tax Differences		The figures in this section apply to both federal and state tax calculations
Permanent Differences - GL-related - Revenue		
Revenue - Permanent Item	$0	From 1600 - Entity trial balance. (e.g. tax-exempt interest)
Permanent Differences - GL-related - Expenses		
Expense - Permanent Item	$20,000	From 1600 - Entity trial balance
Times: M-1 Statutory Disallowance %	50%	This percentage is an example only (e.g. a meals percentage disallowance)
Perm. Difference - GL-related Item - (Fav)/Unfav. Sch M	$10,000	Amount carries to 1000 & 1100 - Federal and state tax provision summaries
Permanent Differences - Special Tax Calculations		
Perm. Difference - Special Tax Calc. - (Fav)/Unfav. Sch M	$0	Reference separate supporting workpapers here (e.g. IRC 199)
Temporary Differences - GL-related		
Liabilities - Accrued Expenses	$20,000	From 1600 - Entity trial balance
Less: Liabilities - Accrued Expenses - Prior Year	$0	This figure is from the prior year workpapers (prior year ending balance)
Equals: Unfavorable/(Favorable) M-1	$20,000	Amount carries to 1000 & 1100 - Federal and state tax provision summaries
		Also carries to 1300 - Pretax Deferred Rollforward
Temporary Differences - Fixed Asset Depreciation		
Book Depreciation	$0	From 1600 & 1700 - Entity trial balance and Fixed Asset Rollforward
Less: Tax Depreciation	$0	From 1700 - Fixed Asset Rollforward
Equals: (Favorable)/Unfavorable M-1	$0	Amount carries to 1000 & 1100 - Federal and state tax provision summaries
Federal-Only Tax Calculations		
Tax Credits - Federal-only		
Tax Credits - Federal-only - (Fav)/Unfav. M-1	$0	From 1800 - Tax credits summary (e.g. the federal R&D credit)

Example #4 - Comprehensive Example (Permanent & Temporary Differences)

1300 - Pretax Deferred Rollforward

US Parent

The purpose of this workpaper is to summarize gross (non-tax-effected) basis differences between book (GAAP) and tax. Positive balances give rise to deferred tax assets (and deferred tax benefits on the income statement) and negative balances give rise to deferred tax liabilities (and deferred tax expenses on the income statement). This workpaper serves as the basis for computing deferred tax expenses/benefits (an income statement concept), as well as deferred tax assets and liabilities (a balance sheet concept). See workpaper 1310 for those calculations.

Description	Beg. Balance[1]	Return to Prov. True-up	Other Adjustments	Adjusted Beg. Balance	Current Activity*	Other Adjustments	Ending Balance	Notes/Explanation
Accrued Expenses	$0			$0	$20,000		$20,000	
Fixed Asset Depreciation	$0			$0	$0		$0	
Totals	$0		$0	$0	$20,000	$0	$20,000	

NOTES

1 - The beginning balance of pretax deferreds should tie to the prior year ending balance of this same workpaper.

Example #4 - Comprehensive Example (Permanent & Temporary Items)
1310 - Federal Tax-Effected Deferred Rollforward
US Parent

The amounts on this worksheet are tax-effected as the federal statutory rate, and they are the source for computing federal deferred tax expenses/benefits (an income statement concept) and federal deferred tax assets and liabilities (a balance sheet concept). Positive balances are deferred tax assets and negative balances are deferred tax liabilities.

Description	Beg. Balance[1]	Tax Rate Changes	Return to Prov. True-up	Other Adj. BOY Balance	Adjusted Beg. Balance	Current Activity	Expiring Tax Benefits	Other Adjustments	Ending Balance	Notes
Accrued Expenses	$0	$0	$0	$0	$0	$5,000	$0	$0	$5,000	From 1300 (tax-effected)
Fixed Asset Depreciation	$0	$0	N/A	$0	$0	$0	$0	$0	$0	From 1800
Federal Tax Credits	$0	$0	N/A	$0	$0	$0	$0	$0	$0	
Deferred Tax Asset/(Liability)	$0 See summary below	$0	$0	$0	$0	$5,000 See summary below	$0	$0	$5,000 See summary below	

Change in Deferred Taxes Analysis

Net Change in Deferreds
End of Year Deferred Balance	$5,000	From above
Less: Beg. of Year Deferred Balance	$0	From above
Equals: Net Change in Deferred Taxes	$5,000	

Breakout of Net Change in Deferreds
Current Temps - Deferred Tax (Exp)/Ben	$5,000	This relates to current year temporary difference activity
Credits - Deferred Tax (Exp)/Ben	$0	This relates to current year tax credit activity
Subtotal: Current Activity	$5,000	Ties to deferred schedule above
Tax Rate Changes - Tax (Exp)/Ben.	$0	From the tax-effected rollforward above
Expiring Tax Benefits - (Exp)/Ben	$0	
RTP True-ups	$0	
Other Adjustments to BOY Bal.	$0	
Other Adjustments	$0	
Equals: Net Change in Deferred Taxes	$5,000	Ties to total net change in deferreds above
	In Balance	

NOTES
1 - On this workpaper, the tax-effected beginning balance is calculated, but this amount should also tie to the ending balance of the prior year workpapers.

Applicable Tax Rate
Current Year Tax Rate	25.00%	From the "Tax Rates" tab
Less: Prior Year Tax Rate	-25.00%	
Equals: Change in Tax Rates	0.00%	Percentage used to calculate the "Rate Change" in the tax-effected rollforward above

"The Missing Tax Accounting Guide – A Plain English Guide to ASC 740 Tax Provisions"
@ 2022 Tax Director Services, Inc.
All rights reserved

Example #4 - Comprehensive Example (Permanent & Temporary Differences)
1600 - Trial Balance or "TB" (1 of 2)
US Parent

The column on the left is the unadjusted trial balance provided by the Accounting Group to the Tax Group for the purpose of computing the tax provision. The unadjusted trial balance is final (meaning pretax book income is final) except for the tax entries. The middle column contains the adjusting entries for tax (from workpaper 50) based on tax provision calculations. The column on the right is the final (or closing) trial balance.

Shaded cells contain formulas; do not enter data
Debits are (+) and credits are (-) unless otherwise noted

Account Description	Unadjusted Opening Trial Balance	Tax Adjusting Entries	Closing (or "Final") Trial Balance	Notes/Explanation
Asset - Cash (after cash income tax payments)	$1,105,000		$1,105,000	Ties to a reconciliation on page 2 of 2
Asset - Tax Receivable - Federal	$0	$0	$0	From 50 - Tax AJE summary | Ties to 60 - Tax Payable/Receivable Rollforward
Asset - Fixed Assets	$0		$0	From 1700 - Fixed Asset Rollforward
Asset - Accumulated Depreciation	$0		$0	Same
Asset - Deferred Tax Asset - Federal	$0	$5,000	$5,000	From 50 - Tax AJE summary | Tie to 1310 - Federal Tax-Effected Deferred Rollforward
Asset - Other	$0		$0	
Liability - Accrued Expenses	($20,000)		($20,000)	Relates to a temporary difference; assumes accrual only, with no cash payments to date
Liability - Tax Payable - Federal	$0	($28,750)	($28,750)	From 50 - Tax AJE summary | Ties to 60 - Tax Payable/Receivable Rollforward
Liability - Deferred Tax Liability - Federal	$0	$0	$0	From 50 - Tax AJE summary | Tie to 1310 - Federal Tax-Effected Deferred Rollforward
Liability - Other	$0		$0	
Equity - Common Stock & APIC	($1,000,000)		($1,000,000)	
Equity - Retained Earnings (beginning of year)	$0		$0	This is beginning of year retained earnings; CY inc. stmt. activity is closed to EOY RE
Revenue - Standard	($340,000)		($340,000)	"Standard" in this context means book revenue equals tax revenue
Revenue - Permanent Item	$0		$0	This book amount is a permanent item for tax
Expense - Standard	$215,000		$215,000	"Standard" in this context means book expense equals tax expense
Expense - Permanent Item	$20,000		$20,000	This book amount is a permanent item for tax
Expense - Temporary Item	$20,000		$20,000	This relates to the trial balance line item above "Liabilities - Accrued Expenses"
Expense - Depreciation - Book	$0		$0	From 1700 - Fixed Asset Rollforward
Expense - Income Tax - Federal - Current Exp./(Ben.)	$0	$28,750	$28,750	From 50 - Tax AJE summary | Ties to 1000 - Tax provision summary (current tax exp.)
Expense - Income Tax - Federal - Deferred Exp./(Ben.)	$0	($5,000)	($5,000)	From 50 - Tax AJE summary | Ties to 1000 - Tax provision summary (deferred tax exp.)
Check Figure (should be zero)	$0	$0	$0	Assets (debits), liabilities (credits), income (credits) and exp. (debits) must foot to zero
	In Balance	In Balance	In Balance	
		From 50	Carries to 5	

Example #4 - Comprehensive Example (Permanent & Temporary Differences)
1600 - Trial Balance or "TB" (2 of 2)

Pretax Book Income Calculation

	From Unadjusted Opening Trial Balance	From Closing (or "Final") Trial Balance	Notes/Explanation
Option 1 - Revenue & Expense Excluding Income Taxes			
Pretax Book Income/(Loss)	$85,000	$85,000	The sum of all current year rev. and exp. items on pg. 1 of 1 except inc. tax accounts
Option 2 - Net Income with Taxes Added Back			
Current Year Net Income/(Loss)	$85,000	$61,250	The sum of all CY revenue and expense items on page 1 of 1
Add: Current Tax Expense/(Benefit) - Federal	$0	$28,750	From page 1 of 1
Add: Deferred Expense/(Benefit) - Federal	$0	($5,000)	Same
Equals: Pretax Book Income/(Loss)	$85,000	$85,000	This amount should tie to the figure above
	In Balance	In Balance	"In Balance" means that Option 1&2 proofs are in balance (equal to one another)
		In Balance	"In Balance" means that tax entries did not impact pretax book income ("PTBI")

Cash Reconciliation

Cash - Beginning Balance	$1,000,000	Original capital provided by investors
Add: Pretax Income/(Loss) for the Period	$85,000	Assumption: All revenue was collected in cash
Add: Accrued Expenses	$20,000	Assumption: Accrued expenses have not been settled (paid in cash)
Less: Cash Income Tax Payments - Federal	$0	From 60 - Tax Payable/Receivable Rollforward
Cash - Ending Balance	$1,105,000	Ties to page 1 of 1

20 APPENDIX – Example #5 – Comprehensive Example – Permanent and Temporary Differences plus State Taxes

The purpose of this example is to build on Example #4, which included a provision with permanent and temporary differences. However, Example #4 employed a simplification in the form of a combined federal and state tax rate. Example #5 also includes permanent and temporary differences, but this time the federal *and* state elements of the tax provision are computed separately and then combined in the financial statement presentation. As a result, this is effectively a "real" (albeit simplified) tax provision.

Note: Some workpapers in Example #5 reference other workpapers that are not included in this example. In those situations, such workpapers were not included to simplify the material being presented and because they contained no data or information necessary to support the overall tax provision calculation.

Example #5 - State Income Taxes
5 - Financial Statements (1 of 2)

This set of abbreviated financial statements and related footnotes are derived from the final adjusted trial balance (see the third column at 1600) and supported by the tax provision (1000) and other workpapers.

Consolidated Balance Sheet

	Amounts	Notes/Explanation/Reference
Other Assets (this includes all non-tax-related assets)	$1,105,000	From 1600 - Closing trial balance (third column on page 1 of 1)
Deferred Tax Asset - Federal & State	$4,990	Same
Total Assets	$1,109,990	Ties to the company's published financial statements
Liability - Taxes Payable	$28,693	From 1600 and 60 - Closing trial balance and taxes payable rollforward
Deferred Tax Liability - Federal or State	$0	
Other Liabilities (this includes all non-tax-related liabilities)	$20,000	From 1600 - Closing trial balance (third column on page 1 of 1)
Equity - Common Stock & APIC	$1,000,000	From 1600 - Closing trial balance (third column on page 1 of 1)
Equity - Retained Earnings	$61,298	See the "Retained Earnings Rollforward" on 2 of 2
Total Liabilities & Stockholders' Equity	$1,109,990	Ties to the company's published financial statements
	In Balance	

Consolidated Statement of Comprehensive Income/(Loss)

	Amounts	Notes/Explanation/Reference
Revenue	$340,000	From 1600 - Closing trial balance (third column on page 1 of 1)
Expenses (Pretax)	($255,000)	Same
Income/(Loss) Before Income Tax Provision	$85,000	Ties to pretax book income per 1600 (page 2 of 2)
Income Tax (Provision)/Benefit	($23,703)	From 1600 (see the "Income Taxes" footnote on page 2 of 2)
Net Income	$61,298	
	In Balance	"In Balance" - Ties to net income per 1600 (page 2 of 2)
Other Comprehensive Income	$0	
Comprehensive Income/(Loss)	$61,298	Ties to the company's published financial statements

Example #5 - State Income Taxes
5 - Financial Statements (2 of 2)

Notes to Consolidated Financial Statements ("The Footnotes")

Income Taxes

The income tax provision/(benefit) for the year consisted of the following:

Current Income Taxes
Current Taxes - Federal	$22,943	From 1000 - Federal Tax Provision
Current Taxes - State	$5,750	From 1100 - State Tax Provision

Deferred Income Taxes
Deferred Taxes - Federal	($3,990)	From 1000 and 1310 - Federal Tax Prov. and Fed. Tax Deferred RF
Deferred Taxes - State	($1,000)	From 1100 and 1320 - State Tax Prov. and State Tax Deferred RF
Total Tax Provision or Expense/(Benefit)	$23,703	Ties to the income statement on page 1 of 2

In Balance

Here, further comments and insights would be made on the income tax expense of the company, such as how it compared against the prior period, whether there were important trends, risks, etc.

Effective Tax Rate Reconciliation

The differences between the effective tax rate reflected in the tax provision and the federal statutory rates are as follows:

Description	Dollar	Rate	
Expected Tax Provision/(Benefit) at the Statutory Tax Rate	$17,850	21.00%	From 1000 - Federal Tax Provision
State Taxes Net of Federal Benefit	$3,753	4.41%	From 1100 - State Tax Provision
Nondeductible Expenses	$2,100	2.47%	From 1000 - Federal Tax Provision
Income Tax Provision/(Benefit) / Effective Rate (ETR)	$23,703	27.89%	Ties to the financial statements and the footnote above

In Balance

Supporting Calculations (NOT shown in the financial statements)

Retained Earnings Rollforward

Beginning Retained Earnings/(Deficit)	$0	From 1600 (column one)
Add: Net Income/(Loss) for the Period	$61,298	Ties to the financials (page 1 of 1)
Less: Dividends and Other Distributions	$0	
Equals: Ending Retained Earnings	$61,298	Ties to the balance sheet on page 1 of 1

In Balance

Example #5 - State Income Taxes
50 - Tax Journal Entry Summary

The purpose of this workpaper is to adjust the period's beginning (or opening) balances to the correct ending (or calculated) balances based on tax provision calculations.

Column three below, the adjusting tax journal entry ("tax AJE"), is one of the key products of the Tax Group's work on the tax provision. When this entry is provided to the Accounting Group and booked in the general ledger (column two of 1600) then the company's trial balance should be final (column three of 1600). When that happens, the company can then prepare its financial statements and the accompanying footnotes (summarized at workpaper 5).

For consolidated companies with multiple entities, tax adjusting entries should be prepared on a separate company basis (as opposed to a consolidated "top side" adjustment). Also, when applicable, tax adjusting journal entries should be prepared in the local currency of the entity (USD or otherwise) because that is how they will be entered into the accounting system.

Account Description	Opening Balance From 1600[1]	Calculated Balance "Plug"[2]	Adjusting (Tax) Journal Entry Carries to 1600[3]	Notes/Explanation/Reference
Deferred Tax Asset - Federal	$0	$3,990	$3,990	Calculated at 1310 - Federal Tax Deferred Rollforward
Deferred Tax Asset - State	$0	$1,000	$1,000	Calculated at 1320 - State Tax Deferred Rollforward
Liability - Tax Payable - Federal	$0	($22,943)	($22,943)	Calculated at 60 - Tax Payable Rollforward
Liability - Tax Payable - State	$0	($5,750)	($5,750)	Calculated at 60 - Tax Payable Rollforward
Liability - Deferred Tax Liability - Federal or State	$0	$0	$0	There are no deferred taxes in this example
Expense - Income Tax - Federal - Current Exp./(Benefit)	$0	$22,943	$22,943	Calculated at 1000 - Federal Tax Provision
Expense - Income Tax - State - Current Exp./(Benefit)	$0	$5,750	$5,750	Calculated at 1100 - State Tax Provision
Expense - Income Tax - Federal - Deferred Exp./(Benefit)	$0	($3,990)	($3,990)	Calculated at 1310 - Federal Tax Deferred Rollforward
Expense - Income Tax - State - Deferred Exp./(Benefit)	$0	($1,000)	($1,000)	Calculated at 1320 - State Tax Deferred Rollforward
Totals / Check Figure (should be zero)			$0 In Balance	Total debits and credits should net to zero

1 - These balances are from the first column of workpaper 1600.

2 - These amounts are calculated (or proven out) in various tax provision supporting workpapers as referenced in the "Notes" column.

3 - These adjusting entries carry to the middle column of workpaper 1600. As noted above, they adjust the trial balance from what it was (the first column at 1600) to what it should be (the third column at 1600).

"The Missing Tax Accounting Guide – A Plain English Guide to ASC 740 Tax Provisions"
@ 2022 Tax Director Services, Inc.
All rights reserved

Example #5 - State Income Taxes
60 - Taxes Payable Rollforward

The purpose of this workpaper is to roll forward the income tax (payable)/receivable accounts in the general ledger (at 1600) to their ending balances. Note that debits are positive and credits are negative unless otherwise noted. A proof at the bottom of this workpaper compares the ending balances of the rollforward with known amounts per tax returns, estimated tax payments, extension payments, and other verifiable balances.

Taxes (Payable)/Rec. Rollforward

	Federal	State	Totals	
Beginning of Year ("BOY") Tax Receivable/(Payable)	$0	$0	$0	Ties to the prior year ending balance sheet
Tax (Expense)/Benefit - Q1 through Q3	$0	$0	$0	From 1600 - Year to date ("YTD") activity from the TB (column one)
Subtotal - Tax Expense/(Benefit) through Q1 - Q3	$0	$0	$0	
Summary of Cash Taxes Paid/(Received)				
Tax Payments/(Refunds) - Q1 Estimated Tax	$0	$0	$0	Ties to estimated tax payments and AP cash disbursements
Tax Payments/(Refunds) - Q2 Estimated Tax	$0	$0	$0	
Tax Payments/(Refunds) - Q3 Estimated Tax	$0	$0	$0	
Subtotal - Tax Payments/(Refunds) - Q1 - Q3	$0	$0	$0	
Subtotal: Net Receivable/(Payable) - Q1 - Q3	$0	$0	$0	Ties to 1600 - Trial balance ("TB") opening amount (column one)
Current Tax (Expense)/Benefit - Current Period (Q4)	($22,943)	($5,750)	($28,693)	Calculated at 1000 & 1100 - Fed. and State Tax Provision Summaries
Other Adjustments	$0	$0	$0	
End of Year ("EOY") Tax Receivable/(Payable)	($22,943)	($5,750)	($28,693)	Carries 50 - Tax Journal Entry

Ending Tax (Payable)/Receivable Proof

	Federal	State	Totals	
Total Expected Income Tax Payable per the Provision	$22,943	$5,750	$28,693	From 1000 and 11200 - Federal and State Tax Provisions
Less: Estimated Tax Payments to Date	$0	$0	$0	From above - Ties to est. tax vouchers & AP cash disbursements
Less: Extension Payments to Date	$0	$0	$0	
Other Adjustments	$0	$0	$0	
Equals: Expected Payable/(Receivable) Per Tax Returns	$22,943	$5,750	$28,693	Ties to ending payable amount above

Example #5 - State Income Taxes
80 - Tax Rates Summary

The purpose of this workpaper is to list federal, state, and foreign tax rates that are used for tax provision calculations. Referencing tax rates from one location in the workpapers is efficient, and it also helps to maintain the integrity of internal checks and controls.

Federal Statutory Rate

	Current Year	Notes/Explanation
Federal Statutory Rate - Current Year	21.00%	

State Tax Rate
Blended State Tax Rate

Gross Blended State Tax Rate	5.00%	This is the average tax rate for all states in which the company operates

The State Tax Rate Net of the Federal Benefit

Gross Blended State Tax Rate	5.00%	From above
Less: Fed. Benefit of the State Tax Deduction	-1.05%	Calculated below
Equals: State Tax Rate Net of the Federal Benefit	3.95%	

The % Federal Benefit of the State Tax Deduction

Gross Blended State Tax Rate	5.00%	From above
Times: Federal Statutory Rate	21.00%	Same
Equals: Federal Benefit of the State Tax Deduction	1.05%	Carries above

Example #5 - State Income Taxes
1000 - Federal-only Tax Provision*

*See workpaper 1100 for the state tax provision.

Calculation of Current Federal Taxes

	Tax Provision	Dollar Amt.	ETR	Notes/Explanations
	Current Year	Current Year	Current Year	
Pretax Book Income	$85,000	$17,850	21.00%	From 1600	The expected tax expense/rate of PTBI at the statutory tax rate
State Taxes				
(Deduction)/Benefit for State Taxes - Current Exp/(Ben)	($5,750)	($1,208)	-1.42%	From 1100 - State Tax Provision
Permanent Differences				
Permanent Difference - GL-related Items - Revenue	$0	$0	0.00%	From 1200 - Sch M Summary workpaper
Permanent Difference - GL-related Items - Expenses	$10,000	$2,100	2.47%	
Permanent Difference - Special Tax Calculation	$0	$0	0.00%	
Temporary Differences				
Temporary Difference - GL-related Items	$20,000	$4,200	4.94%	
Temporary Difference - Depreciation	$0	$0	0.00%	
Tax Return Calculations				
Subtotal: Pre-NOL Federal Taxable Income	$109,250			
Times: Federal Tax Rate	21.00%			From 80 - Tax Rates Summary
Subtotal: Federal Tax Before Credits	$22,943			
Less: Federal Tax Credits	$0	$0	0.00%	From 1200 - Sch M Summary workpaper
Subtotal: Fed Tax Return Prov. - Current Tax Exp/(Ben)	$22,943	$22,943	26.99%	Tax expense/(benefit) on a tax return (cash) basis
Other Adjustments & True-ups	$0			
Subtotal: Other Adjustments & True-ups	$0			
Total Current Taxes - Federal-only //Federal ETR	$22,943	$22,943	26.99%	Carries to the "Summary of Current and Deferred Taxes" below

Summary of Current and Deferred Federal Taxes

Current Tax Expense/(Benefit) - Federal	$22,943	Carries to 5 - Financial Statements
Deferred Tax Expense/(Benefit) - Federal	($3,990)	From 1310 - USP Deferreds - Fed; carries to 50 - Tax JE
Total Tax Provision - Federal	$18,953	

"The Missing Tax Accounting Guide – A Plain English Guide to ASC 740 Tax Provisions"
@ 2022 Tax Director Services, Inc.
All rights reserved

Example #5 - State Income Taxes
1100 - State Tax Provision Summary

State Tax Provision Calculation	Tax Provision Current Year	Notes/Explanations
Pretax Book Income	$85,000	From 1600
Permanent Differences		
Permanent Difference - GL-related Items - Revenue	$0	From 1200 - Sch M Summary workpaper
Permanent Difference - GL-related Items - Expense	$10,000	
Permanent Difference - Special Tax Calculation	$0	
Temporary Differences		
Temporary Difference - GL-related Items	$20,000	
Temporary Difference - Depreciation	$0	
Tax Return Calculations		
Subtotal: Pre-NOL State Taxable Income	$115,000	
Times: State Tax Rate	5.00%	From 80 - Tax Rates Summary
Subtotal: State Tax Before Credits	$5,750	
Less: State Tax Credits	$0	From 1200 - Sch M Summary workpaper
Subtotal: State Tax Return Prov. - Current Tax Exp/(	$5,750	Tax expense/(benefit) on a tax return (cash) basis
Other Adjustments & True-ups	$0	
Subtotal: Other Adjustments & True-ups	$0	
Equals: Total State Taxes - Current	$5,750	Carries to the summary below

State Taxes Net of the Federal Benefit
Calculation of State Taxes "NOFB"

Total Provision for State Taxes	$4,750	From the summary below
Less: Federal Benefit of State Taxes	($998)	Calculated below
Equals: State Taxes Net of the Federal Benefit	$3,753	Ties to 10 - Financial Statement Tie-out

Federal Benefit of State Taxes

Total Provision for State Taxes	($4,750)	From above (with the sign reversed)
Time: Federal Tax Rate	21.00%	From 80 - Tax Rates Summary
Equals: The Federal Benefit of State Taxes	($998)	Carries to 10 - Financial Statement Tie-out

Summary of Current and Deferred State Taxes

Current Tax Expense/(Benefit) - State	$5,750	From above - Carries to 1000 - Federal Tax Provision
Deferred Tax Expense/(Benefit) - State	($1,000)	
Total Provision for State Taxes	$4,750	Carries to 1000 - Federal Tax Provision

Example #5 - State Income Taxes
1200 - Sch M Calculation Summary

The purpose of this workpaper is to centralize and summarize all figures used to compute book/tax differences ("Schedule Ms"). Shaded figures are pulling from other workpapers, and hard coded (unshaded) figures are supported by data and calculations outside of this workpaper (with a reference to the source documents provided).

	Amount	Notes/Explanation
Federal and State Book/Tax Differences		The figures in this section apply to both federal and state tax calculations
Permanent Differences - GL-related - Revenue		
Revenue - Permanent Item	$0	From 1600 - Entity trial balance. (e.g. tax-exempt interest)
Permanent Differences - GL-related - Expenses		
Expense - Permanent Item	$20,000	From 1600 - Entity trial balance
Times: Sch M Statutory Disallowance %	50%	This percentage is an example only (e.g. a meals percentage disallowance)
Perm. Difference - GL-related Item - (Fav)/Unfav. Sch M	$10,000	Amount carries to 1000 & 1100 - Federal and State tax provision summaries
Permanent Differences - Special Tax Calculations		
Perm. Difference - Special Tax Calc. - (Fav)/Unfav. Sch M	$0	Reference separate supporting workpapers here (e.g. IRC 199)
Temporary Differences - GL-related		
Liabilities - Accrued Expenses	$20,000	From 1600 - Entity trial balance
Less: Liabilities - Accrued Expenses - Prior Year	$0	This figure is from the prior year workpapers (prior year ending balance)
Equals: Unfavorable/(Favorable) Sch M	$20,000	Amount carries to 1000 & 1100 - Federal and State tax provision summaries. Also carries to 1300 - Pretax Deferred Rollforward
Temporary Differences - Fixed Asset Depreciation		
Book Depreciation	$0	From 1600 & 1700 - Entity trial balance and Fixed Asset Rollforward
Less: Tax Depreciation	$0	From 1700 - Fixed Asset Rollforward
Equals: (Favorable)/Unfavorable Sch M	$0	Amount carries to 1000 & 1100 - Federal and State tax provision summaries

Made in United States
Orlando, FL
18 January 2024